Working Men's Social Clubs and Educational Institutes

HENRY SOLLY

CAMBRIDGE
UNIVERSITY PRESS

CAMBRIDGE UNIVERSITY PRESS

Cambridge, New York, Melbourne, Madrid, Cape Town,
Singapore, São Paolo, Delhi, Tokyo, Mexico City

Published in the United States of America by Cambridge University Press, New York

www.cambridge.org
Information on this title: www.cambridge.org/9781108036221

This edition first published 1867
This digitally printed version 2011

ISBN 978-1-108-03622-1 Paperback

CAMBRIDGE LIBRARY COLLECTION

Books of enduring scholarly value

History

The books reissued in this series include accounts of historical events and movements by eye-witnesses and contemporaries, as well as landmark studies that assembled significant source materials or developed new historiographical methods. The series includes work in social, political and military history on a wide range of periods and regions, giving modern scholars ready access to influential publications of the past.

Working Men's Social Clubs and Educational Institutes

Social reformer, Chartist sympathiser, advocate of universal suffrage, and opponent of slavery, Henry Solly (1813–1903) was a man driven by the desire to stamp out inequality. As part of his mission to improve the lives of working-class people, he founded the Working Men's Club and Institute Union, becoming its first paid secretary in 1863. The Union encouraged the formation of social and educational clubs where working men could 'meet for conversation, business, and mental improvement, with the means of recreation and refreshment, free from intoxicating drinks'. His tireless campaigning led directly to the formation of the Charity Organization Society, which advocated the principle of aiding those prepared to help themselves. Published in 1867, this is Solly's vigorous manifesto for social reform based around temperance and the formation of social clubs and educational institutes for working men.

Cambridge University Press has long been a pioneer in the reissuing of out-of-print titles from its own backlist, producing digital reprints of books that are still sought after by scholars and students but could not be reprinted economically using traditional technology. The Cambridge Library Collection extends this activity to a wider range of books which are still of importance to researchers and professionals, either for the source material they contain, or as landmarks in the history of their academic discipline.

Drawing from the world-renowned collections in the Cambridge University Library, and guided by the advice of experts in each subject area, Cambridge University Press is using state-of-the-art scanning machines in its own Printing House to capture the content of each book selected for inclusion. The files are processed to give a consistently clear, crisp image, and the books finished to the high quality standard for which the Press is recognised around the world. The latest print-on-demand technology ensures that the books will remain available indefinitely, and that orders for single or multiple copies can quickly be supplied.

The Cambridge Library Collection will bring back to life books of enduring scholarly value (including out-of-copyright works originally issued by other publishers) across a wide range of disciplines in the humanities and social sciences and in science and technology.

WORKING MEN'S

SOCIAL CLUBS

AND

EDUCATIONAL INSTITUTES.

BY

HENRY SOLLY,

LATE SECRETARY TO THE WORKING MEN'S CLUB AND INSTITUTE UNION.

LONDON:

PUBLISHED BY THE WORKING MEN'S CLUB AND INSTITUTE
UNION, AND TO BE HAD AT THEIR OFFICE,
150, STRAND. W.C.

———

1867.

NOTICE.

This Volume is issued in the belief that its publication will materially promote the important objects that the Working Men's Club and Institute Union have in view. The Council wish it to be understood that they do not thereby pledge themselves to agreement with all the views and arrangements that the Volume contains.

CONTENTS.

4

⁎ *The papers in this volume are partly published now for the
first time, and partly reprinted from the Society's other publications,
and from Cassell and Co.'s " Working Man," by the kind permission of that firm.*

Dedicatory Letter

REV. FREDERICK DENISON MAURICE, M.A.,

AND HIS FELLOW-WORKERS IN FOUNDING AND CONDUCTING THE
WORKING MEN'S COLLEGE, LONDON.

———————

DEAR MR. MAURICE,

I wished to put your name at the commencement
of this little work, by way of expressing my grateful sense of
the good you have effected for the great body of operatives, not
in London or England only, but, I believe, in every part of the
world and for all future time, by the principles you have
enunciated and carried into action in the London Working
Men's College. Other persons, no doubt, besides yourself, have
done valuable work for the industrial classes, and you must
suffer me to add, with due humility, that you appear to me to
have also rendered services in other ways to our highest interests
and to our national life, for which future generations will long
be grateful. But now I want to speak of just this particular
service rendered to working men, because it is that which has
chiefly enabled me to be, possibly, of a little use in the special
department dwelt on in this book. There are others whose
names I would gladly mention in connexion with your own ; for
you have drawn around you, from the first, men worthy to be
your fellow-labourers in so great a cause. But it would be
invidious to mention some and not all. To you and to them
let me, then, dedicate this humble contribution to a good cause.

Having been present at the *genesis* and first formative operations of the Working Men's College, and watched its progress
carefully ever since, especially having studied your lectures on
" Learning and Working," I saw in your enterprise what I had
been groping after for years, and what supplied, in the work
which I had long been trying to do myself, precisely those links
without which it must always have been wretchedly inefficient
and incomplete.

I do not say, neither assuredly would you, that your Working

Men's College solves all the difficulties connected with the culture and development of working men as regards their highest—
i.e., spiritual—welfare. Still less does it meet all their humbler
social wants. But while it does, and has done, so much to solve
those difficulties by its direct enunciation of certain principles,
I believe it has done and will effect even far more good to the
industrial population by its indirect action in testifying to the
desire of Christian ministers and laymen to promote the mental
and social well-being of those who, until a recent period, were
regarded too often merely as "hands," as useful machines, or
beasts of burden. And you will easily understand that in
undertaking for a time duties of a different character from those
that had previously occupied me, it was with the hope that, by
promoting the social interests of working men, the opportunities for advancing their far higher spiritual life might ultimately
be secured to them.

Having now done the best I could in the former direction,
and having drawn up this digest of our experience and advice as
a last legacy to the Club movement, may I ask your sympathy
in the efforts, however humble, which I hope once again
to make for meeting some of the religious and spiritual
wants of the working classes? I know that you and others
will think me mistaken in endeavouring to exercise religious
ministrations apart from the Church of England. Let me hope,
that if the larger share of blame for that course is given to my
supposed defective judgment or unrighteous self-will, some
error of that National Institution, either in formula or management, may possibly, in part, account for such conduct. May the
day come when there shall be greater approaches made to one National Christian Catholic Church, embracing all sincere disciples
of our Lord Jesus Christ ; aiming, not at uniformity of doctrine,
but at "the unity of the Spirit," and thus retaining us all "in
the bond of peace." In the meantime, may you and others,
who are enrolled under the Established system, be able to wish
some of us God-speed, as at least a sort of volunteer or guerilla
combatants in the great warfare against Evil, seeing that we
endeavour to be loyal to the one "Great Captain," and are at
all events fighting on the right side ; while it is our very loyalty
to our Lord which alone keeps us (however mistakenly some
may deem it), against both our desires and our interests, in this
"unattached" condition.

In the Appendix you will be reminded of a correspondence
that took place between us several years ago. Although it was
a great disappointment to me at the time that I could not get
the Lancaster working men to accept the name of "College," I
believe the movement is, on the whole, working out far better
for the ends you and your friends had in view when founding

the London College, than if this name had been adopted as the symbol of our work generally. But you will see in other parts of the volume how profoundly important I believe it to be that both the principles and the name of "College" should be kept steadily before the working classes of this kingdom.

I fear there are too many repetitions in the book, but the nature of it rendered this very difficult, if not impossible, to avoid. My comfort under its various imperfections is, that no one can be half so sensible of them as I am myself.

Several subjects of interest have had to be omitted for want of room; but I had the less scruple in at last excluding them, because the Council of the Union intend dealing with them in future "Occasional Papers," which may be had for a very small sum (probably twopence or threepence), at their office, 150, Strand. Among these may be mentioned a paper on "Club Refreshments," by E. Hall, Esq. (Architect), a member of the Council, which I have reason to believe will be very valuable, and another on the "Exemption of Clubs and Institutes from Local Rating." It was also originally intended that I should give several of the Parent Society's published papers in the Appendix, as well as the last Annual Report, or copious extracts from them; and the reader accordingly is referred to them in several passages as to be found in the Appendix. But since they can all be procured at the Society's office, it ultimately appeared more advisable to introduce matter that would not otherwise be preserved. I may add, that for all which appears in this volume, if it is not stated otherwise, I alone am responsible.

An omission in this book less easily supplied than that of the papers now mentioned is, that no justice is done in it to the invaluable and disinterested support which has been given by many members of the Council for various terms of office since the formation of the Union. Where so many have laboured worthily, it would be invidious to specify particular names, with a very few exceptions; but I cannot forbear expressing my grateful sense of the value of the services rendered to the Society and the movement generally by two of our Vice-Presidents, Lord Lyttelton and the Earl of Lichfield, and to three members of the Council—Mr. Hugh Owen, of the Poor-law Board, Mr. John Bainbridge, a mechanic (who have been on the Council from its first formation), and Mr. Hodgson Pratt, formerly Under-Secretary to the Bengal Government, who has acted as Chairman of the Executive Committee for a considerable period, and devoted much time and money to the work, in a spirit of self-sacrifice worthy of the highest praise. To Mr. Bainbridge I owe my first introduction, more than a quarter of a century ago, to the *bonâ-fide* artizans of this country; and the love and respect which he then awakened in me towards himself and his class have increased to them and him with years.

In making this acknowledgment of the services of the Council, I cannot but penitently confess that I fear there is much on my own part for which I have to ask their forgiveness. My only consolation is, that they have been "used up," wearied, and worried in a cause that deserves and rewards all sacrifice and endurance, however wrongfully exacted. It has not, however, been altogether a path of roses to myself; yet it must not be supposed that I have deserted my post in connexion with the "Union" from weariness or disgust at my task. I think I had earned a right to return to ministerial labours ; and if I am doing so somewhat sooner than I had expected or was engaged to do, I believe that I shall be acquitted of all blame by those who are acquainted with the circumstances under which I resigned my office. The Society and myself part in peace, and we shall, I trust all have a blessing on the various ways in which we may henceforth labour respectively to serve our working brethren. In regard to the advice offered and the plans propounded in the following pages, experience may ultimately prove that matters work out best in a very different way from what is there recommended or anticipated. Let me assure you, who have so often exhorted your brethren, and set them an example on this point, that I have no more earnest desire than to find that the best I could do or hope for has been superseded by something far better. In regard to the failures detailed here, you, I know, would be the last to be discouraged by them ; but you will perhaps think danger threatens some of the Clubs mentioned in the following pages because I have praised them warmly. I think so too. It is a great misfortune to be singled out for approbation, and to be set up as an example. But it is one of those misfortunes which must sometimes be endured for the good of others, and which is to be overcome by adequate fortitude and energy. If the members both of the Clubs that have succeeded hitherto and of those that have more or less failed, will learn the lessons of humility and reliance upon One higher than themselves, which you have perseveringly preached to others and practised yourself, they will pass safely through much severer ordeals than my feeble praise or censure, and may one day hear the Voice which says to labouring and suffering mortals, "Faithful servant, well done."

Believe me, dear Mr. Maurice,
Ever gratefully yours,
HENRY SOLLY.

Grove House, Rosslyn, Hampstead, N.W.,
September, 1867.

CHAPTER I.

In tracing the origin and nature of the recent movement on
behalf of Working Men's Clubs and Institutes, we must look
back forty years to the agitation in favour of Mechanics'
Institutes, originated by that true friend of the working
classes, Dr. Birkbeck; and to which the illustrious man who
has led the van in so many great enterprises for the good of
humanity, Lord Brougham, gave such distinguished assistance. That agitation was purely an educational effort, intended originally to teach mechanics the correct knowledge
and principles of their own trades. Then came various unconnected intermittent attempts to provide what were called
" Reading-rooms " for working men, in which the chief
element was the supplying a place where time might be
innocently passed, but where neither education, social intercourse, nor recreation was offered, except so far as reading a
newspaper or book in the same room with other people might
be supposed to afford all or either. Next came the formation
of Mutual Improvement Societies, which met chiefly in school-
rooms, and aimed at Classes, Discussions, and especially at
the preparation of short papers on interesting and improving
topics. There was often a good deal of the sociable spirit in
these little organizations, but they were seldom long-lived.
The writer formed one on a more comprehensive plan in 1842
at Yeovil, Somersetshire, for the working men of the town
generally, which aimed to be a fellowship for mutual benefit
in various ways, but chiefly educational, with very little of
the recreation element in it, and without any of the Club
features properly so called. It was well appreciated and very
useful for a time, but after he left the town dishonest practices
broke it up. In the same year, that excellent institution, the
People's College at Sheffield, was established by a very earnest

and able friend of the people, the late Rev. R. L. Bayly, of that town, which has done great good there, and is still, we believe, as useful as ever.

But the greatest impulse to the movement for helping working men in the particular direction now under consideration, at all partaking of a national character, subsequently to the initiation of Mechanics' Institutions, was given by the Rev. F. W. Robertson, Incumbent of Trinity Church, Brighton, in 1849, by the establishment of the Brighton Working Men's Institute. The large-hearted, Christian sympathies of that gentleman, and his striking eloquence, procured a considerable amount of attention to his enterprise; its influence was felt through the Midland counties and as far north as South Shields, where a Working Men's Institute was formed, shortly after, by working men who had heard vaguely of such a thing doing good to working men somewhere, and thought, therefore, it might do the same in their own locality. Their Institute has continued in healthy and useful existence to the present day. A more direct and acknowledged impulse from the Brighton centre was given in various other towns where Working Men's Institutes were formed, and among others to a few working men and their friends, including the writer, in Cheltenham, where in 1849-50 a Working Men's Institute was established which, like its prototype, aimed at a combination of education and amusement, but which subsequently fell into bad hands and closed ingloriously.

The establishment of Night Schools, and the formation of the Yorkshire and Lancashire Unions, of the Southern Counties, of the South Staffordshire, and of the Metropolitan Societies for promoting Adult Education, have been useful agencies during the last dozen years in the education of the working classes, but the good done has been chiefly confined to young persons, and the results generally have been very far from satisfactory as regards working men.

While, however, all these efforts have been productive of more or less unquestionable benefit, none of them met that which is undoubtedly the first great want of working men after their long day's toil—viz., unrestrained social intercourse, the means of chatting with one another, with or without refreshments. This is the first and simplest kind of relaxation that hard-worked men in any rank of life desire ; but in proportion to mental culture and educated tastes will be the desire, of course, for other enjoyments than mere gossiping chat. All efforts, as far as we are aware, to benefit working men, not aiming directly at their moral, religious, or pecuniary welfare, previous to 1852, appear to have ignored this their primary and simplest, but most urgent want. Hence their very limited success. A few of the *élite* of the working classes benefited by them here and there. But they never reached the masses, who still found the only conditions for the relaxation they desired in the public-house, where they had to pay for it in a way that very often, at all events at first, they did not desire—viz., by drinking for "the good of the house," and to the damage of their families and themselves.

In the year above-mentioned, however (1852), there appears to have been a new element introduced. An institution, we are told, was opened that year in the Colonnade, Clare-market, under the presidency of Viscount Ingestre, which was called " The Colonnade Working Men's Club," and provided amusement and refreshment, as well as newspapers and books, though it does not appear quite certain when it was actually commenced. It continued in existence, however, until recently, and met with a tolerable amount of support ; and though suspended for a time, has been since re-opened as a Youths' Institute.

Laudable, however, as this improved scheme was, it does not appear to have attracted any general attention. In 1855, Mr. Horlock Bastard, of Charlton Marshall, near Blandford, Dorset, without having heard of any similar enterprise, established a Village Working Men's Club in that parish, which still continues its career of humble usefulness, and which, like the Colonnade Club in London, made the means of conversation, combined with opportunity for obtaining refreshments, the primary object—newspapers, books, with chess and draughts, being at the same time offered. Women are allowed to be members of the Charlton Club. A similar Village Club was established about the same time in Hertfordshire on the estate of Mr. Lawes, in conjunction with garden allotments. Beer in limited quantities was sold at this Club to members with the result, we are told, of shutting up the public-house. Soon after, village Clubs were established at Littlemore and Iffley in Oxfordshire, which again gave rise to Clubs at Kingham, Chipping Norton, and Adderbury, Oxon.

Then came one of the greatest, if not *the* greatest, impulses yet given in this country to the movement for elevating working men in the social scale. We mean the establishment, by the Rev. F. D. Maurice and his earnest fellow-workers, in 1854, of the London Working Men's College. This most important enterprise grew out of the wants felt, and desires awakened, by the "Christian Socialist or co-operative" movement, in which those gentlemen had been previously engaged; but the name and idea of a college, Mr. Maurice tells us, were suggested to him by the People's College, Sheffield, which, however, though an admirable institution, has been little more than a system of capital classes.

The specialty of Mr. Maurice's labours in this direction— that which makes them mark an era in the history of the working classes, and exert so deep and wide-spread an influence—is the development and application of the grand old idea of a Brotherhood for the completest culture possible of its members as human beings—*for their whole development as men.* He and his friends came to the working classes, suffering as they do from their imperfect early education, and from their contracted and often deadening daily toil—came to persons, in fact, who are often reduced nearly to the condition of machines—and said, "We want to help you, and want you to help one another, to be MEN; to attain to that humanizing culture and happiness, and to that noble, manly development of mind, and body, and spirit, for which you were created. For this purpose, we must have a true fellowship, mutual social sympathies, regular and earnest educational effort, a Bible-class, gymnasium, library, coffee-room, occasional lectures, *soirées,* and so forth. Will you work with us?" It will be sufficiently evident, we think, how this London Working Men's College, therefore, differed from all Mechanics' Institutions, People's Colleges, Mutual Improvement Societies, &c., that had preceded it. Its influence, which has already been felt through various ranks and in several localities, is evidently destined to increase, like most great vital forces, with the lapse of time. In the remarkable lectures which Mr. Maurice delivered on "Learning and Working" (Macmillan and Co.) in Willis's-rooms in the spring of 1854, he laid the foundations of that influence in truths and principles which "cannot be moved."

The publication of Miss Marsh's deeply-interesting work, "English Hearts and English Hands," though not claiming a distinct place in the record of efforts to elevate the working classes by means of social or educational institutions, gave so great a stimulus to those efforts, and to middle and upper class sympathies with "the sons of toil," that it would be a serious omission if it were not noticed here. Among the most direct and striking results of its publication was the share it had in leading Mrs. Wightman to enter upon her Christian work at Shrewsbury in 1860, which has issued in the erection of a spacious and handsome Workmen's Hall as a material agency, and in an incalculable amount of moral and spiritual good to the working men of that town and elsewhere. There is a very flourishing Temperance Society that holds its meetings at the Hall. But there appears to be nothing now corresponding to a Working Men's Club held there. Penny Readings, &c., were checked.

In 1858, about four years after the establishment of the Working Men's College, a clergyman in Salford, Manchester —the Rev. E. Boteler Chalmer, Incumbent of St. Matthias— formed a Working Men's Club in that parish, which made social intercourse, amusement, and refreshments, the primary object. It has been eminently useful and successful, and attracted more attention than either of the previous "Club" enterprises (see next chapter).

In 1860 two excellent ladies in different parts of the metropolis, and in ignorance of what each other was doing, but both moved to action by witnessing the sufferings and degradation of the wives and children of labouring men in whom they were interested, were busy devising means for drawing these men from the public-house. In the course of the year 1860, Miss Adeline Cooper, after much consideration and labour, succeeded in fitting up premises in Duck-lane, Westminster, suitable for the object which she saw must be aimed at, and in December of that year the Westminster Working Men's Club was formally opened, amid great rejoicing. Fortunately, Miss Cooper saw the value and importance of

calling the institution, thus established, a Club, and by bringing the writer to the same view, has been mainly instrumental
in fixing the right name both on these societies and on the
movement generally—no slight service, seeing the wonderful
extent to which a cause depends for success upon its name.
When names are symbols their power is immeasurable. The
Duck-lane Club has continued to this day in its course of
humble but most remarkable usefulness. During the same
year (1860) Mrs. Bayly was holding several interesting
conferences with the brickmakers of Nottingdale, in conjunction with Mr. Parfitt, an able and zealous City Missionary in the district (see "Workmen and their Difficulties,"
"Mended Homes," &c., by Mrs. Bayly, and *Leisure Hour*,
June, 1867) ; and, in 1861, the Notting-hill Workmen's Hall
was opened in the Kensington Potteries. This institution
also has done an immense amount of good, and, after a
temporary suspension, through the commercial failure of one
of its chief supporters, and through Mrs. Bayly's leaving the
neighbourhood, it is once again entering on its career of usefulness. For further particulars of the history of these
pioneer Clubs, and of the benefits conferred by them, see
various numbers of the *Weekly Record* (Tweedie); also a
very interesting paper read by Mrs. Bayly in 1862, an
abstract of which was published in the Social Science Trans-
actions of that year, p. 527. They were both of them
practically Working Men's Clubs in the sense now given to
the word—viz., societies of working men formed to promote
social intercourse, innocent amusement, mental improvement,
and mutual helpfulness of various kinds ; and their establishment, which was made known far and wide among temperance
reformers, through the *Weekly Record* as well as by Mrs.
Bayly's own publications, gave a powerful impetus to efforts
and inquiries in this direction. The Manchester enterprise
and Mrs. Bayly's led the writer, during the year 1860, to
consider the desirableness of adding the Club element to such
societies for mental improvement as he had previously
endeavoured to promote in various localities. The Temperance Reformation had long engaged the attention and enlisted
the active support of many earnest friends of the working
classes, but it was Mrs. Bayly's and Miss Cooper's efforts that
first led him to see what was imperatively wanted, and might

easily be supplied, to make that great reform permanently
efficient, and, when combined with higher influences and aid,
gradually independent of the teetotal pledge

About the same time the writer, who for twenty years had
been trying in various parts of the country to promote
Mechanics' and Working Men's Institutes, was coming to the
conclusion that a much larger amount of recreation and provision for social intercourse than these Institutes afforded was
required to meet the wants of working men. Having also
worked during the greater part of that period in the Temperance movement, and seen how many reclaimed drunkards
fell back after a time into their old ways, he began to understand that by far the larger number of men who frequent
the public-house go there for the company rather than for the
drink. And when a lady who was devoting herself to the
benefit of the working men in Lancaster, observed to him one
evening at a pleasant social party in a well warmed and
lighted drawing-room, that a friend had written to her only
that day, "The cry comes from all parts of the country,
What are we to do with our reclaimed drunkards?"—a new
view of the work to be done for the industrial classes presented itself to his mind. He had been trying for two years
in vain to get the working men to attend a Mechanics' Institute possessing capital premises, in Lancaster, but without
success ; and he now, therefore, got a number of the inhabitants to consider the whole question at two meetings in the
Town-hall (June, 1860), under the presidency of the Mayor.
Having been warmly interested in Mr. Maurice's labours,
his first idea was to try and establish a Working Men's College (see Appendix), which should also combine the attractions of recreation and social intercourse as part of its
constituent elements. But he soon found that the name of
"College" would repel nearly all the men whom he had
so far interested in the scheme, and still more those whom he
specially wanted to attract from the public-house. After
several meetings and conferences, therefore, a "Working
Men's Mutual Improvement and *Recreation* Society" was
formed, which flourished with considerable vigour and very
useful results for about a year and a-half, until it coalesced
on favourable conditions with the Mechanics' Institute.
About this time an able pamphlet by W. T. Marriott, Esq.,

formerly of Manchester, now of the Middle Temple, was put into the writer's hands, in which, after dwelling on the wants and claims of the working classes, Mr. Marriott suggested the establishment of " Clubs " for working men on the same principle as those used by the upper classes. He had taken an active part in the formation of a capital Working Men's Institute at Hulme, Manchester, in which he had set up a gymnasium, and had also doubtless been an interested spectator of Mr. Chalmer's enterprise in Salford. Some faint rumour of this Salford Club had also reached Lancaster during the agitation there in 1859-60, but unfortunately did not receive from any one the attention it deserved.

In the summer of 1861 the writer, when visiting London and conversing with the Rev. David (now Dr.) Thomas, of Brixton, found that gentleman as deeply interested as himself in the subject of suitable places of resort for working men, and looking precisely in the same direction. Mr. Thomas, urging the importance of immediate and *national* action in the matter, proposed the formation of a Limited Liability Company, with a capital of 3,000,000*l.*, for building Working Men's Institutes all over the country. The writer saw with great thankfulness that such an organization, if only it were made a philanthropic society instead of a commercial company, was the very thing required ; and Mr. Thomas consenting to the change, they set to work at once to draw up a prospectus, and form the Society. The consent of Lord Brougham to become its President was obtained through Mr. Serjeant Manning, who, with M. D. Hill, Esq., the Rev. Dr. Guthrie, Canon Robinson of York, and Mrs. Bayly, signed the request to his lordship ; and this invaluable support once secured, other eminent men were successively induced to become Vice-Presidents. The writer next drew up a paper ("A Glance at the Wants of Working Men"), which was read for him by the Rev. S. A. Steinthal at the Social Science Association meeting in Dublin the same year; but owing to the threatening Lancashire distress, it was thought advisable that no further steps should then be taken. In June, 1862, however, the meeting of that Association in London presented too favourable an opportunity to be lost, and the writer having previously brought the question before a Temperance Conference of clergymen and ministers at the London Coffee-house, was there introduced by Mr. Thomas to the Rev. J. Rylance, Curate of St. Paul's, Lambeth. With that gentleman's very efficient help, he then agitated the matter in several sections of the Association (a large number of prospectuses being at the same time distributed), and obtained Lord Brougham's hearty consent to preside at a meeting to launch the proposed Society. This meeting was held at the Law Amendment Society's Rooms, in Waterloo-place, on the 14th June, 1862, when, among other addresses, two very able and interesting speeches were made by Mr. John Bainbridge, an upholsterer, and Mr. Bebbington, a costermonger and secretary to the Working Men's Club, already mentioned, in Duck-lane, Westminster. At this meeting the Society was duly inaugurated, under the title of the " Working Men's Club and Institute Union," Mr. Rylance and the writer being appointed Hon. Secretaries *pro tem.* Mr. W. M. Neill announced his intention of giving 100*l.* to its funds, Lord Brougham gave 20*l.* on the spot, and the agitation on its behalf went forward with greatly increased vigour, helped on by the paper already mentioned as read by Mrs. Bayly at one of the Social Science meetings, and by Miss Adeline Cooper's valuable counsels.

In the following autumn, after a great many meetings held by the Council appointed at the meeting on the 14th June, the writer resigned the pulpit of the English Presbyterian Chapel, Lancaster, to become the paid Secretary of the Union at a salary of 200*l.* a-year ; rooms were taken at 150, Strand, and its labours were fairly commenced in the beginning of October that year. Its principles and plans of action were thus expressed in a Prospectus which was immediately diffused far and wide throughout the kingdom (see Appendix) :—

OBJECTS AND PLAN OF OPERATIONS.—This Union is formed for the purpose of helping Working Men to establish Clubs or Institutes where they can meet for conversation, business, and mental improvement, with the means of recreation and refreshment, free from intoxicating drinks ; these Clubs, at the same time, constituting Societies for mutual helpfulness in various ways.

It will be the aim of the Council of the Union to assist in extending or improving existing Associations which have in view objects of a kindred nature with the above, as well as to promote the establishment of Clubs or Institutes where no such Associations may now be found. In order to consolidate and strengthen the action and mutual fellowship of these various Associations, Clubs, or Institutes, the Council will invite them to become Registered Members of the Union. In reference to the use of intoxicating drinks on the premises, the Council are strongly of opinion that their introduction would be dangerous to the interests of these Societies, and earnestly recommend their exclusion. They make this recommendation simply on prudential grounds, the reasonableness of which, it is believed, the Working Classes will be the first to acknowledge. The Council also recommend that at least one-half of the managing body should be *bonâ fide* Working Men.

The Council propose to carry out the objects of the Union :—

1. By correspondence with the Officers of existing Associations throughout the kingdom.

2. By personal visits, by their own Officers and by honorary deputations, to such places as may seem to require to be visited. At these visits conferences will be held with the Working Classes, and with others in the locality who may be interested in the object.

3. By the dissemination of tracts, or special papers, on subjects lying within the sphere of the Society's operations.

4. By supplying instructions for the guidance of persons who may wish to establish Clubs or Institutes ; together with rules to define their objects, and to regulate their proceedings.

5. By grants or loans of Books for Club Libraries, Apparatus, Diagrams, &c., to Societies in membership with the Union, in cases where local circumstances may seem to call for such aid.

6. By grants of money in special cases, by way of loan or otherwise, towards the building, enlarging, or altering Club Houses, or procuring recreation grounds, for Societies in the Union.

As soon as a sufficient number of Clubs shall have joined the Union within a given district, the Council will combine them in local organizations, under specified conditions. Half-yearly, or sometimes quarterly, meetings of Delegates from the various Clubs will be held in each district, for the consideratian of matters of local interest, and for the discussion of social questions ; while an annual conference of District Representatives will be held at various large towns in succession, to consider matters of a more general character.

The Council will be glad to receive communications, addressed to their Secretary, from persons desirous of promoting these objects either in their own locality or generally. Information and assistance will be gladly given and received.

Donations and Subscriptions for the Union will be thankfully received by the Secretary, or they can be paid at the London and Westminster Bank (St. James's Square, S.W.), or any of its Branches.

An Annual Subscription of not less than £1, or a Donation of not less than £10, constitutes the contributor a member of the Union.

GENERAL REMARKS.—Notwithstanding all the efforts made to improve the character and condition of the Working Classes in this country, intemperance, ignorance, improvidence, and religious indifference still abound among them to a deplorable extent. One main reason of the want of more complete success is probably to be found in the *incompleteness* of the measures adopted. Vast good, for instance, has been accomplished by the Temperance Reform, but it often fails to retain those whom it has reclaimed from intemperance, in not supplying something to occupy the leisure hours formerly spent at the Public-house. Mechanics' Institutions, also, with efforts of a kindred character, have done a great work ; but they, too, generally fail in not providing *recreation and amusement.* Their aims have been too high for the great majority of Working Men ; hence, while they have attracted and benefited many, the inducements held out have failed to withdraw the multitude from habits and indulgences which all alike deplore. As a result, we find such Institutions now generally given up to the trading and middle classes. Working Men's Colleges, admirable as they are, require some such intermediate step between them and the Public-house as the Societies above described.

Recreation must go hand in hand with Education and Temperance if we would have real and permanent improvement ; while efforts should be specially made to awaken or cherish a brotherly spirit of mutual helpfulness among Working Men themselves, as well as between them and the classes socially above them. The best hope of success is in thus binding people together for worthy ends in a true brotherhood, so that each may be led to give as well as to receive, striving to contribute to the common good. Higher results will follow as these preparatory measures are successful ; and when the temptations to debasing indulgence are removed the way is open for good influences of every kind.

The aim of the Union in all cases would be to help Working Men to help themselves, rather than to establish or manage Institutions for them—this being as essential for the moral usefulness as for the permanent success of our endeavours. Local and Working Class efforts may frequently be fostered and developed by external help with the happiest result, when the establishment of entirely new Institutions, managed by the higher classes in the neighbourhood or by a central Society, would be viewed with jealousy or indifference. The very first step towards forming a Club or Institute would be to interest the Working Men of the district in the undertaking, and to make them feel that, when once started, its management and success must depend mainly on themselves.

The next point in forming these Societies would be to procure suitable premises for the accommodation of the members, containing rooms to be used for conversation, refreshments, recreation, &c.; and others for classes, reading, lectures, and music. A library of entertaining and instructive books, scientific apparatus, diagrams, &c., a supply of newspapers, and some works of art, should be aimed at. The services of efficient teachers, paid and unpaid, should be procured ; Discussion Classes, to awaken thought and a desire for knowledge, should be established ; readings from amusing and eloquent writers, interspersed with music and recitations, should be given periodically ; and, generally, any similar measures adopted for effecting the objects in view. Women should have the privilege, on a small payment, of taking books out of the library, and of admission to the lectures and concerts of the Institute ; also to classes, when efficient female super-intendence could be procured. The very valuable influence of educated women has of late years shown itself in various schemes to improve the condition of the Labouring Classes. A much wider field for this influence may be afforded by Societies such as those now advocated.

The Club Rooms in every locality will form the strongest counter-action to the allurements of the Public House. The desire for social enjoyment and the love of excitement are the impulses that habitually drive the Working Classes to visit the Beer Shop. These instincts also form a great temptation of *reclaimed* drunkards. They remain as strong as ever in their nature after they have become abstainers, and the Public House stands before them as the most available means for their gratification. Music, also, which ought to purify and refine, is now extensively employed as a temptation to drinking and other vices. Until there shall be established in every locality an institution that shall meet these instincts with superior attractions, but without temptations to evil, it is unreasonable to expect a great diminution in the drinking customs of the working population. This want the proposed Clubs will supply. Here the Working Man will obtain, at a charge within his reach, social intercourse and healthy mental excitement—the refreshment he requires or the improvement he seeks.

The extent to which Working Men suffer from their dependence upon the Public House merely *for business purposes* is also an immense evil, and one that is still inadequately appreciated. [See Mr. Tidd Pratt's last Report on Friendly Societies to the House of Commons, page 35, where he remarks "The holding of these Societies at a Public House is also another ground of their failure. . . . In the course of last year the Registrar found that in Herefordshire, since 1793, the number of Societies enrolled and certified were 136 ; of this number 123 were held at Public Houses, and 13 at schools or private rooms. Of those held at Public Houses no less than 42 had broken up, but of those held at schools or private rooms only one had been dissolved." Even where no drinking is allowed during business hours a considerable sum is often spent afterwards, especially by the younger men.] Gradually, however, the proposed Clubs and Institutes will become the Houses of Call for men in search of work, and will be the centres of various Working Men's Societies, such as Friendly Societies, Freehold and Building Associations, Co-operative Societies, Circulating Libraries for the district, Temperance Societies, and of any similar agencies calculated to improve the condition of the Working Classes.

These are no mere visionary ideas. They have been already reduced to practice with most beneficial results in Westminster, Notting Hill, Clare Market, Brighton, Norwood, Manchester, Shrewsbury, Leeds, Farringdon, Liverpool, Carlisle, Southampton, Scarborough, and many other places. The Working Men's Club and Institute Union aims at multiplying such results by *stimulating and assisting local effort.*

The time is evidently ripe for this movement. In all directions earnest and benevolent people are groping after the means or making isolated efforts for elevating the Working Classes above debasing vice and ignorance ; but these efforts often need judicious guidance or timely support, and would be greatly assisted by united counsels and organized power. Our hard-working brethren can seldom find time to initiate, or can rarely obtain adequate support among their own class for local enterprises of this nature. Those best acquainted with them, however, know that they thankfully welcome such help as it is now proposed to afford.

In conclusion. it will be seen that, while the Working Men's Club and Iustitute Union may be useful with the smallest, it will be able to make efficient application of the largest means that may be placed at its disposal—beginning with selected localities, and widening its sphere of action in proportion to the public support it may receive. The Counsel earnestly solicit the assistance, personal and pecuniary, of all who approve their objects ; and, sincerely praying that the Divine blessing may rest upon this undertaking, they commend it to the support of all who desire the true welfare of the Working Classes of this country.

While these preparations were being made for a national organization, two ladies in Southampton (Mrs. Deacon and Mrs. Inglis), two members of the Society of Friends (Messrs. W. and R. Westlake), Sir George Pechell, and other gentlemen, who had been struck with the account of Mrs. Bayly's and Miss Cooper's labours given in the *Weekly Record*, and animated by similar hopes, had commenced, early in 1862, a movement in that town, which resulted in the opening of three Workmen's Halls in the summer of that year, and a fourth, on a smaller scale, in the spring of 1863. The remarkable success which at first attended these benevolent efforts was fully described in a letter by Mr. W. C. Westlake to the *Morning Star*, December 11, 1862, from which, and from the " Occasional Paper," No. 1, published by the Union, the following extracts are taken :—

" Three Workmen's Halls have been opened in Southampton within the past year, situated respectively in Orchard-lane, St. Michael's-square, and Northam. They are designed for the benefit of working and seafaring men ; the management is in the hands of one central and three executive committees— the latter are working men, elected half - yearly by the members ; and the total number of members is at present 400. . . . . The Halls are opened from six to ten o'clock every week evening, and from two to nine on Sundays. Refreshments are supplied at a low fixed rate. Smoking is allowed, but the use of intoxicating drinks on the premises is prohibited. A large number of publications—five daily, and nine weekly London and provincial newspapers, and sixteen weekly and monthly periodicals—are placed on the tables; and provision is made for fourteen games in the Halls and skittle-grounds. There are class-rooms and places for letter-writing at each Hall; and the Halls in Orchard-lane and at Northam are open at mealtimes. A trade register is kept for persons seeking employment. Public readings, recitations, and singing take place every Wednesday, when the members take their wives and families. The subscription required is one penny per week, and a single payment secures admission to all the Halls. Admission free was given for the first month after opening. The experience of the promoters of these Halls has brought out some very interesting particulars. In reply to the question, "Could not beer be sold at the Halls, as at other Club-rooms?" one of the Vice-Presidents writes: 'We think it undesirable to do so. But few of our members are teetotallers, and as we have had sometimes 150 to 180 men at once in the Hall, it would be too much for one woman to keep order (as she now easily does) if men could have a 'finishing pint' on our premises. We also find that if men do not drink beer they are less induced to bet, and less quarrelsome. . . . . We were often told that no one would play at skittles without beer, or without betting. We resolved to test the assertion, and the result so far is that, while our 'skittle alley' is thronged every evening, those of the public-houses around are almost deserted; and we are as noted for good words and good temper as most others are for the contrary." A skittle-ground, under proper regulations, we may here remark, is a very valuable adjunct to these Clubs, especially in large towns, where working men cannot easily get to cricket grounds or recreation fields.

"The distribution of trades among the first 700 members was as follows: One-fourth, or 172, were labourers, hawkers, porters, etc.; 109 bricklayers, masons, and carpenters, etc.; 103 boiler-makers and smiths, etc.; 61 shoemakers, curriers, etc.; 54 engineers and seamen; 99 painters and mechanics, etc.; 26 tailors; and the remainder were shopmen, agents, carriers, etc.

" Everything added to the substratum of recreation, and occupation is on an ascending scale. There are classes for reading and writing, large elocution and singing classes, a harmonic club, a benefit society, and a lending library at each Hall. Political discussions are excluded. Order is maintained in accordance with the simple rule, "that every man must be his own policeman."

The further steps taken and the principles which guided the original supporters of the Union will best be seen by the following extracts from a paper read by the present writer at the Social Science Association's meeting held at Edinburgh in October, 1863. But it may be well to state that Lord Lyttelton, who at the request of Lord Brougham became a Vice-President of the Union in October, 1862, and has ever since been one of its staunchest and most valuable supporters, made an emphatic protest early in 1863 against any attempt to impose restrictions on Working Men's Clubs in regard to the sale of malt liquors to members, and a special meeting of subscribers to the Society was called in consequence. The result was to rescind a rule originally passed prohibiting the admission of any Club into the Union which allowed the sale of such liquors, and substituting a simple recommendation, expressed in the second paragraph of the above Prospectus. It is also desirable to remark that great stress was laid at the inaugural meeting on the importance of combining educational facilities in the programme of all these Clubs ; and, on the motion of E. G. Clarke, Esq., the name of " Institute" was at length carried as an addition to the name " Club," to signify this inclusion of the educational element. Hence the idea of combining the essential elements of a Working Men's Club and a Working Men's College under the significant and comprehensive title of " Working Men's Club and Institute " was constituted the indestructible and vital principle of this movement, differentiating it from all other similar enterprises, and giving it the conditions and the guarantee, it is believed, for permanent as well as wide-spread usefulness.

"The present movement in favour of Working Men's Clubs and Institutes takes its rise in a perception of the privations and evils of various kinds to which the working classes of this country are exposed, first, from the limited nature of their domestic accommodation, and secondly, from their imperfect education. These two causes have led them to seek social intercourse and pastime in the public-house to an extent as injurious to their moral as to their pecuniary wellbeing. A third evil has been the want of places where they could meet for business purposes ; leading to the same calamitous results. Hence, various efforts to provide rooms where they might enjoy that social intercourse and rational amusement, with those opportunities for mental improvement and business meetings which the wealthier classes possess in their own homes and in various public institutions. The Mechanics' Institutes have done vast good, but not generally to the working men. The Clubs and Institutes which are now being formed in so many directions, aim at supplying all the advantages of the public-house without its evils.

"But for the establishment of such Clubs, and especially for their formation on sound principles, a stimulus *ab extra* is frequently needed, and advice, information, and experience almost always required. A central propagandist society, therefore, to give that stimulus on the one hand, to gather up and diffuse the results of reflection and experience on the other, appears to be necessary ; a society which might bring the friends of this movement into helpful relations with each other, and at the same time collect their pecuniary offerings for successive undertakings where pecuniary help is required. To meet that want the Working Men's Club and Institute Union, which I now have the honour of officially representing as its Secretary, has been formed.

" The measures which we took to carry out the foregoing objects were, in the first place, to issue circulars to the Secretaries of the various Mechanics' Institutions and Temperance Societies, to editors of provincial newspapers, and to persons known to be interested in social progress, enclosing a prospectus, and inviting co-operation in our enterprise. Various papers and pamphlets were then prepared successively, and circulated extensively in reply to inquiries, in preparation for public meetings, or in aid of local efforts generally. Several thousand copies of these publications have been thus distributed. But while we thus aimed at bringing into organized activity as large an amount as possible of benevolent zeal, we were fully convinced that we could be of permanent use to the working classes of this country only so far as our help stimulated and strengthened them to help themselves; our chief aim, therefore, has been to awaken an interest among working men in the formation, maintenance, and management of these Clubs. Our motto has been "Supplement, not supersede." And we have found working men in every direction ready to give a cordial welcome to our efforts as soon as they understand our plan and principles.

But working men cannot in general provide those funds themselves, which is perhaps fortunate, as it gives wealthier people the occasion for rendering them help of an elevating nature, and of strengthening the bonds of good feeling between different classes. From 25*l.* to 50*l.* will generally be required to furnish and fit up the Club-house, the rent of which, varying from 12*l.* to 60*l.*, the members cannot individually guarantee, while few landlords would accept their collective responsibility. It is in meeting these preliminary expenses, and in giving this guarantee, that pecuniary help is required. When fairly started, the Clubs in large towns at once, in smaller towns by-and-bye, may be made self-supporting by judicious management, coupled with a determination on the part of the members to pay their contributions as regularly as to their Friendly or Benefit Society. One Club, recently established at Wednesbury, in Staffordshire, under our impulse and guidance, has from the first resolved to be bravely independent of all assistance from their wealthier neighbours, and the Secretary informed me the other day that they have kept and intend to keep their resolution. Their Club received 320 members during the summer months, paying twopence per week, and they paid the preliminary expenses by a subscription among themselves. The receipts amounted to 17*l.* 16s. 2½d., the expenses to 15*l.* 11s. 2½d. Wednesbury, at present, is the only instance with which we are acquainted where, from the beginning, the Club has been entirely independent of extraneous help. How, then, are these needful expenses to be met in the great majority of cases?

"The Working Men's Club and Institute Union has always aimed at getting the requisite funds for starting these Clubs by stimulating local zeal, because they have felt that such an institution should be rooted in the sympathies and cherished by the support of all classes in the neighbourhood—must be developed, as it were, from the soil where it is to grow, not be planted there as an exotic merely by foreign influence.

"But in appealing for local support for any particular Club, we know that the best way of obtaining legitimate help for working men is for themselves to show they want it, and will make good use of it.

"For this reason we have dwelt much upon the value of holding a public meeting at the outset of district agitation, and getting a provisional committee formed thereat, or shortly after, consisting chiefly of working men. We have also advised the circulation of forms, to be used by influential operatives in getting the adhesion of their shopmates and acquaintances to the proposed undertaking, and which forms, when filled up, should be shown to the persons whose donations or subscriptions are requested. Whether a private preliminary meeting of persons of the wealthier class to raise the requisite funds should precede or follow the public meeting must depend on local circumstances. But working men often need counsel and guidance as well as money. Moreover, in a great number of cases they ask for, or heartily recognize, the necessity for some amount of supervision in conjunction with their own self-government and freedom. They see the necessity of fundamental rules, and they generally desire that the guardianship of these should be placed beyond the interference of members of the Club. Persons also who subscribe their money to establish an institution naturally desire some guarantee for its objects being faithfully carried out. Hence one of the most difficult problems has been to reconcile a certain amount of supervision and control with that independent action and self-government generally by the members which we all recognize as so vitally important. The plan of having two committees, one of gentlemen, and the other of working men, or one appointed by honorary members, subscribers, and donors of 10s. and upwards to hold the purse and manage all financial matters, we believe to be essentially unsound and pernicious. 1st. Because it gives rise to jealousy, collisions, and discontent, among the members, who feel that they are being treated as children, mistrusted, and deprived of one of the most important functions of government. 2nd. Because it prevents the members from acquiring experience in financial management, and from learning how to make their

Club self-supporting. 3rd. Because it checks any desire to make it so, and shifts the responsibility of keeping it out of debt from the shoulders of those who are enjoying its benefits to those of wealthy patrons, and thus inevitably tends to pauperize the members. We believe that we have, to some extent, solved the problem by recommending the appointment of three or four trustees chosen by donors and honorary members who shall hold and expend such donations and subscriptions as their constituents may contribute, and be at the same time responsible for the observance of certain fundamental rules agreed on by the persons who desire to establish the Club, but which said trustees will have no right of interfering further in its general management, or have anything to do with the ordinary members' subscriptions. Working men are accustomed to the authority of trustees in their Friendly and other Societies, and do not feel such control as the above to be at all irksome or inconsistent with their rightful liberties. Where the trustees or any other parties are responsible for the rent and taxes of the Club-house, it is, of course, right and desirable that they should have the first claim, if they desire it, upon the current subscriptions, honorary or ordinary, and have control over them to that extent. In some cases it may be necessary that all the funds should go direct to the trustees, or persons guaranteeing rent, &c., and that they should vote at monthly meetings such proportion thereof as they find they can afford, to be spent by the managing committee.

"As soon as the existence and objects of the Union became known, applications came to the office from various parts of the country for advice and information, for pecuniary help, for a visit from the Secretary, or for social influence to help in awakening a local interest for the establishment of a Club; and from the gratifying success which has hitherto attended our labours, we cannot but hope that our Society is meeting a great want of the age, and that we are becoming a not unimportant fact in the history of our country's social progress. Persons of rank, of social position, and high culture, no less than the *élite* of the working men, members of every Church, and sect, and political party, especially benevolent and accomplished ladies, in every quarter of the kingdom, have come forward to welcome and uphold us in our work. Resolutions in favour of our movement have been passed by no less than four important Conferences of representative men—viz.: The Annual Conference of Delegates from Mechanics' Institutes in connexion with the Society of Arts, held at the Adelphi, London, last May ; the Annual Conference of the British Temperance League, held at York, in July last; the Annual Conference of the West of England Temperance League, held at Bristol, in August ; and the Annual Conference of the South Staffordshire Adult Educational Society, held at West Bromwich this present month.

"Not to dwell longer on the methods we adopted, or the help we received, the immediate results are to be seen in the thirty-two Clubs and Institutes we have been instrumental in establishing in the space of twelve months, containing on a rough calculation about 7,400 members, and, as we have reason to hope, in the improved working of about twenty more, which we have assisted with information, advice, and deputations. There are also many other Clubs in process of formation, and every week brings us tidings of their establishment by benevolent friends in conjunction with the working men in different parts of the country.

" The principles which we have kept steadily in view and recommended to others as the only sound basis on which to establish these institutions have been—

1st. That they were to be managed chiefly by the working men themselves.

2nd. That they were to make facilities for social intercourse, amusements, and rational recreation, the primary object.

3rd. That they were invariably to aim also at combining with those facilities a quiet reading-room and classes for those who wished to improve themselves.

4th. That they should aim at having frequent entertainments, lectures, &c., which might be attended by the wives and daughters of members.

5th. That no intoxicating drinks, betting, or gambling, should be allowed on the premises.

6th. That boys, and youths under the age of eighteen, should not be admitted to membership.

7th. That smoking should be allowed, but in a separate room if required.

8th. That the Clubs should be not merely places to which men may go, but Societies to which they should belong.

9th. That the Clubs should be thoroughly unsectarian, socially, politically, and religiously.

For want of attending to one or other of these points many unfortunate failures have taken place, and earnest benevolent people been discouraged, so that a great and sometimes lasting hindrance has arisen to prevent a similar enterprise on wiser principles being attempted again in the same locality.

"The necessity for developing an *ésprit de corps*, a genuine spirit of fellowship, I regard as absolutely indispensable, not merely as an essential means for keeping the Clubs in existence, but as a most important end in itself, to be gained by the establishment of the Clubs.

"Experience daily confirms us in our conviction of the wisdom and importance of rigidly preserving the non-sectarian character both of this movement generally and of the individual Clubs. They are intended for persons of all sects and parties ; they occupy a common ground on which men of the most varied shades of social, religious, and political opinions may meet in pursuit of common objects in a friendly spirit and for mutual benefit. Hence they must not be employed as machinery for promoting sectarian views of any kind. Teetotallers can cordially support them because they will greatly promote sobriety ; but they must not be made into Total Abstinence Societies ; no man must be excluded from office, still less from membership, because he believes himself justified in taking a glass of wine or beer. A member of Friendly Societies can give them hearty support, because, by offering an alternative as a place of meeting to the public-house, they will greatly promote the success and benefits of those valuable organizations. A Trades' Unionist may support these Clubs for the same reasons, but neither will he be committing the Club to Trade-society views by belonging to it, nor must he endeavour to convert the Club into a means of enforcing those views. Conservatives and Liberals of all shades can promote these Clubs and Institutes, because they promote the general well-being, morality, and happiness of the working classes, help to dissipate the alienation and misunderstanding sometimes existing between different ranks of society, afford opportunities of mutual interchange of benefits and kindly courtesies, tend to dissipate that ignorance and apathy which foster so fearfully the evils which enlightened politicians of every party labour to remove. Men of all religious persuasions can give these Clubs their zealous co-operation, because whatever promotes sobriety, provident habits, health, intelligence, courtesy, self-respect, rational recreation, and mutual helpfulness, is preparing the way for higher influences and spiritual good, as well as directly promoting many of the objects which all good Christians heartily desire to accomplish.

"Hence, if sectarianism must be thus carefully avoided, it is quite clear that the Clubs cannot in general legitimately or safely be used for directly promoting either religious or political improvement, because the members, in almost all cases, or those who might wish to become members, would differ as to what was truth or improvement in those directions, or as to the proper persons for proclaiming that truth. We must be very careful, however, to repel the notion that therefore persons joining such institutions thereby show their indifference to religious or political truth. As one of our Vice-Presidents, Lord Lyttelton, observed at our last annual meeting, a man may join the Athenæum, the Carlton, or Reform Club, without ever being asked what are his religious opinions, and he will continue a member of such Club for all his life without in any way promoting, or aiming thereby to promote, particular religious views or religious practice, but he would be very much astonished if he were, therefore, to be told he belonged to a godless society, or manifested an indifference to religion.

"In most cases a Temperance, Co-operative, Loan, or Friendly Society might be formed among members of the Club, and hold its meetings at suitable times on the premises without giving occasion for any hostile feeling. So with a Trade Society, or a prayer-meeting, a religious service, or, possibly (but this is more doubtful), associations connected with matters of public importance. But in all such cases it would be necessary to keep the organization thus formed, and the proceedings connected with it, entirely independent of the organization of the Club, and in strict subordination to the general comfort, feelings, and wishes of the great majority of the members.

"Finally, the work which now lies before the Society, and which, as I have said, is increasing daily in magnitude and importance, consists :—

1. In aiding to give the impulse, and to awaken the local efforts, requisite for establishing Clubs, and especially to give the guidance needful in most cases for establishing them on sound principles.

2. In giving advice or material help requisite for sustaining or renovating Clubs already established.

3. In developing the full capacities of the Clubs for usefulness, doing this especially by means of the organization which unites them together in our central Society."

A further and fuller view of the essential principles that should be regarded as constituting the nature of these Societies, is to be found in the following passages taken from the same paper as that from which some previous passages have been quoted, read at the Social Science meeting in 1864.

We have said that the fellowship or brotherhood of its constitution and the completeness of its aim constituted the speciality and vital idea of a Working Men's College. But so far as the Clubs are to be a permanent and powerful element in the elevation of the working classes of this country, these will form, as we have also said, *their* vital force likewise. We may have Reading-rooms, Night Schools, Lectures, Mechanics' Institutes, Mutual Improvement Societies, on the one hand, and we may have Recreation Shops, Talking and Smoking-rooms, Penny Readings, Concerts, and Free-and-Easys on the other. And we may have all or any of these combined under one roof, calling the establishment a Workmen's Hall, a Working Men's Institute, or a Working Men's Club, and the said establishment, or any of the separate agencies, will undoubtedly do more or less good while it or they continue. But to start or promote them, however useful and laudable in particular cases and as preliminary steps, is not the real work now before the social reformers and friends of the working classes of this country. That work is to help bring into being organic bodies with a living soul in each, all forming part of a larger organization which should be filled with a yet higher vital force. We want societies, brotherhoods, inspired with the same noble idea as that which has been attributed to Working Men's Colleges, aiming at the completest culture and development of the mental, physical, and spiritual of the life members which may be possible under the given conditions, yet beginning with the humblest and simplest agencies, meeting the actual social wants of the least cultivated, while offering the means of gradually increasing cultivation as they may be willing and prepared to receive it. So far as we aim at less than this, so far as our movement fails to be inspired with this idea, all who promote it, we firmly believe, are only working for a little temporary good, and are preparing successive failures which will exert a disastrous influence on all subsequent efforts for the benefit of working men. The reasons for this belief are given at some length in the paper on " Industrial Colleges," also read at Edinburgh (to be found in a later part of this volume), and in the one read at Dublin in 1861.

If all this be true, it is evident that Working Men's Clubs and Institutes, when rightly constituted, may be viewed as Working Men's Colleges " in the forming," with the constituent parts in different degrees of development, as in all growing organizations. The social element, and next to it that of recreation, must always be made the principal features of a Working Men's Club in its earlier stages of existence. Free-and-easy sociability, without any interference of masters or teachers, is the very first and absolutely essential condition for the life and usefulness of the Club. But woe to that Club which aims at nothing more ! In proportion as working men obtain comfortable and roomy homes, and give up drinking habits, they will see their friends at their own homes, just as the upper classes do, and the Clubs will be proportionately less required for social purposes. But their higher uses will always be needed ; and a hundred years hence the number of Working Men's Colleges will probably far exceed that of Working Men's Clubs.

This view of the matter attributes, it will be said, rather a complex organization to what some have fancied was an extremely simple affair. True. But the higher any existence may be in the scale of creation—the greater its power and the more enduring its life—the more complex we find its organization to be, and the more complete its development. This is as true of communities and institutions as of individual beings. There was a stage in the existence of all of us, when, as in the case of certain animalculæ, the stomach was the principal and most active organ in our system ; but the laws of development and the principle of growth have carried us to higher and more perfect conditions, not in spite, but *in consequence* of such partially exaggerated development of that organ in infancy. The basis of a Working Men's Club—viz., the talking and smoking-room—is simple enough, and with the recreation department will be the principal feature in it for a long time. Nevertheless, that basis may nourish and prepare for higher forms—*will do so inevitably, if the Club lives.* At the same time, when a Club and Institute begins to outgrow the wants and tastes of the lower class of working men in any neighbourhood, another for purely Club purposes should immediately be formed, and thus a succession of suitable agencies for the gradual elevation and culture, as well as for the immediate enjoyment, of the working classes will be duly provided. All that we insist on is that, in securing the rudimentary, we must never lose sight of the higher and ultimate results. If we care only for certain excellent, but very limited objects, or for ephemeral and feeble institutions, do not let us trouble ourselves about Working Men's Clubs and Institutes. Be content with Adult Night Schools, Penny Readings, or Recreation and Refreshment Rooms. If we desire to see organizations capable of permanently aiding the working classes to attain that full culture and humanizing development which we have the highest authority in maintaining they were created to enjoy, then let us accept the ideal standard now offered. We may be quite sure that the best efforts will fail to reach it fully. But, unless we have both a true and a lofty ideal, the reality accomplished will be miserably inferior, both in quality and permanence, to what we should otherwise have attained. On the other hand, the higher influences will certainly fail to reach the great mass of working men unless the humbler attractions and advantages are first offered.

Next in order to the need for a genial welcome, and for providing attractions to the Club, as set forth in the "Occasional Paper" No. IX. (see Appendix), comes the necessity, hinted at above, for cherishing and developing the "society" spirit —the need of brotherhood, in fact—that spirit which has been at the heart of all true civilization and of all successful *corporate* action from the Dark Ages when men had to form leagues for mutual protection by the sword, down to the age of Friendly, Trade, Temperance, and Co-operative Societies. But to get this spirit of cohesion and of mutual helpfulness in a Working Men's Club and Institute, on what are we to rely ? Persons who have seen the power with which it has been manifested in Religious, Political, Trade, and Temperance organizations, say we never can awaken it in these Clubs, because there is no common bond of interest and sympathy, no motive power strong enough to arouse enthusiasm and zeal. Well, if there is not—if they are merely places where the members may go for a little individual or selfish amusement and rest—we grant they never can become real societies. But then we must equally grant that, in a great majority of cases, they are destined to have but a brief existence. Twenty years hence, in a few large towns, they may exist on the same footing as the gentlemen's West-end Clubs, but they will not take root *now*, on that footing, among the great body of the working classes, nor probably at any future time. Can we find no true and natural living bond of union for them—some principle and object that shall be capable of cherishing and unfolding that divine spirit of fellowship and sympathy which is mightier to bind men together than all their selfishness and discords are to rend them asunder ?—something that shall make them *societies* to which men may belong, and not merely *places* to which they may go ? It would be weak and shameful to doubt it.

That uniting and inspiring principle will be found, we believe, by reflecting on the various social, mental, and moral privations under which the working classes at present labour, and on the means offered by these Clubs for supplying those wants, as set forth in the foregoing remarks relative to the aim of Working Men's Colleges (p. 12). Who will deny that here we find a principle and an object capable not only of binding men together in a permanent organization, but of inspiring them with that earnestness — even enthusiasm — which we not only admit, but earnestly contend, must be called forth to make a great enterprise successful? And considering how vast and deep must be the nature of such an organization as is described in the above passages, we must not wonder that a grand, far-reaching principle and aim should be needful to fill that organization with life and power.

But it will, very probably be asked, Why are Clubs for

working men to be so much more complicated, and to aim at so much more, than gentlemen's Clubs? Evidently because of the difference in the circumstances and condition of the two classes. The gentlemen who compose the West-end Clubs in London, for the most part, have had the means of gaining tolerably complete culture at school and college. They have, moreover, far greater means and leisure for continuing that culture at home or in the world, and their occupations often have more of a humanizing and educational character than the mechanical handicrafts of the working man, while their homes admit of that social intercourse and interchange of visits from which the working men, at present, are precluded by their very limited domestic accommodation. They are, in fact, in a position to make their Club minister to higher culture when they join it. Working men, on the contrary, often need the very culture which alone would make their Club profitable to them. Hence there is a far greater number of wants requiring to be satisfied by these Clubs, in the case of the working men, than in that of the gentry. On the other hand, a proportionately greater vital force is required to lift working men, and to help them lift themselves, out of the various evils, temptations, and hindrances—social, physical, and moral— which now oppress them, than is needed merely to supply certain simple wants, already felt and recognized by persons perfectly able and willing to help themselves. That force can only be found in great principles working through suitable and varied organizations. Possibly the Clubs of the upper classes may yet find that they have an important lesson to learn from those of the working men. It is said that many of them are already beginning to feel the want of more sociability among the members, of some more definite bond of union.

There are two practical applications of these views, which are comprehensive and important.

First,—In relation to the government and practical conduct of Working Men's Clubs and Institutes.

In every enterprise and institution there must be some governing principle, as well as some inspiring idea. Where there is organic harmony and connexion between the constituent parts, this principle, to which all questions not of mere expediency should be referred as to a ruler and judge, will be found to originate in the fundamental idea. It is so in the case of Working Men's Clubs and Institutes. The governing principle is mutual helpfulness for the culture, advancement, and enjoyment (which indeed is only a species of culture) of all the members. Hence, if any question gives rise to difference of opinion concerning the management and operations of the Club, the principle says, "Do that which will best promote the largest amount of culture and happiness compatible with the *common* consent of the members. You are not to do that which will best promote those objects *according to the views of particular individuals or sections* of the Club-members, but must remember that it is a fellowship formed for *mutual* benefit, and that there must, therefore, be mutual concession to promote the *common* good. Have the largest amount of agencies and appliances for recreation, education, and social advancement that can be obtained by common consent and the constitution of your Club, but do nothing that would destroy that harmony of aim and of feeling, that balance of effort and condition, which is requisite for complete culture and associated life."

Second,—In relation to the maintenance and usefulness of the Club.

Here the fundamental idea of a Club clearly demands the application of the principle of CO-OPERATION, which we take to be that of *united contributions for proportionate profits—* but, in this case, profits for others, and not for oneself alone. Money, time, strength, education, talent, and skill, must all be brought to maintain the existence and develop the usefulness of a Club. No one must belong to it merely for the good he himself is to get out of it, but also for the good he is to bring into it. On the other hand, care should be taken that every one, in proportion to his contributions, whatever they may be, and to his capacity for receiving, should be benefited by being a member of the Club to the utmost of its capability for good. All sorts of agencies will thus be brought into operation ; on the one hand, to obtain for the Club from all classes general sympathy and help ; on the other, to make it self-supporting ; but, in any case, to give it the widest usefulness and the most permanent existence.

If, in conclusion, it be objected that we have made the maintenance and management of these Clubs too complicated and difficult to secure their efficient operation, and have set the aim and meaning of them far too high to obtain for them general support, we answer—

First,—That the best means for attaining any end are those which, whether complicated or simple, grow organically out of the fundamental conception of the enterprise, institution, or machine, and which, therefore, are in harmony with its parts and adapted to its objects.

Second,—That Working Men's Clubs and Institutes, in our judgment, must be such as we have described, or they will ere long be *nothing at all;* that if they have merely a body without a soul, they can have no enduring life, and are as certain to die as any of Owen's or Fourier's Phalanxes; but that if they *have* life they will inevitably *grow;* and then in time they will become what, perhaps, we rightly shrink from imagining them in their earlier stages.

Third,—That if loftiness of aim, or difficulties of execution, will preclude any important enterprise from obtaining the sympathy and support either of the higher or the working classes of this kingdom, we have entirely misread the history of our country, and misjudged our national character.

Concluding here our sketch of the history and general principles of the movement, we propose giving in the next chapter an account of various individual Clubs, with a glance at the causes of their failure or success.

CHAPTER II.

THE following extracts from the "Occasional Papers," Nos. I., II., V., and VI., published by the Parent Society in 1863-4, will afford the best indication of the kind of work done by the Society during its earlier stages, and the immediate results :—

"DERBY.—The Derby Working Men's Association was founded by the Rev. J. Erskine Clarke, in August, 1856. It has excellent central premises near the Market-place. It is governed by a Committee, consisting of seven workmen, elected annually, and a president, hon. treasurer, and hon. secretary, who, not being benefit members, do not submit themselves to election, but hold office so long as they are willing to do so. This constitution has been found to work well at the Lichfield Working Men's Association, which was founded (likewise by Mr. Clarke) in 1854, and which is still [1863] in a most flourishing condition. 'Our Derby Association,' wrote that gentleman, however, in 1863, to the Secretary of the Parent Society, ' has not made as much progress in the way of attracting members of the hard-working orders as it ought in so large a place—our average number of benefit members since the commencement has been about 120.' The following account was then given :—

" ' The members pay 6d. a-month. The reading room is spacious, well warmed, carpeted, well lighted and furnished, and in winter there is also a conversation room. The only recreative appliances are six tables, with squares for draughts and chess painted on them, which are almost always in use, and some solitaire boards. There is no smoking room. The question was discussed at a general meeting of the members, and the non-smokers were the majority. [We fear that the want of concession in this respect, judging by wide experience, accounts in some measure for there not being a larger number of members.] The housekeeper provides coffee, tea, and simple refreshments, if required. There is a library of about 700 volumes, which is much valued and used.

" ' One of the largest and best bodies of Odd-Fellows have just, of their own accord, transferred their lodge from a public-house to the premises of the Association, and other lodges are moving for the same change. A Co-operative Store rent part of the premises, but are in no way connected with the Association, except as tenants.

" ' Attached to the Association is the Derby Penny Bank, which, we are told, has been of vast service to the poor of the town.

" ' For three winters the Committee conducted Saturday evening entertainments of music and reading in one of the large halls of the town, which were most successful, and attended by vast numbers of people, largely of the labouring classes, with a remarkably large proportion of grown men. A full account of these was given by Mr. Clarke, in *Fraser's Magazine* of October, 1861. Various classes have been attempted at the Association, but, we regret to hear, with very small success, both teachers and scholars being so hardly worked during the day, that they seem to have lost energy by the night-time.'

" On the above account we ventured to comment as follows in our ' Occasional Paper ' No. II. : ' The last sentence furnishes another illustration of the necessity for making classes for instruction spring out of, and continue a close connexion with, amusement and conversation, in the way suggested in our pamphlet, " Hints and Suggestions," &c., p. 13. Many working men have enough energy left of an evening for a discussion class; others for an elocution class, which leads to a study of English literature; others, again, according to natural aptitude, for a class on natural history, English history, or even political economy, when bearing on strikes, machinery, &c., an interest having been first aroused by the discussion class.

" ' Possibly the usefulness of this excellent Society, founded by one who during the last seven or eight years has given a great impulse to such efforts for improving the condition of the working classes, might be increased by having an *un*-carpeted room open for conversation and games all the year

round, and by placing in it two or three bagatelle-boards;
also by having a separate room for smoking, and, if possible,
a skittle-alley, which may sometimes, as our friends at Soho
remind us, be made in a cellar, and during winter evenings
proves very attractive. Could not weekly payments of 1d.
or 2d. be tried ? We agree that 120 is far too small a number for such a town as Derby.'

" ' The following rule, also, while excellent for a professedly
Christian Church organization, is clearly a great barrier to the
adhesion of working men generally :—

" 'Persons wishing to become members must be proposed
and seconded by members, and are then balloted for by the
Committee. No member is eligible for election who does not
acknowledge the Bible as the rule of life.'"

" The comments made on the Derby organization, in the
above passages, were cordially welcomed by its principal supporters, and the Secretary to the Union was invited by the
Rev. J. Erskine Clarke to go down and address a public meeting in Derby on the subject generally. This he did in November last [1863], when the mayor presided, and a good attendance of working men was secured. The various suggestions
offered by Mr. Solly were at once acted on, and the results
are given in the following extract from a letter received by
the Secretary a few weeks later :—

" ' You will be pleased to hear that our Clubbified Association is going on famously. We have had about 300 penny
members weekly, and that without making it known by hand-
bill at all—for we were afraid of too *many* coming before we
had power to manage matters. We have now got that, or
shall have it on Monday, as we have engaged a hall-keeper to
live on the premises, and do nothing else.

" 'We have bought another larger bagatelle-table than the
one you ordered for us, and both are in constant use.

" ' If you are coming this way again I shall be very glad
of a visit, and to show you how we have profited by your
visit. We find, as at Scarborough, that the smoke room is
now comparatively *little used,* the games being more attractive,
and we don't allow smoking where the bagatelle tables are, in
the large lower room, which you remember. Of course, there
are draughts, chess, &c., in the smoke room.' [For reasons
which Mr. Clarke would explain at length to any one desirous

of hearing them, this useful and promising Society has not been able to continue in existence.]

"HOLLOWAY.—[The following account was communicated to the Council by the promoters of the Club in this district, in March, 1864 :—]

" In the winter of 1859, some gentlemen interested in the mental, social, and moral improvement of working men, commenced some classes for instruction in reading, writing, and arithmetic (in connexion with a Bible-class), in the Holloway ragged school.

"In the course of the three following winters, there were added to these classes—lectures, a temperance association, a singing-class, a provident fund and coal club, a free library of about seventy volumes, and a Sunday evening service. These various operations were managed by a Committee, of whom some were *bonâ fide* working men, and all the members were banded together as 'The Holloway Working Men's Christian Association.'

" A certain amount of success attended the movement; but the good accomplished, as well as the difficulties encountered, showed that much more benefit would be the result under more favourable circumstances. By the kindness of the Ragged School Committee, the use of their rooms was allowed at a merely nominal charge, and were opened every evening in the week ; but, although this was a great boon, it was found that the mere fact of meeting in a school was prejudicial to the work. Many men would not come to the place, simply because it was a schoolroom ; and, beyond that, it was practically impossible to make the rooms comfortable and inviting ; nor could more than one thing be attempted on the same evening. There could be no comfortable reading room always open ; smoking, necessarily, could not be allowed, nor could refreshments be supplied. The Committee often debated the desirability and possibility of taking premises expressly for the purpose they had in view, but they were men of no great standing or influence, and were doubtful whether they could raise the means necessary for what, in their neighbourhood, at all events, would be an experiment. Just at this time their Hon. Secretary [Mr. Tattersall], when attending the meetings of the Social Science Congress, in the Guildhall, had put into his hands, by the Rev. H. Solly, the prospectus of a proposed

C

'Working Men's Club and Institute Union.' It embodied all that their three years' experience at Holloway showed was wanted by working men.

"In the spring of 1863, the Hon. Secretary put himself in communication with Mr. Solly, and the result of the useful information and practical advice given him by that gentleman was to convince him that it was as practicable to establish a Working Men's Club and Institute in Holloway as in other places—in some respects, almost more so, for there was a fair number of working men already strongly in favour of such a movement.

"On the 20th April, 1863, a meeting was held, and a provisional committee elected, the whole of whom, with the exception of the Secretary, were working men. The first thing to do was to secure the co-operation of working men, and then the countenance (by their names, their support, and their money) of the clergy and ministers of all denominations, and some of the more influential laymen of the neighbourhood.

"A 'Form,' supplied by the Working Men's Club and Institute Union, setting forth the objects of the proposed Club, was circulated, and the signatures of about one hundred working men, who pledged themselves to join such a Club when established, were obtained.

" A public meeting was then held (1st June), at which about sixty men were present, when rules were made, and a permanent Committee (two-thirds of whom were working men) and other officers elected.

"Suitable premises were obtained, and on September 21, 1863, " The Holloway Working Men's Club and Institute " was opened—the first week free, subsequently at a charge of one penny per week.

" It has now been open five months, and during that time to 27th February, 1864, 505 men have joined the Club. Of course, a great number joined from mere curiosity ; others ceased to attend as the blush of novelty wore off, and it has been found necessary to suspend a considerable number of youths ; but there are now 220 members in more or less regular attendance. The average number paying weekly during the five months has been 151, and the average daily attendance 73. About Christmas there was a very marked falling off, but that has been partly recovered ; and for the last six weeks the weekly payments have varied very slightly from 130, and the average daily attendance has been steadily about 70.

" The premises are open from 8 A.M. to 10 P.M., and are provided with a good supply of newspapers, periodicals, and games. A bagatelle-table is making. A library of nearly 400 volumes has been collected, and is in much request. Classes for instruction in reading, writing, and arithmetic, meet twice a-week. A discussion and elocution class meets on another evening. A drum and fife band has been formed, as also a " bank and coal club." Lectures or readings are given every Thursday, and a social concert, very well attended, is held every Saturday evening.

" Good refreshments—coffee, tea, ginger beer, and cake— are supplied at a low price, and yet leave a small margin of profit. No single article is charged more than one penny, yet in five months 16l. 14s. 8½d. has been received for refreshments."

" WANDSWORTH.—Towards the end of 1862 ten gentlemen in this locality subscribed the money requisite for procuring, as premises for a Club, a public-house, paying in equal proportions as follows :—

Lease for twenty-one years and Fixtures, together with sundry expenses on entering...	£200
Repairs, Papering, Tables, Stools, Crockery, &c.	75
Games and incidental expenses, about ...	25
	£300

" The *locus standi* being thus secured, the Secretary to the Union met the subscribers and a dozen working men, when a constitution was agreed upon, for the most part in accordance with the principles and plans recommended by the Union. In little more than a month the Club was formally opened by a tea meeting, followed by a crowded and enthusiastic public meeting in the Assembly Rooms, presided over by G. F. White, Esq., President of the Club, and addressed by the Rev. Hugh Allen, Rector of St. George's, Southwark,

Rev. J. H. Rylance, of St. Paul's, Westminster-road, George
Cruikshank, Esq., Dr. Longstaff, Mr. George Howlett, and
the Rev. H. Solly. At this time the management and responsibilities of the Club, under the Fundamental Rules,
were given into the hands of a Committee of twelve working
men, with a President, Vice-President, Treasurer, and Secretary, all to be chosen annually; and in addition there is " a
Council of gentlemen (formed of the landlords of the Club
[the ten named above] and of any liberal donors to its funds),
who shall confer with the Committee on all matters requiring
grave deliberation." One hundred members enrolled their
names immediately after the opening meeting, and the number
afterwards rose to 205. The members pay 2d. a week, and
none are admitted under eighteen years of age. Each receives
a card of membership (price 1d.) and any member is at liberty
to introduce one friend to the benefits of the Club on ordinary
occasions by the payment of a halfpenny. All discussions on
controversial theology are excluded from the meetings and
classes of the Club. The rooms are not to be used for
ordinary Club purposes on Sundays. On Saturday evenings
they have readings for the members, occasionally accompanied
with vocal and instrumental music. Some of these meetings
have been attended by as many as seventy working men. A
class for reading, writing, and arithmetic, &c., is also held on
Tuesday and Thursday evenings, and the members have
formed a Cricket Club among themselves, which is prosperous.
The games that take best are draughts and chess ; the skittles
have been used mostly by the younger members. A discussion class meets on alternate Friday evenings. The
managers of a Mechanics' Institute in the neighbourhood,
considering that the Club was carrying out the objects for
which they had founded their Iustitution unsuccessfully, determined to close it, and to hand over its library, containing
more than 1,000 volumes, to the Club. These books, increased by Sir Walter Scott's works and other British
classics, have been very much used by the members. The
Vice-President of the Club writes : " The publicans are complaining of the loss of their customers, as many of the members of the Club used to drink a great deal, but are now becoming very steady."

" This Club has done and is doing much good, but its success has not been so great as could be desired, owing, first, to the want of a large hall for weekly meetings, and, secondly, to the want of a better and more active management during the first few months of its existence. Members got into arrears, and there were no steps taken to draw them back to the Club. Readings were given from valuable works, but perhaps not of a sufficiently varied and interesting character. "Chat meetings" could not be held for want of a room large enough for the purpose."

[This was one of the Pioneer Clubs, which has at length succumbed to the apathy of the working men in the neighbourhood and the want of the large room above referred to, as well as to other wants, concerning which we have since gained more experience.]

"Soho (London).—Early in last year [1863], a leading article in the *Builder*, favourably noticing the Union, was read by several working men in the neighbourhood of Soho, and they resolved at once to write to its Secretary. The result was a conference between them and a deputation from the Council, at which they stated the wants and wishes of the working men of their district. They were none of them total abstainers, and some had been hard drinkers, but they described the longing which working men felt, after a hard day's toil from six o'clock in the morning, for the refreshment of social intercourse ; and among the younger men for some kind of games during some part of the evening ; dwelling at the same time on the want of accommodation in their own homes. They referred to the practice so prevalent among them, of standing at the street corners for a little chat, often till their toes were half frozen, rather than go into the public-house, or when their money was all gone ; and said they knew of scores of men who would gladly join a Working Men's Club at once, and pay 2d. a-week, giving their labour to fit it up, if only they were helped by having the materials found for them, and the rent of a house guaranteed. Ultimately, a member of the Council agreed to guarantee the rent (45*l.*) of a suitable house, which they named, at 24, Crownstreet, Soho, and gave them 10*l.* towards the preliminary expenses. A strong recommendation of the undertaking to the support of gentlemen and tradesmen in the district was drawn up and signed by members of the Council and the secretary, armed with which, and a little help from the secretary in canvassing the neighbourhood, the additional sum of 23*l.* was collected. This enabled them to make tables and benches, fit up conveniently and floor an outhouse for a smoking-room, colour-wash the whole house from top to bottom, purchase crockery and a few games, knock down and put up partitions, and introduce gas-fittings into every room. They worked so heartily, that, within five weeks from their interview with the Council, they had the Club in full operation, with about 140 members. A discussion class was formed, and proved to be the mainstay of the Club. A member of the Council presented them with about sixty interesting volumes, and Mr. Cassell kindly added a present of his valuable Pictorial History of England. The money requisite for purchasing a large bagatelle-table, greatly coveted by them, was lent by the Union; several public-houses in the neighbourhood having capital bagatelle-boards, and constant use for them.

" The management was vested entirely in the hands of the members, who elected their own Committee, President, Treasurer, and Secretary; but in the very first interview with the Council, the originators of the Club expressed their strong desire that the Fundamental Rules recommended by the Union should be made its basis, and that Trustees should be appointed, who would be responsible for their due observance.

" A skittle-alley was very much wished for; and there being no back-yard, they laid one down in the cellar as soon as they got the requisite funds, making up for the shortness of the range (25 feet) by increasing the weight of the bowls, but, unfortunately, this had to be closed, partly from the damage done to the walls, and partly from the difficulty of preserving sufficient order.

" On Saturday nights the house at first was very full; and a thoroughly unobjectionable ' free-and-easy,' consisting of a meeting for songs, recitations, &c., when concertinas were brought, was held in two rooms with the partition removed. It was greatly enjoyed by men who formerly thought such enjoyment impossible, or found it unattainable, except under influences of a depraving or expensive character, but for want of elocution and glee classes, as well as from other unfortunate circumstances connected with the management of the Club, there was not a sufficient supply of new recitations, songs, &c., when the first stock was worn threadbare.

" The use of a large hall in the neighbourhood for weekly entertainments, to which the members should be allowed to bring their wives and daughters, was to be obtained during the winter months, and one or more excursions were intended to be organized during the summer.

" Considerable reliance was placed on the help to be obtained by these weekly entertainments in drawing persons to support the Club ; but the members were disappointed in their expectation of being able to obtain the hall. About three months ago, however, a smaller hall in the immediate neighbourhood was procured by the assistance of the Council of the Union, and a series of penny readings, kindly commenced by C. H. Plumptre, Esq., was at first tolerably successful, but, owing to the want of time on the part of the secretary, bills announcing the readings for the ensuing week were not ready for distribution at the close of each entertainment. This greatly hindered the success of the experiment. Members of the Club and of the Working Men's College choir, Great Ormond-street, with other friends, kindly supplied excellent singing between the readings.

" Altogether, the Soho Club has not thoroughly prospered; and it must be frankly confessed it is at present a failure. Difficulties and drawbacks must, however, be expected in all new undertakings. They must not discourage us when we can see their origin, and guard against them in the future.

" The fundamental deficiency in the Soho Club, as admitted now by the members themselves, was the want of two or three gentlemen of business habits, to work on the Committee with the other members, who were all of the working class. One or two of those most anxious for the Club, and taking a prominent part in its establishment, were not equal to the position and duties they assumed. There was not enough knowledge of each other among the managing members generally, nor sufficient friendship between them. Jealousies and dissensions crept in, and errors were made in various ways, which would probably all have been either avoided or rectified, had there been two or three persons of influence and business faculty among them to act as mediators and counsellors, and whose opinions would have been deferred to without difficulty by the working men. This is the view taken of their past trials by themselves, and it is entirely confirmed both by our own observation and by that of intelligent members of one or two other Clubs who have mingled with them. There is often much less coherence and good understanding among working men in the heart of London than in country towns, making the establishment and maintenance of a Club far more difficult, and the need of help in working it from men of a higher social position the more necessary. This help, however, every month's experience proves more convincingly, is generally of great value, and in most cases it is essential for success.

" Efficient supervision by the Managing Committee is also extremely important, and the want of this has been another prominent cause of defective results at the Club in question.

" Brighter days, however, we hope, may yet be in store for it, and we trust that past experience and the energetic efforts of remaining members and of new and zealous friends will be crowned with success.

" The particulars of expenditure in opening this Club were so moderate, that it may be interesting to our readers to have them in detail : Timber, gaspipes and fittings, nails, hooks, colour for walls, whiting, &c., 19l. 4s. 6d.; printing bills, circulars, cards, &c., 2l. 3s. 6d.; games, 7l. 14s. 6d.; household articles and utensils, 3l. 1s. 4d.; forms, table, and cupboard, 1l. 16s.; newspapers and books, 18s.; stamps and stationery, 19s. 6d.; new stove, 8s. 6d.; sundries, 12s. 6d.

[The hopes expressed above were not realized. Dishonest management, qnarrels, and very objectionable practices, ultimately ruined an enterprise apparently so well begun, and which, while it lasted, had been productive of such beneficial results. Even since the foregoing account was written, striking evidence has been received of the good which this Club had been the means of accomplishing. But in the more recently-formed " St. James and Soho " Club we see how the experience gained by a failure may promote subsequent success.]

PRESTON.—The following account of the Preston Club was kindly communicated to the Secretary of the Union by the

Rev. R. Macnamara, late of "All-Saints'," in that town, in a letter dated 18th February, 1864:—

"The Committee, which was formed on the night of your address at Mr. Clapham's schoolroom, has been very active ever since. We took a large ten-roomed house near the Market-place, and opened on the 1st of the present year. The outlay for furnishing and painting the place has been about 300*l.* All of this has been collected from people connected with Preston (excepting about 30*l.*, which we still owe). We have 600 members. We charge twopence per week, or one penny a-day. We have a good refreshment-room, to which non-members can come and have soup, tea, coffee, pies, and cold meat, at a reasonable fare (not quite so cheap as at the cheap dining-rooms!); or people can bring their own refreshments, and be accommodated with hot water, cups and saucers, &c., at 1d. a-head. This will suit the market country folks when it is fully known and understood; and by this means we hope to send them home richer and more sober than the whiskey-shop keeper does. We have an excellent gymnasium, which is used by our young men up till time of closing, 10.30 P.M. This you should look at if you come to Preston, in order that you may make it one of the main things you recommend in your addresses. . . . It has been a most pleasing thing for me to think of, that I was the humble means of launching this very useful movement in that large and important town. My little Club has become almost absorbed in the central one (Lord-street). Mr. Chapman's (St. Peter's) has also 400 members, and is doing very well." [This gentlemen left Preston shortly after, but the Rev. W. C. Squier, who had taken part in the formation, threw himself energetically into the enterprise, and materially contributed to its success.]

Additional interesting particulars were given by Mr. Livesey in letters to the Secretary, from which a few extracts are given, and in Liverpool and Manchester papers. The refreshment and dining-rooms department makes the Club self-supporting:—

"We have now 600 members. Our Club embraces the following departments: Instruction, including a newsroom, small library, and classes for writing, discussion, elocution, and chess-playing, and other classes will probably follow; amusement, including chess, draughts, dominoes, and, above all, a bagatelle-table; physical exercise in a small gymnasium in a ground adjoining; refreshments, consisting of tea, coffee, soups, pies, &c., but no intoxicating liquors. All these combined keep us very busy, and bring in a return more than sufficient to cover expenses."

" Good management and suitable attractions are sufficient to make a Club pay, provided, of course, the building is a suitable one and in the right place. This management cannot be expected in most cases by placing it entirely in the hands of working men, and here it is that many, I fear, are likely to make a mistake. Few of them can give the time requisite, and still fewer can incur any pecuniary responsibility. A committee of working men alone will seldom be found to agree, and it is not to be expected that their experience can give them the best ideas of what a public institution requires, and of those adaptations on which success will often depend." [Our own experience fully confirms the general tenor of these remarks. Further particulars concerning this capital Club will be found subsequently.]

We next offer for consideration some more recent experiences, communicated in the spring of 1866 to Cassell's *Working Man*, with the lessons they teach us. Before quoting them, however, it is important to bear in mind what we then urged on the friends of this movement—viz., that a Club may have been eminently successful in one sense—viz., in benefiting its members and improving the condition of the whole neighbourhood, yet have failed to make both ends meet in its financial department. On the other hand, a Club may be quite self-supporting, yet be doing very little good. This latter case might occur when a building has been presented rent-free to the members, or when the profits from bagatelle-boards, skittle-grounds, or entertainments of a low character might bring in a good deal of money, while the Club was doing little to promote the well-being of its members. We would especially recommend this consideration to the attention of those persons who imagine that the great test of a Club being wanted, of its being on a healthy basis, and likely to last, is, that it should, from the beginning of its career, or very soon after, be supported entirely without help from any but its ordinary members. Unquestionably, where this can be legitimately accomplished, it is a great point gained, even as it is always an object to be earnestly striven after. But most of us had to be carried, we suppose, before we could walk; and we must not wonder if these societies, which will necessarily work a great change in the habits and tastes of those whom they are meant to benefit, should not at once receive all that support from working men which alone could make them independent of other help. We are not speaking now of the capital requisite for preliminary outlay. This, of course, must generally be found by wealthier parties than weekly wage men, although, when the latter can be induced to come forward in sufficient numbers, either to subscribe for shares in a Limited Liability Company for building a Club-house and establishing a Club, or to give donations for the purpose, we need not say this is the best possible basis for its formation.

Honorary members' subscriptions, however, or occasional levies on friends, to meet even current expenses, have been hitherto generally found necessary. That pioneer Club established by the Rev. E. Boteler Chalmer, in Salford, Manchester, has needed and received such support, we understand, from its commencement in 1858; but the amount of good it has accomplished is remarkable.

In like manner the two Clubs which followed Mr. Chalmer's in order of time—viz., Mrs. Bayly's, at Notting-hill, and Miss Cooper's, in Duck-lane, Westminster, have been successful to an extent as striking as it is gratifying, in benefiting their respective neighbourhoods; but both have required continual help from honorary subscriptions, and the supporters of the latter have no desire or intention of making it self-supporting. The weekly subscription there is only a halfpenny, and although many of the members would willingly pay a penny, yet, as it is greatly used by numbers of the very poorest working men—costermongers, scavengers, crossing-sweeps, &c.—Miss Cooper has always objected to increasing the subscription, in order that no one should be excluded on that ground, and because she finds no difficulty in raising the considerable sum required to make up the deficiency. No Club in the country is probably doing more good than this and the one at Notting-hill, and good of a kind which leads and enables the members in various ways to improve their own pecuniary, as well as mental and moral, condition, so that it would be impossible to give money to help other people in a way that more directly assists them to help themselves. All this is equally true of the very large and flourishing Club at Leeds, established by Mr. Darnton Lupton, and which costs him a comparatively large sum every year, as well as of various others through the country, which at present require honorary members' subscriptions to make both ends meet.

Moreover, in the case of Clubs, many, if not most of them, only require extraneous help for a time. In the spring of 1865, the Union received returns from seventy-seven Clubs, thirty-seven of which stated that they were self-supporting; but only a small proportion of these had been so from the first, while some of them would not continue to be able always to claim that distinction. Owing, in part, often chiefly, to the needful system of allowing weekly payments where they are preferred, most Clubs are liable to great fluctuations of prosperity, especially during the summer months. About 100 Clubs sent no returns at all, and it is to be feared a large proportion of them had no great success to announce in this direction; yet, unquestionably, like the thirty which returned themselves as non-self-supporting, they were nearly all doing much good. We now give results obtained down to 1866.

Among Clubs that are distinguished by having been at once self-supporting and extensively useful, we know of none that excel, few that equal, the Camden Town Working Men's Club, in King-street, Camden Town, London, N.W., commenced in 1863. Several have been as useful, and others as pecuniarily successful; but few, if any, have equally combined success in both departments. One cause has undoubtedly been excellent premises, including a concert and lecture hall, in a central situation. Another is to be found in the determination of the promoters and managers, from the first, to make the Club something more than a place for mere recreation. They have fostered both the educational and commercial element, while they have, at the same time, been untiring in their attention to the recreation department. But the main secret of their success, humanly speaking, has lain in the devoted, self-sacrificing zeal and judgment of its committee and secretaries; while a still more noteworthy, because more important and rarer, element of success is to be found in the fact that, in the concluding words of their report, as a

committee, they have always " sought wisdom and strength
where alone it can be found." It is not, indeed, often that a
Club committee can be found in which, as in that of Camden
Town, the persons composing it are all of them prepared and
willing to commence their weekly meeting with united prayer.
But we must be permitted to say we think it would be a wonderful blessing, and the surest guarantee of success, if they
could do so, and that, where that was not found practicable,
if those who were thus disposed could either meet together
at some other time to ask for help or guidance, or would each
individually do this before coming to the meeting. It must
be distinctly observed, that neither this course, nor that which
the Camden Town Committee have followed, in the slightest
degree compromises the strictly neutral, unsectarian character
of the Club, which, indeed, cannot be too jealously maintained.
If any of the members of a Club, whether when meeting for
business or any purpose, *unanimously* desire to engage in
united prayer in a room where for the time being they have
the sole right of access, no other person's liberty of conscience
is affected, no principle of the Club is in the slightest degree
violated. But, of course, all depends upon the desire being
unanimous.

One ground for apprehension with regard to this Club—
but it is a serious one, and requiring constant attention—is,
that it has been so good that tradesmen in the neighbourhood
use it, and the class of working men by whom these Clubs are
especially needed is not so fully represented as one could wish.
This drawback is probably increased by the ground-floor
rooms being frequently occupied by classes and friendly
societies, instead of being kept for sociable chat and the inevitable " weed." The best room in the house is given up to
a " reading-room." However, there is no doubt as to the incalculable good the Camden Town Club has been instrumental in effecting. The members last year formed a Limited
Liability Company, and, with the aid of friends, purchased
the whole of the premises. This spirited proceeding places
them in a very advantageous position as regards rent, &c.,
and will probably prove eventually a source of profit, even to
the shareholders. [Since the above was written this Club
has experienced a severe check to its prosperity. But having
purchased the premises, the Club not only holds its ground,

but is beginning to recover its former position. It is much
to be hoped that the committee will encourage the attendance
of the men who now go to the public-houses in the neighbourhood for sociable intercourse, and give them the best accommodation the house affords. Some time ago we heard of
a hard-working man going to this club one night, to spend an
hour or two there [and see what it was like. He was very
anxious to stay, but found it so full he could not get a seat,
and he told the Secretary subsequently that he went away to
his old haunts, and spent eight Shillings that same night
in drink and " treating !"]

A few other Clubs should be specially mentioned as honourably distinguished, in the same way as Camden Town, for
combining usefulness and financial success—viz., those at
Wednesbury, Staffordshire; at South Shields and Sunderland, in Durham ; at Preston and Buersill, in Lancashire ; at
Guildford, in Surrey; and at Essex-road, Islington, London.

The Wednesbury Club is also distinguished by owing its
success almost exclusively to *bond fide* weekly-wage operatives, the only person a little above that rank among their
managers being a clerk, whose position, character, and influence, however, have been a most valuable element in the
enterprise. These men have raised more than 200*l.* among
themselves (about 7*l.* only having been contributed by other
parties), and the Club has been inspired from the first with
that corporate, brotherly spirit on which special stress was
laid in the first chapter.

The same description applies to the society at South Shields.
The Club in this town is also specially deserving of notice,
from having been founded as a " Working Men's *Institute* "
so far back as 1850, and having worked on quietly and use-
fully ever since. The members decided on adding the features
and name of a Club, after a visit we paid them in 1864, and
their prosperity and usefulness have largely increased. They
numbered, in January last, 653 members, and during the last
year they have been self-supporting, for the first time in the
course of their existence. They have a library of 1,298
volumes. Classes for arithmetic and writing, shorthand,
French, and German. Six entertainments and six lectures
during the six months ending December, 1865. But, since
there is no restriction as to the age of admission, there is a

little reason to fear that the men may be in danger of being swamped by the youths. Probably, however, as there is very good management, that evil may be guarded against by having separate rooms for the juveniles and adults. We shall have something to say on this head in speaking of unsuccessful Clubs. It is utterly impossible to have a Working Men's Club, if youths are admitted to it, without the provision of separate rooms.

At Preston, in addition to an energetic and public-spirited committee and officers, the Club has been fortunate in having its refreshment and dining-rooms admirably managed; while, by turning its excellent situation (near the market) to good account, and throwing open the refreshment-room to the public, it clears 50l. a-year. Of course no other rooms in a Club should be open to the general public without payment; and we believe that admitting casual visitors to them systematically at a penny a visit is in general a great mistake. There are exceptions, however, where the plan works well. Some Clubs make a good deal of money by it, but it tends to impair, if not to destroy, the Club principle. To the refreshment-rooms, however, public admission is quite a different thing. The Preston Club has lately held, in conjunction with the Literary Institution of that town, an Industrial Exhibition, whereby it will clear for its share of the profits 1,000l.!

By its second annual report we see that the large sum of 720l. had been received during the year for refreshments, while the cost of provisions, &c., was only 561l. No intoxicating drinks are sold, and it is gratifying to observe how large a profit may be made in some localities by good management, without taking any steps towards bringing the Club to a level with the beershop. The average weekly number of members was 132; the previous year, 314; but the falling off during the latter part of last year may fairly be attributed to the attractions of their very successful exhibition. There had been sold during the year 3,410 tickets at 2d., and 3,784 at 1d., figures which represent a great amount of good conferred on workmen and their homes. No mention, however, is made in their report of classes; and for want of a hall they are unable to have entertainments, readings, or lectures. This, no doubt, is a great drawback. The hall, however, they hope shortly to procure by alterations of their premises or building, and the money they have gained by this exhibition ought to put them in possession of one capable of seating 600 people. With regard to classes, we would ask the managers of the Club to consider the suggestions made in a former chapter respecting the importance of promoting educational improvements in Working Men's Clubs, and some of the ways in which gentlemen's help may be so valuable for that purpose.

The Buersill Club is to be marked with special honour, as having originated and been supported *entirely* by weekly-wage operatives (a few Sunday-school teachers, &c.), in the darkest days of the cotton famine. The feeling and principle of fellowship, self-help, and reliance upon a higher blessing, have nobly distinguished the cotton-spinners of this Lancashire settlement. It should be mentioned that the sympathy and encouragement of the vicar were of great value to them.

At Guildford and Essex-road there has been wise and vigorous management, combined with considerable attention to the educational element, while recreation has been actively cultivated. [This last Club has had a check in its useful career, in consequence of having to leave its commodious premises and remove to less desirable ones. But we trust it will soon once more acquire a suitable habitation.]

In the *Sunderland* Club we find from their returns (though not personally acquainted with them) that there has been an excellent discussion class; French and drawing ditto, moderately well attended; elocution ditto, poor attendance; harmonic meeting every Saturday night, crowded. All this has, of course, been both cause and effect of their prosperity. A good discussion class is one of the best signs of a healthy state of things, and a great aid to it. Few things more effectually promote mental improvement and intellectual life. Theological topics should, however, be invariably excluded, as their discussion is almost certain to break up the Club, besides being objectionable on other grounds. The number of members in this Club last January was 750, and the average throughout the year was between 500 and 600. This is a very high average. Independently of other advantages, there must be capital management here, and a good spirit of fellowship among the members. The elocution class, however, ought to be better attended, or the harmonic meetings will, perhaps, suffer from want of new recitations and readings. [A

Limited Liability Company has been formed by the committee for the purchase of a more commodious Club-house, with more space for out-door games. The purchase was completed in January, and the Club was then shortly to remove.

The following letter, received in May, this year, describes some of the measures that have made the Club to which it refers one of the most successful in the country :—

" . . . I believe that in many cases the failure of these excellent institutions is attributable to a want of *life* and *spirit* in the management. When we were making arrangements to open ours it was freely observed on all hands that "it would never do." Similar attempts had been made before, and none of them succeeded, so this one must fail. One very shrewd townsman asked me, I remember, if it would last six months ; so that we did not begin under the most encouraging circumstances. . . . The superiority of the accommodation we offered to anything to be found at the public-houses had much to do with our success. Having got the house, we set about furnishing it ; and *that* we did in a thoroughly substantial and *comfortable* style. The floors were all matted, and so were the stairs ; in the reading rooms every reader had an armchair, as good, if not better, than he would find in a reading room at 21s. a-year—in fact, our motto was, " It is no use half doing the thing," and experience has proved that it was a politic course. . . . The Club was opened according to announcement, and *remained open, free*, for a week, during which there were some thousands of visitors ; and open it has remained ever since, in spite of the gloomy prognostications surrounding its birth, except for three days, when it was closed for removal to its present much more commodious premises. Of course there was a large amount of prejudice against it at first ; but I don't think it has many enemies now, except a few publicans. . .

It has not yet, however, nearly so many *active supporters* among the intelligent working men as I could wish, but no doubt that will come ; they *will*, in time, outgrow the habit of going to the public-house to hold their social intercourse ; and the Committee of our Club, while longing for that time, are thankful for the measure of success they have already had, and determined to spare no effort to increase it. . . . It has now been determined to hold an Industrial Exhibition in connexion with the Club in August or September. Will you be north about then ?"]

The *Newcastle* Working Men's Club is distinguished by zealous and efficient management, excellent entertainments, good discussion and drawing-class, and a first-rate singing-class, the latter consisting of between sixty and seventy young people of both sexes, and in which the presence of females has been thoroughly beneficial. Their able and genial-hearted teacher received a present of a watch from them last Christmas, for his kind and disinterested labours. This Club has excellent premises, in a very good locality, yet it is not supported as well as it deserves to be; only numbers about 350 members, pays its way in winter, but is not self-supporting, owing to the falling off in summer time. The age at which members are admitted, however (seventeen), is far too young, and must have something to do with the defective support of *men*. The best room in the house, also, instead of being devoted to social intercourse, as it should be, is given up to newspapers and silent reading. The Club has depended rather too much, perhaps, on recreation and continual excitement for success; too little on cherishing steady sociability and good fellowship among its members. This is not an uncommon mistake, but it is a serious one. However, the Newcastle friends have done, and are doing, an admirable work, and have great reason to be thankful.

The original Club and Institute at *Leeds*, which was established by Mr. Darnton Lupton, J.P., in 1863, and which has been one of the most flourishing and useful in the kingdom, though very far from being self-supporting, averages between 900 and 1,000 members through the winter months. Its eminent usefulness has given a great impulse to the establishment of Clubs in the district. They have one or two entertainments at least, and one lecture, every week through the winter months, the latter sometimes varied by a discussion; also reading, writing, arithmetic, and singing classes. A natural history society meets in one of the rooms. A religious service, conducted by ministers of various denominations, is held every Sunday afternoon, and is very well attended. An excellent " Branch " for boys has recently been opened by Mr. Lupton, at Kirkgate, which is doing considerable good, and relieves the men's Club from the damaging presence of lads. Several hundreds pay every week, there, for admission.

The Duck-lane Club, Westminster, like the very interesting undertaking in St. James's Back, Bristol, deserves a more detailed account than we can give room for here. For the present it must suffice to say that for a long time after its first commencement, in 1860, it averaged between 500 and 600 members. The good which it has accomplished is very striking, and in some respects it is a model for these societies, but being intended for rather a limited range of labouring men, it does not aim at embracing that variety of agencies necessary for most Working Men's Clubs and Institutes.

Its wonderful success has been mainly owing, humanly speaking, first, to the untiring Christian benevolence, good judgment, and tact of its foundress, but, secondly, to an excellent committee. The Club also owed much of its successful start to the wisdom, kindness, and firmness of its first secretary, Mr. Bebbington, a costermonger. A religious service has always been held in this Club on Sunday evenings, and a few of its members have frequently met on week-days, in their dinner hour, for united prayer.

Mrs. Bayly's, Mr. Parfitt's, and Mr. Varley's no less admirable and useful labours at *Notting-hill,* London, should also have a paper to themselves. The whole movement owes more, in its origin, to these two societies, and the ladies who commenced them, than to any other single cause or individual. In addition to what was said respecting the Notting-hill enterprise in Chapter I., we may here add that its most useful career suffered a serious check about three years ago, partly owing to insufficient accommodation for the numerous members who flocked to it, and partly from a dispute in reference to smoking. A secession took place in consequence, and for a short time the undertaking, which had wrought incalculable blessings to the neighbourhood, threatened to prove a failure. Energetic and judicious measures, however, speedily re-established a prosperous state of things. The Club, as such, was dissolved by common consent of the members, and the building was thrown open to the public without any charge, the current expenses being defrayed by the sale of refreshments, and by letting the smaller rooms, as well as the lecture-hall, to various Provident, Temperance, and other Societies, of which the members have formed several, all very flourishing, since the hall was originally opened. These societies form a bond of union amongst the frequenters of the Club, besides doing great good in various ways. A religious service is held there one evening in the week, as well as on Sundays. After the new plan had been adopted the place became self-supporting, which it used not to be under the old system.

The Club at *Holloway* deserves honourable mention. 1st, on account of the zeal and devotedness of the honorary secretary, who originated it, and of the committee, who have so ably worked with him; 2nd, because of the harmony and judgment with which the few gentlemen on the committee and the working men there have pulled together; and 3rd, because of its indefatigable and genial steward, who, by the warm interest he takes in the Club, his delight and pride in making all the members comfortable, and his firm opposition to anything like disorder or infringement of rules, has most materially contributed to the success which this very useful Club has been privileged to obtain.

In the *Rotherham* Club we must notice the cordiality with which a clergyman, a Dissenting minister, and a number of working men have co-operated, the brotherly spirit manifested by the members, and the large amount of usefulness resulting therefrom. Their premises and situation, also, were good, and were turned to the best account. Unfortunately, a railway ejection has compelled them to turn out, but it may be hoped they will soon procure some equally good, perhaps by a Limited Liability Company, now that the working men have learnt the value of the Club, for they earn excellent wages, and might have a first-rate Club-house if they chose. The committee remark, with justifiable confidence, that they believe " the Club has established itself in the affections of a large proportion of the upper crust of the working men of Rotherham; and from the steady increase in its numbers, it is fair to predict much greater results than have been accomplished." This we fully believe. Nevertheless, it would not be satisfactory to find that the average number of members at the beginning of January this year was only 200, were it not that we see the age of admission then was fourteen years. As this is at least seven years too young, and the Club would probably double its number of grown men if none were admitted under at least twenty-one years (though twenty-five would be far safer), no doubt the anticipations above-mentioned will be amply fulfilled in the course of another year.

The Club at *Heywood* is but in its infancy, having only been established the autumn of 1865. It has, however, shown such remarkable vigour and judgment, that we may confidently predict for it a very honourable and useful existence. It has already held a most successful Industrial Exhibition, by which it cleared about 50*l*., and it actually conducts a monthly magazine, price 1d., full of interesting matter.

The *Honley* Working Men's Club is another most promising Club, numbering 320 members; but it is, perhaps, hardly fair to mention these juvenile specimens, stalwart and hearty as they be, until they have had a little longer trial, else we might refer to many other hopeful babies of about the same age. [It is still continuing its prosperous career. See Appendix.]

The *Guildford* Working Men's Institute, however, is of venerable estate, compared with most, having been formed *as an Institute* in 1856. It deserves attention and honour from the great success which has almost uniformly characterized its career, and from being by far the most flourishing society, hitherto, in the Southern counties—for a considerable time averaging 600 members. It has owed much to its wise and zealous librarian; also to the judicious separation of youths from the adults, thus receiving and preparing the lads for subsequent full membership without their annoying and driving away the men in the meantime. It had not been quite so prosperous the last year, but the managers are adopting several practical suggestions, and it will probably rise to even greater prosperity and usefulness than ever, should the same spirit of wisdom and good-fellowship continue to animate its members which they have hitherto evinced. [This hope has been confirmed. See Appendix.]

The Working People's Association at *Pendleton*, near Manchester, and the Charleston Institute, in the same place, are specially noteworthy for the large amount of good they are doing, and the unremitting devoted labour with which they are worked. The former includes a Working Men's Institute only as one of its agencies, and has an extensive organization for missionary, temperance, and Scripture-reading purposes. Capital entertainments are given every week; large and well-supplied reading and recreation rooms are filled nightly by the factory operatives, and the indefatigable honorary secretary has reason to be very thankful for the result of all his zealous labours. The Charleston Institute is a *bond fide* Working Men's Club, and its members enjoy the use, rent-free, of a first-rate building erected for them by B. Armitage, Esq., who has spared no cost of time and money to promote the welfare of the industrious workers in his great factory-hives.

We have not been able to include among the foregoing Clubs any of those in Scotland, because no returns have yet been received from them ; but, from the first annual reports of the Edinburgh and Glasgow Clubs, it is evident that they are exceedingly useful and prosperous. [One more Club, called the Chalmers Institute, has since been established in Edinburgh, and three more in and near Glasgow. Besides these, Clubs have been opened in Aberdeen, Inverness, Dundee, Greenock, and several other places, we believe. But our Scotch friends, with the exception of Mr. Wilkie, Hon. Sec. of the first Edinburgh Club, seem reluctant to inform us of their good deeds, and hide their light under a bushel.]

The task of pointing out Clubs that have been successful and others that have failed, with a glance at the causes of either result, is an important duty, but it will be already clear to the reader that it is by no means an easy one ; for, with a few exceptions, the fate of each Club has been a chequered one, as we might expect in the early stages of all such undertakings. Frequent mistakes are sure to be made, and very rare must be the cases in which have been found a combination of all the elements requisite to ensure success. Several large and very well-managed Clubs have suffered from adverse influences or unavoidable hindrances during their career, which have retarded for a time their prosperity, or even brought them very low. Yet both these and much smaller institutions, which have never attained any great prosperity or suffered serious check, have been effecting a large amount of good, not merely by their direct benefit to individual members, but also by the leavening influence they have been gradually exerting on the working population in the neighbourhood. [This is remarkably true, also, of the in-

fluence that has been exerted even by Clubs that have entirely
failed and been shut up. We have been greatly struck with
this fact on several occasions.]

Bearing these considerations in mind, let us now glance
at a few more of these Club experiences.

In January, 1865, forms to be filled up with various interesting particulars were sent to all the Clubs whose
existence was then known at the Central Office, amounting to
about 180, and returns were received from 77, the number of
ordinary members in which amounted to 18,327, giving an
average of 238 members to each Club: 37 of these Clubs, at
the time of making their returns, were. self-supporting ; 32
are returned as having lectures ; 29 as having classes ; 23 as
having Provident Societies of some description connected with
them ; only one mentions a Bible-class ; 17 state that Friendly
or Trade Societies rent a room at the Club for their ordinary
meetings.

The number of Clubs now on our register (January, 1866)
is 302. The number of those that have failed, as far as we
are aware, during the last three years is 19, which, added to
those now in existence, give 321 formed since 1858, only two
of that number having been formed previous to 1860 ; this
gives only about 6 per cent. of failures, although a considerable number, unquestionably, are not at present in a very
flourishing condition. It may, however, be fairly calculated—-
both from the above returns, and from those that are now
coming in, in reply to questions sent out at the beginning of
this year, as well as from other sources of information—that
an average of 240 members to each Club would be about the
mark, giving a total of about 75,000, every one of whom,
probably, is making at least three people, young or old, more
or less the better and happier for his belonging to the Club
instead of the public-house, giving a total of about 300,000
benefited by this important movement. [We have now reason
to believe that 240 was too high an average; 200 would have
been nearer the truth probably, as several of the Clubs then
newly formed were not on a sound basis, and lasted but a
short time.]

When we turn to the consideration of the causes of *failure*,
partial and total, in these societies, we find them of course,
very various, and, for the most part, either closely con-

nected with the particular circumstances of each individual Club, or to be classified under the head of infringement or neglect of the general principles we pointed out in a former paper as being, according to experience, essential to success. There is, however, one source of mischief to Clubs, from which they have so universally and seriously suffered, that it must be noticed *in limine*, and with all the emphasis which so ruinous and fatal a mistake requires ; we refer to the practice of admitting youths as members. The mischief caused by this practice to the Club movement generally has been incalculable. It was generally supposed, at the outset, that at eighteen youths were sufficiently aged to be suitable members of a Working Men's Club. Sorrowful experience has proved this to be a mistake, and, moreover, that large numbers have no scruple in declaring they have reached even that age long before it is the case. It seems a great pity to have to exclude those who press in so eagerly ; but common sense might have taught us, sooner than experience, that grown men will not sit down for a quiet chat or game where a number of lads are listening to them, or "larking." The men don't complain much ; they simply stay away, return to the public-house or the street-corner, and give the Club a bad name, remarking that " *they* don't want to be among a lot o' boys." Of course not. Do gentlemen admit juveniles into their Clubs, or take their evening's relaxation or amusement in the company of lads, not members of their own family ? The grown members of a Club do not object to the company of youths when listening to a lecture, concert, penny reading, &c., nor to their partaking with them in general in out-door sports ; nor is there any reason against the presence of youths in a silent reading-room ; but in conversation, smoking, and recreation rooms, it is simply fatal to obtaining the attendance of men.

The best course to adopt, and the reflections which these facts suggest, must be left for the present. We have now simply to implore all persons interested in Working Men's Clubs and Institutes, whether of the upper or the working classes, to accept and act on the results of universal and invariable experience. It is melancholy to see a great movement like this continually checked and maimed by one gross, palpable error, which has been exposed and denounced a hundred times in every possible way. But it is *so* hard to be wise by other people's misfortunes, and most of us insist on buying our own experience of evil, often at a terribly costly price.

Considering the unscrupulous way in which youths are found to falsify their replies as to their age, we believe, now, that the general rule for admission to Working Men's Clubs should specify *twenty-five* as the age necessary to be attained before they are eligible. It was hoped, recently, that twenty-one would be sufficient, but we fear it is absolutely necessary, if the Clubs are to be for *men*, that the former should be the limit, unless the arrangements can be made in a Club-house spoken of elsewhere.

The following are various cases of Clubs and Institutes that, although they have had much energy, money, and self-sacrificing zeal bestowed upon them, and have done great good, have not attained that marked success which they would seem to have deserved, and which characterizes those above mentioned. In general, the initial letter only will be given of any Club whose defects or failures are thus commented on; enough to show that a particular Club is being specified, and not merely a hypothetical case. But the Club at *Bolton* has been, and is doing so much good, so near becoming a magnificent success, that we need have no scruple in referring to it by name, and specifying what, after a lengthened discussion with its friends and managers, we believe to have been its difficulties and mistakes. They are few, but very instructive.

This *Bolton* Club, then, let us say, possesses the best indoor and out-door premises of any Club with which we are acquainted. They have some excellent men on the committee, both working men and a few of the class above them, all working harmoniously, and, above all, they have an able and active secretary. They began (February, 1864) with great *éclat*, originating at a very large and enthusiastic public meeting the previous November, and, for a time, had remarkable success. During one of their first half-years they had 307 quarterly members, paying 1s. 6d. a-quarter, 4,396 weekly payments of 2d. each, and 10,509 visitors' payments of 1d. each (for a single night). Two amateur concerts or entertainments were given every week. Several Provident and Trade Societies removed their meetings from public-houses, and rented rooms at the Club. Their eighteen rooms, including the dining and refreshment room, were thronged night after night. The gymnasium and skittle-ground were in constant requisition.

A year after (January, 1866), we found the numbers returned were 100 quarterly and 80 weekly, with 300 visitors per week. These are figures high enough to show what an amount of good the Bolton Club is still doing, and unsatisfactory only when we compare them with the former amount, and consider what this society, with its eminent advantages and earnest promoters, ought to be accomplishing. Let us see, then, what have been the hindrances to their greater prosperity.

The first error we would refer to as committed by the Bolton friends is simply that on which we have just dwelt, and in which nearly all other Clubs have kept them company —viz., that of admitting youths. The nominal age fixed was eighteen, but large numbers, considerably younger, pressed in. The usual evils ensued.

The next was confining those members who wished to smoke as well as talk, to one room, not very large, *and at the top of the house.* We may be allowed here to say that we fully share the strong convictions which many persons entertain as to the injurious effects of smoking, especially in youths and persons following sedentary occupations. But it is quite certain that if Working Men's Clubs are to answer the purpose for which they are established, smoking must be allowed in the common club-room appropriated to conversation and refreshments, and that this room should be on the ground-floor, or easily accessible, and at least as thoroughly comfortable and inviting as a public-house taproom. We are aware that the managers of the Bolton Club were hampered in this matter, and could not, at first, well make any other arrangement. We only mention this among other hindrances to their greater success. Another serious drawback during their first year was that they were unfortunate in their steward. But, like the previously-mentioned evil, this has been since rectified. A fourth great difficulty (though, had all other things gone well, it might not have been a mistake) was getting saddled with a debt of 700*l.* for furnishing, fitting-up, alterations, &c., in addition to the interest (about 60*l.* per annum) on the remainder of the purchase-money; for this debt bears a very heavy interest, and has been a mill-stone round their necks. A fifth hindrance has been that with all their large and commodious premises they have not got a room large enough to hold more than 130 people, whereas they ought to have had one that could accommodate, for their weekly entertainments, at least 400 or 500, including the members' wives. Next must be noticed the absence of classes and means of mental improvement. And lastly, the admission of anybody, who liked to pay their penny a-night, to all the advantages of the Club.

Now in talking over the whole subject with the Committee, the other day, they said, " Ah, Mr. S., you drew such a beautiful picture of what a Club should be, at the public meeting, that we were too enthusiastic, and started on too grand a scale ! " " No," we replied, "Emphatically no. You did that which was right and true ; and I did not—could not well exaggerate what the Club should do and be. Only you did not fully carry out the scheme as I proposed it, and which you rightly, at first, viewed in such bright colours." For instance, we laid great stress on the Club being also an Institute—on its doing something to promote the intellectual life and growth of its members ; but when we reminded our friends that this had been almost entirely omitted, they replied that they had not wished to interfere with the Mechanics' Institute, and admitted that they thought the Club should be confined chiefly to purposes of social intercourse and recreation. We urged what we have already laid before our readers (see Chap. I.) on that point in speaking of the great principles that should guide the managers of these Societies. Then, again, we reminded them that at the public meeting we also dwelt upon the necessity of cherishing a strong corporate " society " spirit among the members, but that these penny admissions of strangers interfere fatally with that. A number of persons come in who have no interest in the Club, no bond of union between themselves and one another, or the members of the Club. If the somewhat degrading and decidedly unspiritual, but marvellously attractive and tena-cious bond of the " pewter pot " is taken away, we must certainly see that some other, equally powerful, if possible, is substituted in its place. In too many Clubs, while the attrac-tions and *nexus*, the uniting principle, of the public-house have been righteously discarded, the higher elements have not been sufficiently introduced. No public spirit, no warm and deep attachment to the Club has, in consequence, been evoked. The vacuum has not been filled up which yawns in most working men's minds at the end of the day's work; nor have their animal, social, and intellectual cravings been satisfied. No wonder that Clubs have not been a uniform success.

But the Bolton men would have been working quietly and successfully through all these drawbacks but for that heavy debt of 700*l.*, at eight or nine per cent. And there we cannot help thinking, with all deference, that both the working men and their employers were somewhat to blame. If, when the first enthusiasm for the Club was felt, and its great advantages thoroughly appreciated, the members had tried, and been encouraged by the capitalists, to raise the required sum in shares instead of borrowing it, might not this have been accomplished? The men would have been putting forward self-help, and wealthier people, seeing this, ought easily to have been induced to do more than they did. About 1,200*l.* was generously raised among the middle and upper classes, but if the men had put their own shoulder to the wheel, doubtless a few hundreds more would have been willingly given. Now, we think that one main reason why more was not attempted by the members of the Club was because they had not enough of that corporate spirit above referred to. Had they felt as many working men do when they have formed a Friendly, Trade, Co-operative, or Temperance Society, the Bolton Club would long ere this have been all it ought to be. Had they merely knocked two rooms into one, or run up a temporary " lean to," for their entertainments, which the masons and carpenters among them ought to have been able and willing to do very cheaply after their day's work, they would have taken several pounds a-week during the winter months, and be rapidly paying off their debt. Let them see what those Buersill spinners and weavers did in that same county, and while labouring under the same difficulties arising from the cotton famine.

On the other hand, many Clubs might learn from the Bolton managers and promoters a lesson of liberal giving and devoted work, which might, perhaps, have been all that it was necessary to draw from their history, had they not been "as a city set on a hill," and had they not done so well that it is impossible to help regretting they have not done better. [Since the above was written the encouraging account has been received of this Club, which will be found in the Appendix.]

The only other case of partial failure that we shall refer to by name is that of the *Southampton Working Men's Halls;* and we mention their name, first, because the earnest and benevolent promoters have publicly expressed their own views on the matter, with which ours, for the most part, coincide; and, secondly, because they were commenced so brilliantly, and attracted such a large amount of attention, that, unless their want of greater success can be satisfactorily explained, the faith and zeal of many friends of the movement may be much impaired.

The first of these Halls was opened in September, 1862, just before our own society got under way. So great was its popularity, that the gentlemen who established it were led to open two others shortly afterwards. This they now consider to have been their *first* error, for there was not enough working power to conduct and control all three. None of us at first understood how much continuous work is required to make a Club succeed ; and although some of the gentlemen, and several of the working men who originated the halls, laboured most zealously, they were not adequately supported. They early saw, but not soon enough, that their *second* error was the universal mistake with regard to the age of admission. Lads and youths rushed in, monopolized the bagatelle-boards and other games, keeping the halls too often in a state of excitement and noise utterly subversive of a grown man's notion of comfort and relaxation. *Thirdly* must be ranked the absence of solid mental improvement. The halls were little more than mere recreation places ; and hence no earnest growth of interest in the undertaking, nor gratitude for benefits conferred by it, continually added new recruits to the ranks of its devoted supporters. *Fourthly* must be noted the cardinal error of having merely Halls (places to go to) instead of Clubs (societies to belong to). On no point does experience, as well as broad views of the needs and tendencies of human nature, speak more plainly than as to the necessity of binding the members into a true and brotherly fellowship, if these Clubs are to live and prosper. And, in the *last* place, the very serious but much less usual mistake was committed at the outset of the Southampton enterprise, of having a double committee system. A gentlemen's committee, appointed by the donors and honorary members, had supreme authority, and each hall had its own Working Men's Committee acting in subordination. Now, it is quite right, of course, that when gentlemen give money to start a Club, they should have some security for the due application of their funds; but if the Clubs are to be supported by working men, *they must belong to and be managed by working men.* This is clearly one of the main and fundamental principles of the movement—one on which we have not yet had occasion to dwell, but on which it is impossible to lay too much emphasis. As a shrewd artisan observed at one of our conferences, "Working men have masters all day long, and they don't want 'em at night." We should think not. Change of attitude is indispensable, as necessary for growth as for comfort. Unless the Club is really their own, of course they will not go near it. But this does not imply that they object to fair and reasonable conditions of membership, or to being bound by two or three fundamental rules, or to persons appointed by those who find the money having authority to enforce such rules. All this is very different from having an irresponsible committee over their heads, with power to veto any of their proceedings. Hence we have always urged the appointment of trustees, in whom should not only be vested the property of the Club purchased by donations, but who should have power to maintain the fundamental rules, to prevent the use of the Club-house for improper purposes, and even to close it if the objects duly defined were not being carried out. Working men in most places, but at all events in Great Britain, are remarkable for their respect for law, and are especially used to the authority of trustees in many of their societies. Ample security is gained by this plan, without needless and ruinous interference, *or power of interference*, on the part of those who may be in a higher position, and who have contributed of their larger means to establish the Club. We have given full information on the whole of this subject in one of the publications of the Working Men's Club and Institute Union.

But the friends at Southampton had to grope their way in this matter, and to buy their experience rather dearly. They offer it for the benefit of others, and say with us, Do not have a House of Lords and a House of Commons. Either unpleasant collisions will take place, or the independent working men will throw up their share in the business, and go their way. Generally the latter will be the result of those inevitable conflicts of opinion or action. The only possible exception may be found in the case of a Club established and conducted in rooms forming part of church or chapel buildings, and where a very judicious committee of persons connected with the property *may* exercise the required control without collision or offence; but, at the best, it is a hazardous and, as we think, objectionable experiment. One great advantage of Clubs is the opportunity and call they give for persons of different ranks cordially to work together; and while we strongly contend that it is a great benefit to the working men that they should have the advice and co-operation of two or three gentlemen (using the word in a very wide sense) in conducting their Club, as all experience proves, we are quite sure that it is far better, as a general rule, they should sit in the same committee with the working men, and not have a separate committee of their own. They will always command sufficient influence if they are the right sort of men; and if they are in a very small minority, and are at the same time impressed with a conviction of the importance of leaving the working men sufficiently to themselves, there would be no danger of their having undue weight in the committee.

In five Clubs this plan of a double committee has been tried, and it has been fatal to four of them. The fifth case is of the exceptional character above referred to, the Club being held in rooms under the school-rooms adjoining a large district church, and it has not been very long in operation. It may possibly work well there—*i.e.*, not be positively injurious. But under the most advantageous circumstances we should still believe it would be better that two or three of the gentlemen should sit on the working men's committee *rather* than in a separate committee of their own. If, however, the property belongs entirely to the working men, and they alone are answerable for the rent; or if the gentlemen to whom the said property belongs, and who guarantee the rent, are not willing to have any share in the management beyond seeing that fundamental rules are observed, then they had better occupy, as before said, the position of trustees. This is, practically, the plan of administration in the Duck-lane Club, where the committee has always been composed exclusively of the labouring classes, but where Miss Cooper has been the ultimate depository of power and court of appeal.

Two out of the three original Workmen's Halls at Southampton have always preserved a small but vigorous element of life; and after reaching the lowest stage of exhaustion, the surviving members, with true British pluck, willingly accepted the responsibility offered them of taking the management entirely into their own hands, and last year entered on a new and independent career, though, of course, in a very humble way, compared with their former commencement. They have still had the valuable advice and influence of the Messrs. Westlakes, and are working along in a thoroughly sound and, so far, satisfactory manner. A Coal Club, formed by the Winchester - terrace Club (late Orchard - street), has been eminently successful, and a considerable help to the Club in several ways. It numbers 480 members. The parent Club itself has about 72 regular members, with about 20 occasional ditto. The other Club, at Northam, suffered much, not only formerly, from dissensions between its own committee and the gentlemen's committee, but even since being placed on an independent basis, from the conduct of its late secretary. Its last return, however, shows about 77 members, and it is about two-thirds self-supporting, with a rent of 20*l.* The other Club is quite so, but has only two rooms at present, at a rental of 10*l.* [The Northam Club has since found itself unable to pay its rent, being unable to recover from the injury sustained through its late secretary, and trusting, of late, too much to the excitement of dramatic entertainments to keep it open. It has accordingly been closed. But there were a few earnest, excellent working men who stuck to it faithfully to the last.]

There is another small hall at Portswood, in the same town, more recently established, from which we have not yet received any returns, but we believe it is leading an humble and useful existence.

The history of every human enterprise contains, more or less, a record of failure. Those whose success alone is manifest to the world have had many secret disasters or checks. The people who succeed in this world appear to be those who *learn* from failures, *without being discouraged by them.* One more striking instance of this truth may be found in the following account of the Club now called the *St. James and Soho.* It was originally formed at a meeting held in the spring of 1864, under the presidency of Sir J. V. Shelley, after the failure of the Soho and St. Martin's Clubs. It has had a checquered and instructive existence. The Provisional Committee, appointed at the said meeting, contained several earnest, intelligent working men, the Rev. Harry Jones, Incumbent of St. Luke's, Berwick-street, and the Secretary to the Union. They held innumerable meetings in a school-room lent by Mr. Jones; but while they accomplished, after due discussion, the framing of a constitution for the Club, they were utterly unable to find any premises at all suitable. Both the defunct Clubs just mentioned had suffered greatly for want of sufficient room, and the Committee of the new Club felt it would be useless to start again without this indispensable condition. At last something considered by the working men sufficiently commodious was discovered. But, alas! their middle-class friends were out of town, no one was able to guarantee the rent, the landlord could not wait, and the premises were soon taken by other parties. The Committee, some weeks later, after waiting nearly ten months to find rooms in the heart of London, then accepted a kind offer from Mr. Harry Jones of the use of rooms under his church, and the opening of the Club was at length inaugurated by a tea meeting, tolerably well attended, and addressed by the Rev. F. D. Maurice, the Rev. Harry Jones, Thomas Hughes, Esq., M.P., W. T. Marriott, Esq., the Secretary to the Union, and several working men. The new arrangement, though much enjoyed for a time, did not work well, and the Incumbent found that the bagatelle-table, the extra noise occasioned, &c., made it objectionable to several persons connected with the church. The Committee, therefore, looked out again for premises, and at last found they might rent the first-floor, consisting of three rooms (the largest only about 15 feet by 9), over a Cooperative Store, in Broad-street. Here the Club and its brave leaders made a desperate struggle for existence. But all in vain; and when their numbers were reduced to something like twenty, and the landlord was going to put in the brokers, there appeared no further hope. But help, timely and effectual, was at hand. The Secretary of the Union, who had attended nearly all their committee meetings when in London, had by this time thoroughly interested the Treasurer of the Union, Henry Hoare, Esq., in the Club. This gentleman accompanied the former one evening to a meeting in the Club-rooms, which was expected to be the last. The few who still clung to the wreck were utterly disheartened to see nothing before them but a distraint and dissolution after all the year and a-half's weary labours they had undergone. But the two gentlemen cheered them, and chaffed them, and took counsel with them, and Mr. Hoare ended by lending them 5l. to keep their furniture and pay the landlord. Very shortly afterwards comparatively excellent premises were heard of in Rose-street, Soho—three rooms, with a good-sized hall, just what they wanted. But the rent was far beyond what any of them or all collectively could undertake to pay. Mr. Hoare hereupon kindly guaranteed the rent, the Club immediately removed into its new premises (about a year and a-half ago), and it has had an exceedingly useful and prosperous existence ever since. The men who had stuck to it so faithfully had got well accustomed to their work, and to each other, during their long "march in the desert." One of their number, who had been tried and proved, has made a capital steward (his wife being equally efficient), and the Club has not only been a wonderful blessing to its members, but has paid its way, and is entirely self-supporting. A moveable gymnasium is erected in the hall, when it is not wanted for other purposes. A bagatelle-table occupies one corner of the hall, a piano another. A second bagatelle-table is to be found in a room on the basement. A quiet reading-room, furnished with newspapers and a box of books from the Parent Society, is generally well filled. Another room, for sedentary games and chat, is always occupied. A convenient refreshment bar is in constant requisition. An elocution class was conducted successfully through last winter and spring; and a very good discussion class would have been formed if the Club could have afforded to pay seven shillings a-week more, for the use of a room upstairs on the first-floor. For want of this sum, however, unhappily, the discussion class has not been formed. Altogether, this is the most satisfactory Club in London at present (1867), and deserves both honourable mention and due consideration. If the members will cultivate a little more of the educational element, get the use of that upper room for discussions and for other classes, and, above all, hold together in a firm brotherly spirit, they may become a " model Club," and long continue to be a bright example to others, as well as an immense benefit to their neighbourhood. The street in which this Club is placed (Rose-street) runs from Greek-street to Crown-street, Soho, and is convenient of access for anyone wishing to see a Working Men's Club in the heart of London. Doubtless there is still room for great improvement as far as the premises are concerned, and if they could only raise enough money to improve, repair, cleanse, and beautify them, it would be of great advantage. But it would be equally wrong to doubt that, having so far prospered, they will be helped and will help themselves to get more complete success.

Several interesting lectures have been given by various friends to the members of this Club, and been well attended. The plan of having music and singing to precede and follow lectures has been successfully carried into effect here.

Having remarked on various successful Clubs, and on some partially so, let us now glance at the reasons given in some instances for failure on a large scale, and complete enough to end in closed doors. About twenty such had come to our knowledge up to 1866, out of 300 Clubs established, making little more than six per cent., which was a wonderfully small proportion, considering how we have all had to grope our way, and learn by (often) trying experience.

One night in December, 1862, two zealous friends of the working classes were sitting together in the town of S——, deeply deploring the amount of intemperance and vice among the active workers around them, and feeling utterly disheartened at the powerlessness of all efforts to check it. At the same time we were posting to one of them the prospectus of our Union. On receiving it the next morning, our friend ran with it to his companion of the previous night, and in high glee exclaimed, " This is the very thing ! The problem is solved for us. Let us get to work immediately." They did so with their characteristic energy—distributed our

D 2

papers widely, collected funds, got up a capital meeting, which was attended by the members for the borough, several of the clergy and influential inhabitants, and a great number of working men. Before long they had established a large and prosperous Club in admirable premises, and had enrolled from 1,000 to 1,200 members. What they did and how they did it will be learned from the following extract taken from the " Occasional Paper " (No. V.) before referred to:—

"Several builders and tradesmen gave materials, and the working men freely gave their labour gratuitously in fitting up and making the premises suitable for a Club, and on February 28 one of the largest and most successful Clubs in the country was opened free to the public for a week, about one thousand persons entering each evening. The following week 1,241 penny weekly tickets were sold, and the regular issue for some time averaged about seven hundred.

" The accommodations provided by the Club are—a smoking room, a recreation room, containing chess, draughts, dominoes, &c.; a gymnasium; a reading room and library, supplied with about forty daily and weekly newspapers, magazines, &c.; class rooms for writing, arithmetic, chess, singing, &c.; a lecture room, for vocal or instrumental concerts, lectures, discussions, readings from popular authors, and various entertainments.

" The results, for the most part, exceeded the most sanguine expectations of the promoters. Mr. T———, writing to the Secretary of this Union, 9th April, says: ' Our Club— although it has been in operation but for a few weeks—has wrought such a blessed result, that there is scarcely a street or a poor man's home in S——— but what has felt its cheering, happy, and peaceful influence. Here are two significant facts: *The wives of our labouring population are rejoicing in the establishment of the Clubs;* and those who thrive on the vices of the people are praying that the Club may soon be burnt to the ground. . . . I have examined the books of the Police-office, and find that, from the time our Club was opened, on the 28th of February, up to the 9th of April, there has been but one case of " drunk and disorderly;" while before that time scarcely a day passed without one or more, and during the corresponding period in last year there were no less than twenty-six cases.'

"Mr. M————, a working man, and one of the original active promoters of this Club, in writing to the *Times* well observes : ' What, it will be asked, are the advantages to be gained by being identified with these Clubs ? The blending instruction with recreation and amusement. Among the great number of men who thus congregate together are to be found the better class of workmen, the indifferent, and those who previously spent their spare time in drinking and loose company, with some even of the offscourings of society.'

" To accomplish the various objects of the Club, the Committee, in addition to the various entertainments and accommodation enumerated above, established a discussion class, and classes for reading, writing, arithmetic, music, and chess, attendance in all of which is included in the penny a-week. No fewer than eighty men, varying in age from sixteen to thirty-six, joined the arithmetic class as soon as it was opened. Some have even asked for spelling and elementary reading classes. Mr. T———— wrote : ' We purpose developing our Educational Department as there is need, or as we have opportunity. The popular entertainments, concerts, readings, recitations, &c., are very successful, and are attended by the wives and daughters of the members in large numbers.'

" First in importance for success in establishing and conducting a Working Men's Club, of course, come the character and abilities of the men engaged in the undertaking. But suitable premises, probably, rank next, if the requisite funds have been provided; and it may be well, therefore, to mention particulars with regard to those secured by this S———— Club. They were built for a cabinetmaker, have 58 feet frontage, and 30 feet depth, and consist of dwelling-house and shop. The rooms are appropriated partly to classes and committees, partly to the steward and his wife, who have charge of the Club. The shop, having a frontage of 28 feet, has been fitted up as a recreation room ; the gymnasium, which contains all appliances for muscular development and amusement, including a leaping bar and climbing ropes, with 8 or 10 inches of sawdust on the bottom, has a frontage of 15 feet. From the playroom runs a well-staircase to the reading room over, and same size as the recreation rooms, in which 100 readers can be comfortably seated. On this floor, and over the gymnasium, is a long room used for classes and other purposes. Above this and the reading room is the lecture hall, 43 feet long, in which is a piano, and where smoking is allowed when no lectures or other entertainments are going on. At other times the room over the gymnasium is opened for smokers; 'but,' adds Mr. T———, 'the great bulk of them prefer putting out the pipe to giving up the intellectual entertainment in the lecture room.' The cellarage will, perhaps, be fitted up for a bowling alley, quoits, 'brasses,' &c., which would be an excellent plan. But, like most other human enterprises, the S——— Club has had its discouragements and mistakes—the former arising from the latter, which chiefly consisted in having two Committees. Its constitution was thus described in our former 'Occasional Paper':—

" 'The management of the Club is in the hands of a Finance and an Executive Committee: the former consisting of a president, two vice-presidents, treasurer, corresponding secretary, and six members, being elected (annually) by and from subscribers of ten shillings and upwards per year; and the latter consisting of twenty members, with a minute secretary, elective half-yearly by and from members of eight weeks' standing. The general business of the Club is transacted by the Executive; while all matters of finance, or affecting the character of the Club, are determinable only by the Finance Committee.'

"This double-action system of two Committees, however, naturally tends to foster jealousies and dissensions. Gentlemen subscribing their money to establish a Club have a right to some guarantee for the due application of the funds so raised; but if they wish the Club to be self-supporting, or even to continue to exist at all, it must on the one hand be chiefly managed by the working men themselves, and on the other be conducted in accordance with certain Fundamental Rules. These objects are to be obtained in the way described in one of the Society's Papers, entitled "Information," &c.; but they are only referred to here because of the illustration afforded by the Club in question of the evils attending a different course. Its constitution has since been altered, in accordance with the recommendations of the Secretary of the Union, and it has again attained to a prosperous condition, as the following returns, given in January, 1864, will show:

'No. of members, 500. Entertainments, consisting of music, readings, lectures, magic lantern, &c., twice a-week; admission for the public, 1d. and 2d. Attendance from 500 to 800, including from 100 to 400 non-members.' "

The subsequent fate of this most promising Club is full of warning. For by the summer of 1863 there were "roots of bitterness" springing up within the Club, while radical defects of organization also began to tell on its prosperity, and in about a year after the Club was closed. In the autumn of that year, 1864, we visited the town for the first time, and met, by invitation, its principal supporters and managers, among the gentry, the tradesmen, and the working men. At two conferences (the second being more largely attended) the whole question of the causes of its break-down was very fully gone into, and the following were generally admitted to be the chief reasons of failure :—

1st. The double Committee system—one of gentlemen and another of working men.

2nd. The admission of youths and lads.

3rd. A steward who got drunk.

4th. Introduction of Theological questions at the Discussion meetings.

5th. Not enough management and supervision by the Committee.

In addition to these formidable elements of mischief, many speakers alluded to the unhappy jealousies that sprang up between different leading members, and the factions that were consequently formed. All agreed that there was not enough of the corporate or "society" spirit. There seemed no bond of union among the members; comparatively few who seemed to be animated by a disinterested desire to promote the common good. The following are a few of the remarks made in the course of the two conferences :—

" We began with too great expectations, and, therefore, on too large a scale. The rent of our premises was very high (more than 60*l*.), and the rate of subscription (1d. per week) too low. Hence it could not be self-supporting."

Comment.—This last opinion, we think, was mistaken; for their premises were large enough to accommodate the average number—say, one-third—who would attend at any one time on ordinary nights, and the two-thirds, or three-fourths, likely to be present at entertainments, even if they had retained 800 or 900 weekly members ; for that would have given them an income of about 180*l*., amply sufficient in itself, with good management, to have paid all ordinary expenses. Then, the same good management would have got a considerable profit from Penny Readings, Concerts, &c., and also from the sale of Refreshments.

" We had too much success at first. We thinned the public-houses to such an extent, that their owners took the alarm, and used a great many new devices to compete with us." No doubt this was true. See what is said above.

But there can be no doubt either as to the great amount of good which this Club accomplished during its brief career. After it had been shut up some time, a working man coming up the street, sorrowfully asked a member of the late committee when it would be opened again, adding, " I never used to spend less than twelve shillings a-week in that public-house (pointing to the one across the street) till the Club was opened."

The remarks were continued thus :—

" Jealousy and ill-feeling showed itself between the two committees as soon as the first difference about spending money arose."

Comment.—We have already dwelt fully on this fatal mistake of having two committees.

" There was great opposition shown to the Club before long by the religious bodies of the town, both Church and Dissenting."

" The religious discussions did us great harm. One question was, ' Is the Bible the only proper rule of life ?' and this raised a great stir among the Roman Catholics, both in the Club and out of it."

" When the Committee, by a majority of one, stopped the discussions, the Club went down at once. Scarcely any came to the discussion meetings afterwards."

" The Committee ought to have excluded sectarian publications if they excluded religious discussions."

" The Club had gone before those discussions began. There was enough to ruin it without that."

" There wasn't enough supervision as to the subjects for discussion generally. No limit, either, as to the time for each speaker."

Comment.—While we believe that Discussion meetings are of the highest value in these Clubs, so long as theological topics are excluded, there is no doubt that, independently of higher grounds, the introduction of those topics is most mischievous, from the strength of feeling, not to say passion, aroused by them, with the inevitable result of members becoming irritated with one another, and leaving the Club from the unpleasant feelings thus engendered. There can be no " good fellowship," which is the basis of these Social Clubs and Institutes, unless men consent to keep their strong antipathies or hostile convictions in abeyance while meeting on a common social platform, and make their Club thoroughly unsectarian in every sense of the term. But it does seem very sad that large numbers of the religious bodies in the town, when they saw practices going on in the Club to which they justly objected, should have manifested the active hostility to it which they appear to have done, instead of helping its better-disposed members and devoted friends to improve its constitution and management. They would have had abundant power to do this had they given sympathy previously. There is too much reason to fear that many of the followers of Christ in this town lost a great opportunity of serving their Lord when they joined in denouncing and closing, or refrained from assisting, the S—— Working Men's Club and Institute. To return.

" We (the Committee) were always a crotchety lot—we could not agree very well together, and then we consulted the opinions and prejudices of the outside public too much. Working men must manage their own Club, and go their own way, without minding what is said about them."

" There were men in that Club from the first who meant death to it."

" When the religious discussions were stopped, the Saturday evening entertainments fell off. Some of our best singers stayed away."

" Ay, but the chief cause of their falling off was that the pianist, whom the Committee had engaged at 2s. per night, was offered 5s. by a publican, and left the Club."

" Well, but the Committee offered him anything reasonable to come back, and then found he had been promised a situation in addition to his pay. We tried everywhere, in vain, to get another in his place."

" The expenses being so heavy, a great deal had to be done in the way of getting up entertainments. But all that took up a vast deal of time—more than the Committee could afford. And no regular and suitable chairman was appointed, either for the ' Free-and-Easy,' or for the Discussions."

"There was sometimes great uproar and confusion . . . a general want of good management, in fact."

One of the principal founders and managers, after summing up the discussion and admitting the correctness of most of the foregoing remarks, concluded by saying : " But all these difficulties and disasters might have been lived down had not the expenses been too great for the income. Nothing else would really have broken up the Club."

Comment.—No doubt the deficiency in the balance-sheet finally caused the Club to be closed; but the expenses, as it appeared to us, were not at all out of proportion to what the income could and would have been with efficient management. The real, essential defect, next to the double Committee, was, first, too much dependence on excitement, instead of quiet sociable Club life ; secondly, and chiefly, the disproportion between the magnitude of the operations, *and the staff to conduct them.* There was much zeal and judgment, much disinterested and efficient labour, but not enough for the undertaking ; and a good deal of what there was does not seem to have been always applied in the right place. If a few of the gentlemen who formed the Upper House had sat instead on the Working Men's Committee, winning their confidence and just supplementing their efforts ; if other gentlemen outside the Club, belonging to the various religious bodies, had shown cordial sympathy, and given judicious help, in all probability a very different result would have been obtained. The fact must never be lost sight of, that to manage and work a Club and Institute a very considerable amount of time and energy must be devoted to it, proportioned to the scale on which its operations are conducted.

But the effort was not in vain. It left some good results which will not soon pass away. And many of those who, through the melancholy failure of that Club, are now gone back to their old wasteful and demoralizing ways, or sunk again in stupid apathy, will occasionally be the better for remembering that they once rose out of that state into one better and happier. "No effort is lost," says one of England's greatest men ; least of all an effort bearing such good fruit for a time as the one above described. May its benevolent promoters keep up heart and hope, learn by experience, and go to work again at the fitting season with renewed energy.

A letter from the late President of the Club, just received, says, in answer to our inquiry, "There is a Temperance and Benefit Club now in S——, doing part of what a Working Men's Club would have done better. Some of the most useful men in the town, however, have joined it."

In a former note he expressed a great hope that they might be able to begin once again on a smaller scale; but hitherto they have not seen their way to this. [We have since heard that a flourishing Co-operative Store has, however, been established in the town, which provides a good reading and smoking-room, hereby strikingly illustrating the truth of the foregoing remark, that the effort had left enduring results.]

The next case of failure it may be well to look into occurred in the town of B——, where a Club and Institute was commenced under very favourable auspices, and on rather a large scale.

The movement was inaugurated in the year 1863, by a large and enthusiastic public meeting, at which the Mayor presided. It was addressed by influential inhabitants, by working men, and the Secretary to the Union. A good provisional committee was appointed, and premises were soon engaged, which, on the whole, appeared tolerably well suited for the object—the best, in fact, to be had, though by no means perfect. They consisted of a large hall and gallery, capable of seating at least 1,000 people, and three or four Club-rooms partly formed out of one end of the gallery by wooden partitions.

A large number of members were soon enrolled, and for a time everything looked most prosperous; but, unhappily, the same fatal mistake was committed here as in the last case, of having two Committees. In the spring of 1864, we heard of these two bodies having come into collision on the question of Dramatic Entertainments, and were shortly afterwards invited to go down and discuss the state of affairs. This we did, and also attended another meeting about a year after the Club had closed, with a view to its re-organization. On this last occasion, the causes of its downfall were very fully gone into, and we will now give the views of its chief supporters, as then expressed, reserving any comments we may have to offer till the end. They were as follows:—

" The first difference of opinion that arose between the two Committees was in regard to keeping the Club open on Sundays; but that was amicably settled after some discussion, it being unanimously agreed that it should be open for a limited number of hours; that the newspapers should be withdrawn, but the periodicals left. The heavy rent, however (100*l.* per annum), soon began to tell against the Club. It was more than the Club could properly bear. Then a great mistake was made in admitting members as young as sixteen years. The premises, also, were not suitable. It was a great error having two Committees, but might not the same difficulties have arisen with Trustees? The worst part, however, was that the Elocution Class became a Dramatic Class, and then regular Dramatic entertainments, with scenery and dresses, were introduced, not at good long intervals—which would have done no harm—but once a-week. After this, the whole life of the Club seemed swallowed up in these entertainments; couldn't keep up any classes—not even the Discussion Class, or any other sort of entertainments. After a time, the dramatic entertainments, themselves, became disreputable, little better than a ' Penny Gaff.'

" No doubt we did wrong in having two Committees, but we didn't know any better. The General (Gentlemen's) Committee decided against the dramatic entertainments, and then the break-up began. The gentlemen ultimately withdrew, and gave up the Club entirely to the other Committee, who tried to carry it on for a time; but the chief part of the working men had left by this time, and though the dramatic performances were often crowded, the Committee soon found they couldn't meet their rent, and the whole thing was given up.

" The lad who sat at the door to look at the tickets as members came in, was only fourteen years old. Saw hundreds of lads admitted without their ever being questioned as to their age; and even many young girls." (This last, we think, must refer to the entertainment nights.) Various other remarks were made; but the foregoing sufficiently represent the general tenor of the discussion.

Comment.—As to the double Committee and the first founders of the Club "not knowing better," that was clearly their own fault (as in the previous case at S——), in not asking us what experience had taught us on the subject. It is the special function of our Society to collect this experience, and many of the failures that have taken place might, probably, have been avoided if the promoters had sent us a copy of their proposed rules before finally passing them, or otherwise consulted us.

The same remark applies to the early age named in the rules of this Club for admission, as to the double committee system.

Then, in regard to the dramatic performances. Without pronouncing any opinion as to the propriety, in the abstract, of such entertainments, which it would be out of our province to offer, we must urge, as we did at every meeting we attended in B—— after the "vexed question" came up—first, that if people think it desirable to have dramatic entertainments, they had better form a society especially for that purpose, not convert a Working Men's Club into such a society ; secondly, that there is a great difference between an occasional dramatic entertainment being given, say two or three times in the course of the year, and having them every week. A private family may get up such an entertainment, say at Christmas time, and invite friends to witness it, without any evil consequences ; but if it were repeated every week, the household would soon be thrown into disorder. There are many amusements which, coming very rarely, are simply beneficial, but which, from the very interest they awaken, and their exciting tendency, would be decidedly injurious by frequent repetition. Dramatic entertainments and balls stand in this category. Daily and weekly recreation in a Club is needful and good ; but if it be of too stimulating and exciting a character, it tends to absorb all the life and energy of the Club into itself. Classes are given up—even ordinary amusements are voted "slow ; " quiet, steady men drop away from the Club, which is no longer the sort of thing they want, and a break-up inevitably ensues. Clearly, the great majority of working men do not want incessant dramatic entertainments, which, if carried to excess, are, therefore, a palpable perversion of the objects for which the Club was founded. And, as one would expect, in the B—— case, the great majority of the audience at the theatrical exhibitions were under twenty years of age.

As to the rent, it was certainly very heavy, and we agree with one of the speakers above quoted that the premises were not very suitable. But they were the best to be got at the time, and with good management would have answered very well till better were procurable. For in the midst of so large a population as that of B——, the Hall could have been advantageously let one or two nights every week, on an average, and have paid half the rent itself. But when there was so little judgment or proper attention, as to allow of a lad of fourteen being placed at the entrance to examine and take tickets, one sees enough to explain other weak points in the management of the Club.

Answering the question of one of the above speakers, we think the same amount of collision and alienation would not have arisen between a committee and trustees as between two committees—first, because, though trustees certainly ought to have vetoed the constant theatrical representations, their authority would be much more readily recognized by working men than that of a second committee of gentlemen; and secondly, because if some of the latter had been sitting on the Working Men's Committee, they would have talked the whole thing over in a friendly way before the evil had grown, as it were, to a head, and by judicious and conciliatory counsel would probably have nipped the mischief in the bud.

We are thankful to state that, after an interval of about a year and a-half, another Working Men's Club and Institute has been formed in this town on a much sounder basis, with every prospect of a long and useful career. It would have been established sooner but for the difficulty of getting suitable premises. Some of the best men connected with the former effort, to whom great praise is due for the sacrifices they made to establish and maintain it, have cordially put their hands to the plough again; and others, equally efficient, both gentlemen and working men, have joined them. We visited the town twice in hope of reviving it, and on the second occasion a public-spirited manufacturer got together an excellent little tea-meeting, which set the enterprise again on its legs. [Since this was written, the Secretary of a large London Trade Society stated incidentally at a meeting held at the office of the Working Men's Club and Institute Union, last June, that he had lately been at this B—— Club, and he had never been among a pleasanter, more sociable set. Working Men's Clubs, he said, in general were not half sociable enough, but the one in question was all that could be desired, and very comfortable.]

The following statements were made to us at a small Conference held in the autumn of 1866, respecting the causes that led to the failure of a Club in a very densely populated district, the said Club having at first had very liberal support from some of all classes. We have every reason to rely on the general accuracy and trustworthiness of the remarks then made, but cannot vouch for them personally. The men who made them were highly respectable, steady men, connected with some of the principal works in the neighbourhood, but in some points may have been biassed :—

" The first Secretary [an excellent and zealous man, mainly instrumental in starting the enterprise] was a Temperance Missionary, and hence an impression from the first that it was a ' Teetotal move.' This, of course, was strengthened by the rule excluding beer. Then because Messrs. —— [partners in one of the largest works in the neighbourhood who took a warm interest in the scheme, and whom we may call the Messrs. T——] took it up it was called ' T——'s Club.' The first President (a pawnbroker) was elbowed out to make way for Mr. A. T——. Too many of T——'s men were on the Committee. Gambling was introduced in the shape of playing for cigars, so that it cost some men more than the public-house. If a man did not want to smoke he was not allowed to play at bagatelle. The steward or manager of the Club had the profits from sale of refreshments and cigars, and so was tempted to encourage the gambling and push the sale of cigars, &c. The tea and coffee were very bad. At —— [naming a Club in the neighbourhood] they are very good, but there the Committee don't seek to make any profits. The subject of gambling was brought before a meeting, but the voting was taken unfairly. The position of the Club was bad, being too far from the homes and workshops of the men. Five-sixths of them had to walk more than half-a-mile to the Club. The manager of the Club was not judicious, and, though of a jolly disposition, often irritated the men. At—— Club (the same referred to above), they have done wisely in appointing a woman to be manager. She is not so likely to give offence as a man. The committee business was often done in T——'s works instead of at the Club. Then, again, it was a mere recreation place. There was no education; even the reading-room was scarcely used. Then the age for admission was a great deal too low— sixteen—and the Club was swamped with boys. A Club takes a deal of working. The 'Free-and-Easy' held at the Club was very successful for a long time, but afterwards a beer-shop keeper succeeded in drawing many away to a rival Free-and-Easy. The shooting-gallery nearly paid rent."

These were the principal complaints made, as taken down at the time and given for the most part in the exact words of the speakers. One added that he knew a man " who had been in the habit for thirty-five years of attending the public-house and spending a deal of money there, and who gave up drinking altogether, without the influence of the Teetotal Society, and joined the Club. He taught himself to read in six months, and became quite reformed." Another man stated that during the whole time he belonged to the Club " he never heard a man swear or quarrel there. But the men wanted the Club to be nearer to them." It was of a member of this Club that we heard, some time ago, he told the Secretary it had saved him 40*l.* during the first year he belonged to it. All the speakers were of opinion that it would be very desirable to let men have a couple of glasses of beer at the Club, but that the quantity should be restricted to that amount. The work there makes the men very thirsty, and they must go where " they can get their pint."

We will only remark on the foregoing statements, first, that the causes of failure, as there mentioned, were enough to have killed half-a-dozen Clubs; and, second, that there is abundant encouragement for the working men and their friends in the neighbourhood to make another start; furnished with all this important experience, they would, in all probability, be able to make another Club eminently successful. We cannot help deeply regretting that the Council knew nothing of the critical condition of this Club until it was too late, and that all the important information now given was not received till after the Club was closed.

Let us next consider the following case, as pourtrayed in a valuable letter written some months after the catastrophe. It is not necessary to vindicate the absolute correctness of every statement or of every opinion contained in it. We may—to some extent must—receive it rather as an *ex parte* view of the matter. But we must also accept it as the impression left on the mind of a thoroughly impartial, truthful, and reliable witness, while unquestionably the writer was in the best possible position for judging clearly and fairly of the whole proceeding. His views, also, have been generally corroborated by the Treasurer of the Club. This, then, is his account of the business :—

" The Rev. ———— has handed to me your letter respecting the closing of our Club, desiring me to reply to it, and give you all the information I can. I do so with the greatest regret, I may add with great pain, almost disgust ; for, after having worked as hard as I and a few others had done to establish it on a firm basis, I certainly did feel annoyed that it should be so abruptly brought to a close. It is difficult where to begin. There have been several causes, trifling, perhaps, of themselves ; but the indifference of the working men themselves, together with their petty jealousy of one another, has gone a great way towards its downfall. As you observe in your note, the last account you had was that it was flourishing. You are also aware that domestic affliction has prevented me giving so much time as I would have liked (for I may add I never went into anything with so much heart and soul as this, believing, as I did and still do, that it was the very best thing possible that could be provided for working men). Hence I was at last compelled to give up my office. I left them with a good surplus in October, 1865 ; and with the winter coming on— the very best part of the year—I felt sure there would be no difficulty in getting on. The winter of 1864-5 had been a very good one, and the fortnightly concerts realized a hand-some sum. They began, as usual, at the latter end of October with the concerts, with a new Committee, elected in September. Well, one or two of the Committee who were good singers, &c., took upon themselves to get up concerts on their own account for their own individual profit, using the Club's name, taking our singers and gymnasts, whom we had got together

at very great trouble and expense for the Club, hiring the
Hall in our name and on the night before ours ; so that, as a
matter of course, ours was a failure, and led to the matter
being brought before the Committee, when the offenders were
obliged to leave. But, as you must see, the mischief was done.
We tried to repair it, but of course with such selfish opposition it was not likely to make any profit. This was the first
cause of rupture, and a most disgraceful one it was. . . .
About the same time (November, 1865), we changed our
steward, and got a very zealous, but hot-headed man, who
was soon at variance with the members, and lost us a great
deal; this happening at the same time as the concert annoyance, made it still worse, as he was a stranger to all the
singers. The result of it was, the winter half-year, ending
March, 1866, instead of making a profit to stand against the
summer, had absorbed all our surplus. Then another objection made use of was the admission of boys. They certainly were not admitted into the news-room or game-room.
Again, during the summer, the Exhibition held in our town was
considered to have thinned their numbers. This I cannot
answer for, as I could not possibly attend myself. One thing
I always remarked which was very creditable, only the number was limited from the size of the room, that the news-room
was well attended ; and on this point I was continually urging
its enlargement, but it never got done, although I got it
carried in committee to be done. If I had time, I could name
other causes—change often and again ; still worse, rooms
neglected, nothing carried out, &c.

" Well, September 1866 came, a fresh Committee elected,
who were to set vigorously to work and make it prosper.
Mind you, at this time (September, 1866) the Club was very
little in debt, not worth mentioning. We got the enclosed
paragraph inserted in all the papers. Our new Secretary drew
up a good circular to the working men themselves, of which
2,000 were delivered.

" —— WORKING MEN'S CLUB.—The Committee, we learn, have
issued circulars soliciting honorary members and donations in aid of this
Club, which, it appears, is not self-supporting during the summer
months. It would be a source of regret, as well as a reflection on the
city, to allow this society to fail in its object for the want of a little
pecuniary help. It is obvious that an institution which enables work-

ing men to congregate together in a social and friendly manner to acquire information on the current topics of the day, and to indulge in rational and wholesome recreation ; where they undergo a training in habits of self-restraint, respect for order, and regard for the rights of others, the rules of which provide that the language used in their intercourse one with another shall be free from all that is profane and offensive ; where games of chance and gambling of any description are forbidden, on the penalty of expulsion, and where intemperance is not tolerated ; an institution which affords more than all the attractiens of the public-house, without any of its evils—must exert a most important educational influence, and commend itself to the sympathies of all who have at heart the welfare of the working classes or of the community at large. We therefore trust that the appeal of the Committee will meet with a ready and cordial response."

" I urged repeatedly a public meeting, precisely as you mentioned—in fact, the circular to the men states that a public meeting would be held, but I am sorry to say it never was. Before I got so thoroughly crushed by our troubles, I actually got a proof of a bill printed and arranged for the speakers, &c., but it was stopped on account of the principal speakers not being able to attend. I revived it (*i.e.*, the proposal for a public meeting) at the end of the year, but unsuccessfully. Their (the Committee's) argument was that the working men had had a fair chance, and had not responded to the circular sent out to them; that it was they who were indifferent, &c., &c. I stood alone in opposing its closing so abruptly, and without a public meeting being called, giving them another chance. The new Committee set to work, and got up a series of concerts, which were an entire failure, a perfect blunder, or worse, which lost more in one month than had been lost all the year. The number of members also fell off very low indeed—so bad that, familiar as I was with the working of it, I could not comprehend it. But they had not appointed a secretary in my place permanently, consequently there was great irregularity. . . . I thought I had written you all, but on reading it over, I find I have omitted the closing of it. I had not been able to attend so much last year, but a meeting was called to consider the propriety of closing it at once. This was the last Saturday in December. The Trustees attended, and some of the Committee, although it was midday, and very inconvenient. After discussing it in every way, it was proposed to close it at once, so as to avoid any further debt. I am sorry to tell you that I was the only one out of seven who opposed its being closed so abruptly. I contended we had not kept faith with the circular sent out to the working men, &c. ; that we ought to have the public meeting ; then, if they decline to support it, I would give way. But of course one against six could not do anything ; the fact is, they were afraid of being brought in for any liability. I am sorry I cannot lay my hand on the circular sent out, for then you would see what we had done. When I find one I will send it you. Any particular point you want explanation on, if I can give it you, shall be glad do so. If I were to write as much more I cannot express to you my regret at its failure, for I am convinced it might have been avoided. I never was so annoyed. I just remember one argument of the Trustees, &c., was, if we had a public meeting it would only be a flash in the pan, not permanent, and without I would undertake it with some one or two more to manage it, they saw no chance. That they knew was impossible, so I was obliged to give way. It is a disgrace to the town, to the working men themselves, and to the clergy, &c.; for if ever there was a chance of real good being done to the working class, this sort of institution is exactly it. I have not altered my opinion on its usefulness, grieved as I am at its failure. It only wanted properly managing."

Now while most unfortunate mismanagement is manifest enough here, and a great want of disinterested, self-sacrificing zeal on the part of some, if not many, members of the Club, the great error appears to have been in not calling the public meeting so much desired by the writer of the letter, and giving the working men one more chance before so hastily closing the Club. Another strange thing, also, is that no one with sufficient time, business power, and influence to act efficiently as honorary secretary, was found to undertake the rather arduous duties of that office, which the writer had so well performed, and was at length obliged to abandon. On the other hand, it is important to notice that in the newspaper paragraph, which the writer of the letter had a hand in drawing up, there are several expressions extremely well calculated to repel working men from the Club—for instance, the sentence beginning " the rules of which," &c.

We suspect that a large number of Clubs have suffered from this grievous sin of overloading them with restrictions and rules. Can we not understand that after his day's work is done the operative craves to get into the freest possible atmosphere? Rules and restrictions of course are needful, but they should be very few in number, and instead of being paraded in invitations to working men to join the Club, should at all times be kept as much as may be out of sight. What could be more injudicious than to talk to the labouring and artizan class in some of the language of the paragraph in question? We cannot wonder no great accession of members followed from this invitation.

No doubt the Club at ———— suffered, like every other, from want of sufficient separation between the youths and the men, and possibly to some extent from men not being able to get their glass of beer there. But until other refreshments of an excellent quality at a cheap rate have been tried, it is impossible to say in any particular instance whether the absence of beer was fatal to the success of a Club. The *news-room* was very popular, but we want to see the "*sociable*" room more regarded by Committees and frequented by members of these Clubs. We trust that here, as in other places, temporary defeat will be followed by renewed effort and great success. But if anything is to be done, it must be by the working men themselves. It will be long, we fear, before the gentlemen in ———— contribute anything more to the establishment there of a Working Men's Club and Institute.

With the following case of break-down, we leave the subject of "Failures." At the Conference now to be reported statements were made, first by the gentleman who had taken a most generous part in establishing and supporting the Club, and afterwards by members of the Committee and the manager.

Money was readily forthcoming from gentlemen of the town at first starting. A capital bowling saloon was set up and maintained at great cost, but it was monopolized by too rough a class. The regular members could not get at it, and the Club could not afford to keep a person specially to attend to it and keep order. [This points to the evil we have dwelt on elsewhere, of allowing penny nightly admissions to a Club, which are destructive of the Club principle. Weekly payments are bad enough, but often a quite necessary evil.] Classes in French, mechanical drawing, elocution, writing, and music (vocal and instrumental) were established. All the instruction given was gratuitous, except the writing, and by very competent teachers. But, except the music class, none were continuously successful. As the classes were not appreciated by the members, they were thrown open to the public for a small payment, but still without avail. Then, again, there was a deal of work to be done, but the members would not do it unless they were paid. The manager was admirably fitted for his work in every way.

A leading member of the Committee, and a very thoughtful, business-like working man, thoroughly in earnest about the Club, said that the Club was doing a great deal of good, and ought to be kept open by some means or other until the working classes appreciated it. A public-house in the neighbourhood had been closed for a time through the Club. They wanted the means for making their entertainments more attractive, and to keep them going. The success of their entertainments had caused many similar ones to be started elsewhere, and great competition had sprung up. Some of their best singers and reciters had been enticed away. The Committee wanted the means of preventing their performers from being drawn away. During the first year their income was 298*l*. Attendance of all sorts was 28,000. In the second year the income was 220*l*., and the expenditure 254*l*. In the third year the attendance was only 8,000. The raising the subscription from 1s. 6d. to 2s. 6d. a-quarter had driven many away. It would have made a vast difference to the Club if they had had their present manager at first. Their first manager was sadly inefficient.

When the manager came in, he said, among other things, that "the first great drawback to success was that the reading-room was always so oppressively hot, the chimney of some Turkish baths running up at one end of it. They thought the situation was too far from the homes of the better-paid artizans. There were, no doubt, a great many working men living in the neighbourhood, 'but until you get the leaders you don't get the other men.' The former class 'actually prefer paying for a room at the Athenæum for their business meetings, which is much nearer to them, to having a room at the Club for nothing.' A great disadvantage at first starting was the Committee could not pick their men, and the Club used to be very disorderly, whereby they lost a great deal of support ; but now it is quite quiet and respectable. [This points to the value of introducing at first the principle of admission only by ballot after the first fifty or sixty members have joined.] Then there has never been a proper conversation-room till within the last few weeks, when one was opened at the top of the house, and is much valued and well attended. It is true there have been great complaints about the youths, but though there had been a large number of them attending, were they not really the class whom it was most important to care for ? Their habits are not yet formed, and it is the most critical time of life. The older men do not object to be in the same singing-class with boys. He remembered there had been objections made to some of the females who had come to the entertainments, but he believed they were unfounded. In looking at the work the Club had done, he could see it had been very beneficial. A very large number of persons had visited it, and shown that they did appreciate it. It had done a great deal of good in refining many of the worst-behaved roughs, 'making them more gentlemanly.' Then observe the extent to which penny readings, &c., had sprung up in consequence of those given at the Club. True, the lectures had not been successful, but that was the case everywhere, and so of classes. But some of the lectures had been very well attended. He thought there was every reason to believe that if the Club could then be kept open for a time longer it would become well-supported. There was a balance of 6*l.* in its favour at the end of the last current year. A much smaller place in a better locality, even without an entertainment-hall, but with the power of hiring one, would answer well at a rent of about 40*l.* Their present rent was 60*l.*"

A gentleman who had taught the mechanical drawing class confirmed all the previous speakers' statements.

A working man who had formerly belonged to a very successful Club in another town, when he first came to this town was cautioned against coming to the Club there, as it had a bad name. But having attended regularly for some time, he found it was excellently conducted, and he saw that its bad name was wearing away.

We may remark on the above that here also is most abundant ground for renewed hope and effort. But it is plain that, independently of its misfortune in having a bad manager to begin with, it has always, until recently, depended far too much on amusement and excitement. The fact of never having had a conversation-room till lately, and the number of youths, would have been of itself enough to account for the quiet, steady grown-up men not frequenting it. The want of men to do needful Club work without pay showed an absence of public spirit and corporate brotherly feeling which would be fatal to most Clubs. But in this case the difficulties of the Club were discovered by the Council of the Union before it was finally closed; and the result of this conference, and of another meeting held the following day, was to call out an increased amount of public support, encouraging its generous friends to persevere some time. Its very efficient and zealous manager is now conducting it chiefly on his own plans and management, and there is reason to believe he will be able to do so successfully. The suggestions offered to the friends at Bolton, in the letter given elsewhere, would probably be applicable to this Club also.

In concluding our account of various failures in Club enterprises, we would observe that, among all the lessons we have learnt, incomparably the deepest conviction they leave in our mind is that none of these efforts, whether visibly and immediately successful or not, fail to exert an influence for good which shows itself in innumerable forms, and which will be felt when those who made those efforts have long gone to their rest.

CHAPTER III.

GENERAL REVIEW AND PRESENT POSITION OF THE MOVE-
MENT—ITS CLAIMS TO PUBLIC SUPPORT.

WORKING men have had a considerable share of public attention recently. Those who say they have had enough, and wish
to shut off any further consideration, for the present, of their
wants, temptations, weakness, or strength, would do well to
remember that the attention lately given to them has been
forced upon a large number of those persons who previously
had too much neglected the condition of their humble fellow-
countrymen ; and its pressure now is a sign that such neglect
was becoming dangerous. Many questions vitally connected with
the well-being of working men have to be dealt with at once,
perhaps precipitately, which should have been considered and
gradually disposed of years ago. On the other hand, so far
as such increased attention shows that the sympathies and
philanthropic energy of the middle and upper classes are
being devoted to a most important and deserving section of our
own community, and are not entirely exhausted on the
criminal classes and foreign sufferers—so far, moreover, as it
indicates a perception of the true way of dealing with many
of the most crying evils of our day, by improving and redeem-
ing that great class from whose degradation so many of those
evils spring, it must be regarded as one of the healthiest and
happiest features in our present social condition.

Profoundly convinced of the important part which must be
played by Working Men's Clubs and Institutes in that social
progress to which we look forward with anxious desire, and
having already given a rapid glance at particular instances of
success and failure connected with this Club movement, we
now propose to take a general view of it as a whole ; thence
we may deduce some of the reasons on which we conceive the
Clubs to be deserving of general support, and at the same
time discover how far they have succeeded in obtaining it.
So large an amount of time and labour has been devoted to

the subject by the Parent Society, that, although most of the Clubs in existence have been established since its formation in 1862, there is no difficulty in arriving at tolerably accurate results in regard to each of these points.

The fundamental idea of a Working Men's Club, as the designation is now used, we have already seen is not that of a Benefit Club in the sense of a Friendly or Provident Society, but is the same as that on which the Clubs of the upper classes rest—viz., social fellowship. The object is to gain facilities for pleasant social intercourse, reading the newspapers, and obtaining refreshments at a house belonging to all the members in common, not at a house belonging to a host who makes a living out of his guests.

Now to anyone acquainted with the houses of the working classes of this country, it is evident that if the change from tavern-life to Club-life, the transference by the gentry of England of *their* convivial, literary, political, and other social meetings from places of public resort to their own Clubhouses, was good for them, it must be twofold more valuable to working men. The latter have neither the rooms, the servants, nor the money for social intercourse at each other's homes, nor, very often, for that rest and relaxation which a tired man wants during some part, at least, of his evening leisure. Even where there exist the tastes for literary or scientific recreation and culture, the single dwelling-room and narrow resources of the working man afford little chance of his being able to gratify those tastes, except in the rare case of his having large wages, a small family, and no strong proclivities towards the public-house. The Working Men's Club affords an agreeable and inexpensive alternative to the taproom and the street corner, free from temptation, and therefore (as indeed experience proves) highly conducive to domestic happiness, by the improvement it effects in the temper and sobriety of the head of the family, as well as in his financial resources and in the hours at which he returns home. But if good even for the married men, *a fortiori* good for those who are single, who have frequently no home but half a bedroom, or less, and who, under any circumstances, gravitate naturally towards the public-house almost every evening of their lives. The Clubs break those tippling habits, in short, still too prevalent among many of the working classes, and which are the fruitful source of that intemperance, poverty, sickness, insanity, and crime which so many other excellent efforts can only palliate. Hence one of the principal claims of these Societies to general support. In the records of the Club histories published by the Working Men's Club and Institute Union, at 150, Strand (some of which have already been quoted in the preceding chapters), we meet with various facts of the following kind :—

" At a public meeting convened by this Society in February, 1865, held at the London Tavern, G. J. Göschen, Esq., M.P., in the chair,

" THE BISHOP OF LONDON, among other valuable remarks, ' said it had been questioned whether, if they encouraged the working man to spend his evenings in a Club, they necessarily drew him away from family life. Upon that subject he would read an extract from a letter by Mrs. Bayly, a lady who was well known for her efforts on behalf of the working classes at the West of London. Writing to Mr. Solly respecting the remarkable good done by the Workmen's Hall at the Kensington Potteries, she said :—

'One result of this work I must mention as having struck me very much. Several men, constant attendants at the Hall when it was first established, are now seldom seen there, and, in many cases, I find they are spending their evenings in their newly-found homes. Only last week I met two of these men, and in each case I said, "I seldom see you at the Hall now ?" The one replied, "No, Ma'am, you see I have got a home now, which I never used to have, and I stays there now, and teaches my boys, for I neglected them long enough, poor things." The other man said, " Why, Ma'am, I like the Hall very well, but since I have had a good home I find there is no place like it. I have took to reading my Bible a good deal lately- I takes it off the shelf after tea, and I likes it so much I don't care to go out." I said, "You are quite right ; you have found out the best way ; but perhaps you could come to our Bible-class at the Hall, on Thursday evening—it might help you a little in understand. ing what you read." "Well, Ma'am," he replied, "you see my wife can't leave home, and so I reads out loud to her ; and as to the understanding, I believe that only He who wrote the Bible can teach us really what it means, and so I look up straight to Him, and we get on very well." This last mentioned man, two years ago, was, through drink, one of the greatest brutes I have ever met with. Such instances show that these halls help men to stand through the first trying months, whilst the home is "getting up," and then, in many instances, they pass on to something higher and better.' . . . .

" And he was sure it would be granted that there was nothing so likely to allay the misery and affect the poverty which existed throughout the country, as the building up amongst them of comfortable, happy, Christian homes. He would also read them an extract from a letter to Mr. Solly by Miss Adeline Cooper, who established the admirable Club in Duck-lane, Westminster, five years ago :—

'One woman told me it was a blessed place, for now she had no anxiety about her husband, for she knew, if he had a hundred pounds (!) in his pocket when he went to the Club, it would be safe, and he would bring it all home ! Another woman told me that if anything were to happen to shut up the Club, it would be *the greatest misfortune* that could happen to the wives. While another said if I should ever think of shutting it up (which I am not likely to do), there would be a *revolution* among the women, and they would all come in a body to beg me to keep it open. It is a constant occurrence during the evening for wives or children to tap at the Club-room door about supper time when members' names are called, and in a short time the summons is obeyed, and the men go home comfortably to their expectant families. How different before the Club was opened, when entreaties to come home were met by oaths and curses, and often blows. . . And lastly, the men themselves give public testimony, not only at the Club, but at numerous meetings which they have attended, of the value of the institution, it having, by God's blessing, transformed them from selfish and cruel husbands and fathers to kind and loving ones ; their first thought now being for the comfort of those whom formerly they regarded as incumbrances. The *sole aim of these Clubs must be the improving of the homes, by rendering them happy, which I am thankful to say the Duck-lane Club has done in numerous cases during its two years and a-half's work.*'

" He (the Bishop) thought, therefore, that the difficulties suggested were found not to have very much weight, but that the more they encouraged these institutions the more they fostered domestic habits among the working men."

Turning to a different part of the country, about a year and a-half ago, a young man, earning good wages at a woollen manufactory in Yorkshire, married a respectable young woman, and took her to a comfortable little home. Before long, however, he was frequently drinking at a neighbouring public-house, and, by the end of the first year, their cottage was stripped bare of everything, his wife had to return to her parents, and the young man lodged by himself. A Working Men's Club soon after was established in the village by a public-spirited manufacturer and others of both classes, a large public-house having been purchased for the purpose. The young man mentioned above was one of the first to join it, and within a short time he had saved money enough to buy back his furniture, and to bring his wife once more to live with him in a *home*.

A few months after the Wakefield Working Men's Institute had been opened, as its Secretary was walking down one of the principal streets, a paviour stopped his work to say "Good morning" to him; then taking a purse out of his pocket, and shaking it before the face of the secretary, he added: "It's all siller, master, all siller! And I owe every penny of it to your place up yon. I haven't spent sixpence in the public-house sin' I joined it three months agone, 'cept Christmas-day, when a week's wages went; but I shouldn't have gone there then, you see, if t'other place had been open."

We mention this incident just as it occurred, because it illustrates the "saving" power of these Clubs and Institutes, not as *proving* that they ought to be open on Christmas-day.

A clergyman told us recently that a brother-in-law of his established a Club about three years ago in a Yorkshire village where he was the curate, and that the landlord of a public-house said to him lately, "Well, Mr. ——, you have done more harm to my business by that Club of yours than all the vicar's sermons have done during five-and-twenty years."

Talking, the other day, with an ironmaster in the "Black Country," who gives cordial support to the Working Men's Club in his neighbourhood, about the rate of expenditure among the puddlers, rollers, and shinglers employed there, he remarked, "There are many men about here earning their 3l., 4l., or 5l. a-week, who have very little of it left on Monday night." Other ironmasters entirely corroborated the statement.

We happened, some time ago, to be talking to a couple of navvies, who were smoking their pipes at the corner of a street in Camden-town, where we were waiting for an omnibus. As they said work had been slack lately, we observed that the worst of it was that when they did earn money so much of it went to the publican, and referred to the statement recently made (in the *Cornhill Magazine* for April) respecting a Government contractor who hired 300 navvies and a public-house at the same time, asking them how much they thought those men spent per man weekly. "Oh, about 7s. or 8s., I suppose," was the answer. When we said it was 10s., amounting in the aggregate to 7,000l. for the year, one of them observed, "Ah, I've many a time knocked off 15s. on a Saturday night." "And yet," we said, "you don't want all that drink?" "*No, it's the company that does it.*" "May we ask if you are a married man?" "Yes." "Fifteen shillings a-week makes a great hole in a wife's comfort." "Aye, that's true enough," replied our friend, beginning to look rather serious. At this stage of the proceedings we described the Working Men's Social Club in Weedington-road, Kentish-town (which he seemed to think was a sensible sort of affair), and were just recommending them to look it up, when the omnibus appeared on the scene, and cut short our conversation.

The wife of a mechanic in Islington said to one of the committee of the North London Industrial Exhibition that she thought it was a very excellent thing, and wished they had had such things years ago, for her husband had been so busy making something for it that he had been sober for three months, which he hadn't been before for thirteen years. A Club with a workshop in it would clearly have been a great help to this man thirteen years before.

The following relates to a Club in a metropolitan suburb:

"Soon after the Club was opened, a member said to one of the Committee (himself a working man) : 'I was in the Club on Saturday night. I always used to go to the public on a Saturday, but last Saturday I went to the Club instead. I had fourteen shillings when I went in, and when I came out, I'd spent twopence. I haven't felt like that on a Saturday night at ten o'clock, I don't know when. 'Well,' said his friend, 'I hope you didn't go into the public then.' 'No, I didn't,' he replied ; 'I'd got the money in my pocket, so I bought some shoes for the little 'uns, and some flannel for the old woman, and went home.'" See "Occasional Paper," No. 7.

One of the promoters of this Club writes in the same "Paper":—

"Seeing some of the members leaving the rooms one night, after having spent the evening there, I went after them to have a little talk with them respecting the Club, and to ask them what they thought of it ; and they one and all of them, without a dissenting voice, declared that it was the best thing that had ever been begun in Holloway for working men, that it would keep them out of the public-houses, and be the means of putting money in their pockets, and they hoped it would go on and prosper."

"I was at the Club one evening, and was sent for to the door by a poor woman. 'Do you, Sir, know if my husband is here?' she asked. 'Yes, Mrs. ——,' I answered, 'he is upstairs, playing at draughts.'

' Oh ! I am so glad,' rejoined the woman ; ' he has been drinking all day, and I did not know where he was. But if he is here he is all right. Do try and keep him here as long as you can, and I shall be so much obliged to you.' This man says he thanks God for the place."

"Provision is generally made at these Clubs for entertainments of readings, recitations, music, and singing, to which the members are allowed to bring their wives and daughters, and for various excursions or festivals in the summer months. After a time the home becomes benefited also by some of the useful Provident Societies which spring up when working men are rescued from the stupid indifference engendered by habitual drinking at the public-house. But it is impossible to describe all the ways in which the Club is an auxiliary to the home, both when it is needed as the first refuge from the public-house, or the means of escape from one close, crowded room, in which, till the little ones are washed and put to bed, a man's room is sometimes better than his company—and when, in after days, with improved accommodation at home, the Club is still the platform on which he meets with that healthy, improving collision of thought, cheerful converse, or recreation, and all those influences of an elevating and refreshing character *which people in other classes of life need and seek* (however excellent their homes may be), unquestionably to the manifest promotion of the well-being and happiness of those homes.

"As a curious illustration of this tendency of the Working Men's Clubs to improve and refine the manners of those who frequent them, the following fact may be mentioned : After a Working Men's Institute had been opened in the North-West of London about eight or nine months, a publican in the neighbourhood observed to the honorary secretary, ' Well, you have *civilized* these men, at all events.' ' How so ?' was the reply. ' Why, I mean, Sir, that they used to come in with an oath, and ask for their glass of beer , and now there's no swearing, but they say, 'If you please !' It is evident how much the wife and children must benefit by a change which is felt even by the publican."

The strongest and soundest plea on behalf of the Working Men's Club is the benefit it confers upon the working man s HOME, when he has one, and on the safe and improving substitute it offers to him when he does not possess that greatest of earthly blessings."

Further interesting particulars of good effected will be found at the end of the Fifth Annual Report. See Appendix.

Regarding the facilities offered, then, by these Clubs, for social intercourse and good fellowship apart from injurious influences, as their primary idea and their first claim to support, we come next to the provision they afford for recreation and amusement. Here, again, we are naturally reminded how very much more working men and youths stand in need of such provision than the middle and upper classes, not merely on account of their deficiencies in educational resources and cultivated tastes, but because their homes are as deficient in the means of amusement and entertainment as in those requisite for social visiting. Moreover, what amusements are provided for them, at present, by public caterers, almost invariably involve payment by drinking, with the exception of the theatres. But amusement, recreation, all that the Germans understand by the word *Spiel*, being essential, in one form or other, to most human beings, the value to working men of being able to obtain it without pernicious consequences is sufficiently evident. The recreation and entertainment elements, consequently, have been largely developed in Working Men's Clubs; and, considering the deep significance of "Play" as opposed to "Work," its bearing upon national character, and its relationship to man's higher life (too much lost sight of in this country), the claim of these institutions to approval on this ground may be as readily conceded as on the last.

Another primary idea insisted on by the "Union" from its first formation, as essential to the true mission and permanence of Working Men's Clubs, has been the Educational element. Hence its persistent efforts to add the name "Institute" to that of "Club." We have sufficiently dwelt on this feature of the movement in our first chapter, and will therefore only add here that whereas Mechanics' Institutions and adult evening schools were expected to furnish mechanics with the means of adult education, it is a fact too notorious to be denied that they have not been used by the working men for this purpose to any considerable extent. Now, without discussing the causes of that failure in detail, it is obvious that few men in any rank, after a hard day's work, are inclined for a hard night's study. The few working men who have been willing to undergo it are just the men whom one finds here and there scattered over the country, who are occupying a leading position of some kind or other, and who gratefully express their sense of the value of Mechanics' Institutes. But of course they are the rare exceptions to their class.

And when we look into the actual facts brought out in the course of this Club movement, we find other and special objections felt by working men to learning at night. Here, *e. gr.*, is one, so intensely natural, when their daily occupation is considered, that we may marvel it never occurred to the founders of Mechanics' Institutes. We are told in one of the papers of the "Union" that in the course of a Conference on Working Men's Clubs held by the Council three years ago in London, when the propriety of connecting classes with Clubs was being discussed, a working man observed, "We have masters all day long, my lord, and we don't want 'em at night." We should think not. The mental as well as bodily attitude needs to be changed if strength and reason are to be preserved. Yet we fully believe, with many intelligent operatives (and experience is continually confirming this view), that a Working Men's Club without any educational adjuncts, a mere "recreation-shop," has no elements in itself of permanence or stability. It is far too dependent on excitement and novelty. Moreover, it does not attract the finer and more earnest spirits of the working class, who are needful to manage and give life to any enterprise for the benefit of their order. Too often the stimulus of betting and gambling is wanted in such a Club, and is introduced into it. Those who attend a place of that character do not in general become attached or grateful to it, seldom feeling that they have got any real lasting good out of it. But when men, especially young men, are conscious of being mentally and morally, therefore permanently, benefited by any institution, they willingly make considerable efforts and sacrifices in return for the good they have thus experienced. There is nothing, we believe, for which men are more deeply and persistently grateful than for intellectual and spiritual benefits, when they once become conscious of having received them—which, however, is not a phenomenon of everyday occurrence.

But how is this educational element to be developed in the Clubs, if the members so strongly object to having " masters " in their leisure hours? Some light is thrown on the answer to this question in one of the Society's Occasional Papers just quoted, entitled, " Working Men Want and Welcome Gentlemen's Help in their Clubs" (No. 9); also in their "Hints and Suggestions, &c." In these and other papers of the Union the idea is thrown out that a vast deal of information may be communicated, and mental training imparted, in the way in which drawing-room conversation is carried on, without any assumption of tutorial strictness and command on the one hand, or any of the constraint of subjection on the other;

E

while the information may be made as interesting as any reasonable being would expect it might be who considers the marvels to be revealed alike in a chapter of history, a drop of water, the human hand, or an electrical machine. The very name of " Lecture," no doubt, is generally sufficient to scare away most of the members of a Working Men's Club. Both the name and the thing, indeed, are not very attractive in more pretentious institutions. In a subsequent chapter an account is given of a variation on the ordinary " Lecture " successfully attempted in some London Clubs. On the writer's narrating this experiment to the members of the Club at Leicester, one of the Committee, a medical gentleman, offered to devote several evenings to the same subject there, if the diagrams were lent him; and the offer being warmly received, an excellent class for the study of comparative anatomy has been held at that Club throughout the winter. We have heard of a similar *melange* of songs, recitations, and lectures, being also practised successfully at another Club.

In one large and self-supporting Club, where the only deficiency was this very serious one of having no educational element in it of any kind, an enterprising young gentleman (a graduate of the London University) succeeded, with the aid of the Committee, in forming a tolerably large and attentive elocution class, having become highly popular by joining in " the mazy dance" given at the annual tea-meeting of the Club, and on another occasion by taking part in a bout at single-stick. In another Club of a similar character a good English history class was formed, in consequence of a telling sketchy description of the salient features of our history, from the time of Julius Cæsar to the Norman Conquest, given one evening in the principal Club-room.

The fact is, that no class of persons, in any rank or of any age, are more willing to receive information and mental culture generally, than working men, if only they feel it is being given by a *friend*, not by a master, and if it is imparted in an easy conversational style, questions being allowed at proper intervals, or songs and recitations, when the instruction is being given in the form of a lecture or address. The whole secret, in fact, of making the Club and Institute useful in an educational point of view lies in a judicious use of the " *Inclined*

Plane." Begin by meeting their humblest social wants for relaxation and amusement, and you may lift our hard-worked brethren by degrees up to very respectable heights of knowledge and education. But if you begin by presenting the thick end of the plane, in the shape of lectures and classes as the principal inducements for these men to come to a Club or Institute, they naturally reject your invitations altogether. This consideration answers the question often asked, whether Mechanics' Institutes ought to be generally transformed into Working Men's Clubs. The Clubs are needed to prepare scholars for the more systematic and advanced culture which Mechanics' Institutes were intended to supply, and these are, and will be, needed wherever a Club has been doing its fitting work, but has not developed into a College. The Mechanics' Institute should certainly be kept as an educational Institute. If it is performing that function, let it by all means be preserved. If it fails in doing this, either by its own fault or through want of scholars, let it be transformed either into a Working Men's Club, which would enable it to meet the wants of genuine mechanics up to a certain point; or into a Literary and Scientific Institute, to meet the requirements of the tradesmen and middle class.

These are three elements, then, the Social, Recreational, and Educational, among those which constitute the fundamental ideas from which Working Men's Clubs and Institutes are intended to draw support and life—by which they are to be characterized, and for which they claim the goodwill of persons in every rank. The tendency of the whole organization, so far as it approaches its ideal, evidently is at once to remove temptations and evil concomitants from useful and innocent recreation and amusement; and, at the same time, to humanize, refine, and spiritualize those whose daily toil often tends to make them little better than machines or beasts of burden.

There is one other very important feature in the movement, more than once earnestly dwelt on in the publications of the Union. It is explained in the following paragraph, taken from the beginning of one of the first of the Society's publications above referred to :—

" These Clubs should help the working classes towards a social life. By a social life we mean, in the first place,

pleasant company—but not this only or chiefly: we mean also the feelings, the habits, and all the various forms of joint activity appropriate to the whole class of working men, or at least to all those who would realize their actual position of living together as fellow-workers, as neighbours, as citizens, and as men. They must be SOCIETIES, of which the members should be led to feel an interest in one another's well-being, and a desire to promote the common good. In proportion as this corporate brotherly spirit is aroused and cherished, the Club will not only be securing the best chance of permanence, but will be sure to do far greater good while it lasts than could have been effected by the most lavish expenditure of money or by any accumulation of mere teaching or recreative appliances. And assuredly, in proportion as men are thus brought away from mere animal or empty, often debasing, enjoyment—into a state of higher social life, into collision with thoughtful, inquiring minds, and into a manly fellowship with each other—both their intellectual and moral nature will be unfolded, more advanced education will be desired, and the way prepared for that quickening nurture of their higher spiritual life towards which all judicious efforts for the true and enduring welfare of our fellow-creatures necessarily tend."
—*Hints and Suggestions, &c.*, pp. 3 and 4. (See also *Working Men: a Glance, &c.*, pp. 8 and 9, also published by the Union.)

These remarks, our readers may think, point in the direction of Working Men's Colleges, more than in that of Clubs. But the intimate relation, in fact organic connexion, between a College and a true Working Men's Club has been urged in a previous chapter. "If," it was there argued, "the Club be a living organism, not a piece of dead machinery, it will infallibly *grow*, until in the course of years it develops into a College, while still retaining its social Club elements." Always supposing, however, it should be added, that a suitable soil and climate are among the conditions; such—*e.gr.*, as a large town population capable of providing intelligent artizans for students and educated benevolent men for teachers. But it is certainly interesting to note in this connexion that of all the Working Men's Colleges formed in provincial towns on the model and under the impulse of the admirable Institution in Great Ormond-street, the Ipswich College is the only one that has continued to exist; and that, from the first, has possessed and cultivated all the features of a Club as well as of a College. It has, no doubt, possessed very great advantages in its admirable principal, Dr. Christian, in its staff of teachers, and in the support of the Messrs. Ransomes and of the large body of skilled artizans in their employ. But other Colleges have been little, if at all, less favoured in many of these respects, without being able to attract the working men in sufficient numbers to keep the College open.

But this brings us to a difficulty experienced in connexion with Working Men's Clubs and Institutes which has troubled most of the philanthropists of this country not a little—we mean the religious difficulty.

In referring to Working Men's Colleges, in the chapter just mentioned, we observed that their radical idea, as originally laid down by the Rev. F. D. Maurice, is that of a brotherhood or fellowship for the *complete* culture and development of working men as men. Hence among other elements requisite will be a Bible - class. But in Working Men's Clubs the religious element in any shape has very rarely been introduced, partly because the working men generally and naturally as much object to its introduction at their Clubs, as gentlemen would in the Athenæum or Carlton—partly because the movement being intended to embrace persons of all creeds and parties, and standing therefore · on thoroughly neutral ground, it has been almost impossible to connect any kind of religious exercises or instruction with a Club without trenching on its unsectarian character. In those two excellent Clubs, however, already referred to, in Westminster and Notting-hill, where the personal character and influence of the ladies who founded them, and of the city missionaries, gave a form and tone to the Clubs from the first, a Bible-class, prayer-meeting, or short religious service has been regularly and unobtrusively conducted once or twice a-week in a room given up for the occasion, without any ill consequences, and therefore with unmixed, though perhaps very limited, good. But a curious illustration of the difficulty of introducing the same element into other Clubs took place when a deputation went from one of the above-mentioned institutions to invite the Committee of another London Club to have a Bible-class or religious service on the plan they had found work so well themselves. The deputation were very courteously received and listened to. The Chairman of the Committee expressed approval of the idea, hoped it might be carried into effect, and added that he supposed the rector of the parish, the Rev. Mr. W——, would be asked to conduct the service. "No," said another member of the Committee, who also approved of the plan, "we ought to get the Rev. Mr. C——," naming a clergyman in charge of a kind of Refuge in the parish. "He knows a great deal more about working men." "You are forgetting the Rev. J. Mc——," said a third, mentioning a Baptist missionary. "He *lives* among the working men, and they all like him." "Then," cried a fourth, striking the table with his fist—"Then, by Jasus, we'll have a praste!" The deputation retired, and we need not say that no religious service was established. In more than one other Metropolitan Club the attempt to combine religious agencies with a Working Men's Club has proved a complete failure. And even at Notting-hill the Workmen's Hall has not of late kept the hold that could be wished on the working men of the neighbourhood. At Duck-lane there is no missionary directly connected with the Club, and the members, moreover, do not belong chiefly to the operative class, but to a humbler grade. On the other hand, there can be no doubt that many of the agencies of a Club and Reading-room may be, and have been, employed by city missionaries in their arduous labours with great advantage.

Probably the best solution of this important question is found in two remarks put forward by the Parent Society. The first is, that whenever a number of the members of a Club are desirous or willing to have a Bible-class or any religious service, they should apply to the Committee for leave to rent a room at set times for the purpose. This would not identify the Club with any religious party, or commit it to any doctrinal position, just as a room might be let to a Temperance or Trade Society without at all committing the Club to the particular views held by the society. This recommendation was received with great favour by the Conference held at the Whittington Club in 1864. (See "Report of Conference, &c.," published by the Union, pp. 28—30. Also a subsequent chapter in this volume entitled, "The Neutral Position of Clubs, &c.") The second suggestion we must give in the words of an address issued by the Union in its third Annual Report, and quoted in " Facts and Fallacies," &c., p. 10. (See Appendix.)

" It is a universally-recognized and most important principle that this Union, all Working Men's Clubs, and the whole movement generally, must not only be rigidly kept free from religious or political bias, but must scrupulously avoid becoming in any shape or way organizations for promoting political or theological purposes. *On the other hand, it is equally certain that when persons animated by a true Christian spirit, guided and actuated by high religious principle, devote themselves to establishing and working these Clubs, there is the best chance of their having a permanent and useful career.* Nay, experience is continually proving that it is impossible for them to have more than a short-lived or sickly existence, unless they do secure, in one way or other, the services of men, whether of the higher or the working classes, who will devote themselves to this work in a spirit of Christian self-sacrifice and of religious devotedness to duty—who, in the memorable words of a great man, 'will make a conscience of it.' The benefit to those who give such help will often be incalculably greater than that which they confer, as many persons of education working in these Clubs, Institutes, and Colleges gratefully confess ; moreover it is found, as a matter of fact, that where persons of this stamp, of either sex, do so devote themselves, in conjunction with intelligent working men, to making a Club pleasant and useful to the members, and especially to promoting a spirit of genial fellowship among them, there working men not only are attracted in considerable numbers, and are retained in membership, but often thankfully find they are gaining far higher benefits than any for which they originally joined the Club.

" People who have religious objects deeply at heart are entreated to remember that this movement, while abstaining from all direct religious action, powerfully promotes those conditions which are essential to religious life, and prepares men for the reception of all those influences which appeal to them as moral and spiritual beings."

The words we have italicized in this passage express the true theory, we apprehend, of working any movement for

the good of one's fellow-creatures. It may be quite out of
the question, *e. gr.*, to ask persons who have come together to
transact secular business, or even for a philanthropic purpose,
to unite in offering up prayer, but if they have previously, in
the solitude of their own hearts, asked for guidance and a
blessing, we humbly submit that they are much more likely to
transact their business wisely, to carry it forward with perseverance, and to have success granted to them. Again, there
can be no doubt that Christian-minded persons may establish
and greatly promote the success of a Club without ever introducing the religious element into it, and yet, through their
work at the Club, must remarkably promote the religious
welfare of the members and the neighbourhood. The
excellent clergyman who established the Salford Club told us
that when he first went down to his parish there were parts
of it into which he could not go without the danger of being
insulted, and the galleries of his church were empty. But,
within a year or two after he had established the Club,
although he never, directly or indirectly, introduced the subject of religion there, he was sure of a kindly reception in any
part of the parish, and the galleries of the church were filled.
We commend this fact and the foregoing extract to the
attention of thoughtful Christians, whether lay or cleri cal, and
especially of those gentlemen who convened or addressed the
interesting Conference held last January at the London
Coffee-house, to hear the reasons offered by working men for
not being oftener found in our churches and chapels, or connected with religious organizations.

But then it may be asked if the Club is gradually and
organically to grow into a College, at least in large towns,
and if religious culture, to some extent at all events, ought
to form part of the *curriculum* of a true Working Men's
College, how are we to avoid the difficulties now described.
We answer, that in proportion as the Club had done its work
effectually, had so moulded, educated, and enlarged the moral
and intellectual natures of its members, so thoroughly welded
them into a brotherly fellowship for the promotion of each
other's welfare, both secular and spiritual, they would be
prepared to accept religious culture in one shape or another
from the man or men who could best afford it to them, who
could give that culture of the noblest quality, and most free

from sectarian limits. In fact, it is quite possible that the introduction of religious teaching might mark the transition of the institution from the humbler and simpler form of Club organization to the higher and fuller organism of Club and College combined.

On the principles, then, and with the objects that have now been enumerated, upwards of three hundred Working Men's Clubs and Institutes have been established during the last four years. Probably one-fourth of the whole number, being set up entirely by private enterprise, will have aimed at only a very limited part of this ideal. But so far as the influence of the Parent Society has been felt, those principles and objects have shaped the undertaking.

Nearly all the Clubs have originated with a few individuals in each locality ; and, in a considerable majority of instances, a public meeting has been employed to secure the requisite amount of support. But an interesting question, going to the heart of the whole movement, has been recently raised by the advocates of a different course. These persons plead for long preliminary private action, to be carried on by a few earnest like-minded men, animated by a religious spirit, and who should devote themselves to the organization of a Club, without appealing to the public until they have made their own footing good. They maintain that a promiscuous body of men, drawn together in consequence of a public meeting, cannot be expected to have that coherence and those deep mutual affinities which are requisite to sustain the pressure on persons' time, strength, and self-sacrificing zeal required to carry forward successfully so arduous an enterprise as the maintenance and management of an efficient Working Men's Club. For, as we shall presently see, it is by no means an enterprise easy of accomplishment. The change for the gentry of England from tavern to Club life was comparatively easy. For the great majority of working men at the present day it is far otherwise, and for reasons most of which lie on the surface, such as their want of money, and especially of culture, most of all the extent to which public-house life has been wrought into the very fibre of their social existence during the last hundred years. Hence, the need of great and persistent effort on the part of those who try to establish and work a Club efficiently. But while we fully recognize the absolute necessity of the promoters of a Club gathering round them, in one way or other, a little band of devoted workers, the argument for a public meeting rests on the incontrovertible fact that it is often the only way, in a large and populous locality, of making known to one another those who are both fitted and willing to co-operate earnestly in the work. The first three veritable Clubs started in large towns—Salford, Notting-hill, and Westminster—were certainly formed without a public meeting, and by the Christian zeal and love of those few persons first engaged in the movement. They have stood well, on the whole, the test of time. Camden Town Club, again—for a considerable time one of the most useful and successful in the kingdom, originated in the same way, though a public meeting greatly helped it after a time. Buersill, near Rochdale, presents a similar instance. In that busy Lancashire manufacturing village a dozen Sunday-school teachers, in the very depth of the cotton famine, resolved to start a Working Men's Club, and with remarkable perseverance and energy succeeded in their beneficent undertaking. An account of their efforts is given at the end of Chap. V., "Self Supporting," &c.

The Committee of the Camden Town Club (and, we believe, of the Notting-hill Hall and Buersill Club also) have been accustomed to commence their meetings with prayer. At Notting-hill and Duck-lane, a prayer-meeting and Bible-class have been held once a-week from the commencement, for any who chose to attend them. But this is not usual. On the other hand, at Newcastle, Bolton, Preston, Rotherham, Shoreditch, Leicester, and various other places, successful Clubs have been established and the workers chiefly drawn together in the first instance by public meetings. But against these instances several cases of failure might be adduced, where, from want of previous intimacy, and of any vital principle of union among the managers (who had been drawn together only by a public meeting), the Clubs, in the course of a few months, of a year or two at farthest, broke up disastrously. In the case of that Club in the heart of London (St. James and Soho), now thoroughly successful and self-supporting, a public meeting certainly brought together a small number of zealous working men bent on establishing a good Club; but it was not until they had been trained by a year and a-half's disappointments and struggles, welded together by trouble and effort into something like a veteran missionary band, that they obtained success, and which, even then, would never have been forthcoming but for opportune middle-class help. Something of the same process is observable in the Wednesbury Club, though it has not had the same trials to contend against as the London Club just mentioned, but has manifested from the first an admirable corporate spirit among its leading members.

One of the benefits hoped especially from the establishment of these Clubs is, that they will provide a place at which Friendly and Provident Societies can hold their meetings instead of, as at present, almost universally at the public-house. The Registrar of these societies says that he calculates it costs their members, on an average, 5s. for every 1l. they lay by for the rainy day, as the consequence of having their courts and lodges held where they must pay for the accommodation by drinking. Several striking illustrations of this statement, from "Occasional Paper" No. III., are given in a later chapter, and, of course, every one of the Registrar's annual reports contains similar statements and warnings. But the men, hitherto, have pleaded against Mr. Tidd Pratt's remonstrances that they have no other place to go to, except sometimes a school-room, which is cold and cheerless, while they specially seek sociability. But wherever there is a Working Men's Club in the neighbourhood able to let them a room once a-week for a moderate payment, there is no excuse for the present ruinous expenditure; "drinking for the good of the house" may then be exchanged for saving for the good of the home and of the "box" (*i.e.*, their funds). The manager of the Great Ancoats Club, Manchester, stated at a Conference held in that city by the Central Society last autumn, that he was now continually receiving applications from Odd Fellows' Lodges for a room to meet in, which the committee were reluctantly compelled to refuse from want of larger premises. It is also a striking sign of the times that, in many parts of London, the landlords of public-houses are actually giving notice both to "Odd Fellows" and "Foresters" that it does not pay to let them have the use of a room without rent. We have heard of several instances recently, in which these societies have even abruptly had notice to quit. The quantity of liquor ordered by many of the London Societies appears to have marvellously decreased within a very recent period; and this not, apparently, through an increase of total abstinence, so much as from other causes. " Are those men upstairs teetotallers?" asked the landlord of a public-house in Chelsea, the other night, of a " Forester," who had, just come down from his "Court." "No, I should think not, indeed!" answered the man, with a laugh at the absurdity of the question. But the amount of "custom" seemed to be approaching that scale which publicans abhor more than nature ever objected to a vacuum. (See "Fifth Annual Report," p. 15, Appendix.)

The number of Benefit Clubs formed by publicans simply to draw custom to their house, is very large, and constitutes one great cause, Mr. Pratt informs us, of the frequent failure of these societies, as no Friendly Society is really safe unless it have at least 200 members. In proportion as such Societies hold their meetings at Working Men's Clubs and Institutes instead of at the public-house, all these great evils will be more or less remedied.

In these views and noteworthy facts we think our readers will discern the various claims of this movement on behalf of Working Men's Clubs and Institutes to general support. But without dwelling longer on them at present, we must now briefly inquire how far such countenance has been given to it.

There should be no mistake on this point. The work, we believe, has too much national importance for us to be able to afford misapprehension in the matter. Individuals who have noticed only the rise and progress or decline and fall of a few Clubs under their own immediate observation, naturally form an exaggerated notion of the general tendency in one or the other direction. It is only when we stand at the centre to which tidings of the condition of various Clubs are continually coming, and at the office of the Central Society examine the " Returns " and correspondence there converging, that any accurate estimate of the whole movement can be formed.

From that vantage-ground, while we discern various signs of weakness and several cases of failure on which we have already dwelt, and to which we shall again advert, there can be no doubt that many facts are evident for which any lover of his country has reason to be profoundly thankful—facts not only confirming what is generally known, that the middle and upper classes have taken up the movement with remarkable heartiness; but that the working men themselves have welcomed it, if not as fully as was at first expected, yet to the very utmost extent that ought to have been anticipated. On the Tyne, in the busy hives of hardy ironworkers, such as the shipbuilders of Jarrow, Newcastle, Shields, and Gateshead, or in Wednesbury, Birmingham Heath, and Rotherham; in quiet country villages, such as Whitchurch (Dorset), Harting, Kyneton, Whittlesford, Kingham, and Great Baddow; among the artizans and labourers in and about London, as those of Bermondsey, Camden Town, Shoreditch, Soho, Croydon; and in the towns and cities of Portsmouth, Brighton, Reigate, Dover, Bridport, Leicester, Leeds, Guildford, Devonport, Bristol, Edinburgh, Inverness, Glasgow, and Wisbeach; among the "brickies" (*Anglice*, brickmakers) of Shoebury-ness, Chislehurst, and Notting-hill; the costermongers of Westminster and Clare-market; the fishermen and sailors of Bridlington Quay, Weymouth, and Hastings; the plait-workers of Luton; the machine-makers of Ipswich; the colliers and smiths of Wallsend, Sunderland, and Stockton-on-Tees; among the woollen-workers of Saltaire, Bradford, Paddock, Lockwood, and Honley; the cotton-spinners of Manchester, Bolton, Heywood, Buersill and Preston; and in upwards of 200 other places, we find these Clubs existing as so many ganglionic centres of a happier and purer state of existence, radiating out good influences thoroughly inestimable, promoting pleasant social intercourse, innocent amusement, rational recreation, mental improvement, a brotherly helpfulness, and, in every, sense, a higher life for the toiling millions of this empire.

According to the most recent " Returns " furnished to the Parent Society, there are about 280 or 300 Working Men's Clubs and Institutes now existing in Great Britain, Ireland not having yet notified the existence of any in her domains. (A spirited movement has, however, recently commenced in Belfast, which is likely to result in the establishment of one or more Clubs and Institutes.) The greater part of these have been formed under the impulse and guidance of that Society. Of this number, about 35 are within the Metropolitan Districts, about 10 or 12 in Scotland, 3 or 4 in Wales, and the rest in various English towns and villages. It is impossible to give the numbers quite accurately—first, because new ones are continually being formed, while old ones are occasionally dying out; second, because it is always difficult, as even Government officials know too well, to get busy people, such as those who take the lead in useful undertakings, to find the time for sending statistical information to a common centre, or perhaps to understand the value of doing so at all. There is no doubt, however, that the benefits of furnishing accurate information in a movement so new and tentative as the one in question can hardly be over-estimated.

In addition to these Clubs, there are Soldiers' Institutes springing up in various garrison towns, which are doing a vast amount of good. A remarkably successful effort in this direction at Montreal, made when the Guards were sent there in 1861, was narrated by Major-General Lord Frederick Paulet, K.B., at the anniversary dinner of the Union last July. It has led to the formation of the splendid Guards' Institute in Pimlico. (See Appendix).

The Clubs of course vary much in their means of accommodation, attractions, and number of members, from the original Leeds Club, with its 1,400 members, or the Bolton Club, with its twenty-seven rooms and garden gymnasium, down to the humble village Club, with its one or two rooms and thirty members. But, according to average results throughout the kingdom, we might journey on from town to town, and from village to village, night after night for nearly a twelvemonth, visiting a new Club every night, resting only on Sundays, and from the hours of seven to ten every evening we should find in one of these various Club-rooms a party of men chatting and smoking, perhaps playing at draughts or dominoes, apparently as much at their ease and quite as comfortable as in the tap-room of the "Red Lion" or the "Jolly Fiddlers;" in another room there will be found several members reading the newspapers, books, or magazines; elsewhere there will be a group round a bagatelle table, or engaged in skittles in the back yard, or perhaps cellar; in another Club we should find a class engaged in practising elocution or singing, preparatory to the "harmonic" meeting—*i.e.*, "Free and Easy," held every Saturday night; or it may be occupied with a weekly "discussion" meeting. If we look in on the weekly or monthly "entertainment" night, songs and recitations, varied with "readings," will be going briskly forward, perhaps in a large hall (possibly lent for the occasion), in which latter case the wives and daughters of the members will probably be sharing the general enjoyment.

All this, and much more that might be described of a similar character, no doubt presents a contrast as marked as it is gratifying to the interior of most of the public-houses and beershops at the same hour, the contrast being still more striking (as observed in the extracts given page 99). when the husbands, fathers, and sons return to their respective dwellings. According to "Returns" referred to above, there is an average of about 171 members to each Club, giving a total of between 40,000 and 50,000 working men and youths enjoying the benefits of Club life in lieu of public-house life; but, considering that on an average there are probably at least three human beings the better and happier for their husband, brother, father, or child belonging to the Club, the Society seems justified in stating, as they do, that in all probability 200,000 human beings in this country alone are being largely benefited by the existence of Working Men's Clubs and Institutes. The movement has also spread to the Australian settlements, and is beginning to do good service there. A Club has been in flourishing existence at Hobart Town during the last two years; and some generous unknown friend having given 1,600*l.* for the purchase of land and the erection of a building, the corner-stone of the Club-house was laid last February by the Governor, Colonel Gore Browne, in the presence of the Bishop of the Diocese and all the principal inhabitants. A beginning is also being made at Sydney. Benevolent men of high social position from Italy, France, Hungary, Germany, Holland, Belgium, and America, have made inquiries at the Society's office, have procured its papers, and given very favourable reports (sometimes official) on the subject to their countrymen at home. Working Men's Clubs and such social discussion meetings as the Working Men's Club and Institute Union held at Exeter Hall last spring and the year before, are very popular in Switzerland,

and are spreading widely there, both in towns and villages. A very interesting letter on the subject has lately been received by a member of the Council from M. Bouet, of Neufchatel.

At the same time, it must be admitted, as shown in the previous chapter, that there have been many failures, and much to learn by dismal experience. We propose now briefly to review the questions in what way, to what extent, and owing to what causes, these failures have taken place, both by the light afforded from the statements in the last chapter, and from information subsequently received.

Out of about 350 Clubs formed during the last four or five years, about 60, or 18 per cent., have failed and been shut up. Some of these, however, have been re-commenced with the wisdom bought by experience, and are now doing well. With regard to the rest, some have not succeeded in carrying out one part of their scheme, others have failed in some other department. But, as a general rule, the first, or " social intercourse " portion of the programme has been the least successful. Here we come upon the *pons asinorum*, the special besetting difficulty of Working Men's Clubs. They have been eagerly caught at by youths from fifteen to twenty years of age ; but grown men will not sit and chat with one another where youths are either listening to their talk or disturbing them with noise. Hence scarcely a Club in the country but tells the same sorrowful tale, "The men have been driven away by the boys." Yet it is of the highest importance that at the critical age which ranges from fifteen to twenty-five, youths should have the shelter and benefit of these Clubs. " They, of all persons," it is truly urged, " seem most in need of the Clubs, and the ardour with which they have embraced the opportunities so offered shows the exact adaptation of such institutions to their wants." We grant that no class of Her Majesty's subjects more need some such kind of shelter and occupation during their leisure hours than these youths. But it does not, therefore, follow that they should monopolize Working *Men's* Clubs, and totally unfit them for the object for which, often at great cost, they have been established. The true course evidently is either to establish a " Youths' Institute "— on the admirable model originally given by the Rev. Henry

White at Dover, and since worked out with so much Christian devotedness and success by Mr. Tabrum at Islington and Mr. Baker at Bayswater, with the help of a few like-minded friends—or, if there are not the means for this course, then to appropriate separate rooms in the Club for the men and the youths. The same silent "Reading Room" and the "Lecture" or "Concert" Hall can be used by both in common. But it is absolutely necessary, as woful experience teaches, that the grown men should have their talking and recreation rooms to themselves, or they will not come near the Club. At that Club in Lancashire (Heywood), mentioned above, where the adult members were becoming a vanishing quantity, and the youths were literally swamping the concern, the balance was partially restored, and the Club placed on a healthy footing, by the Committee having the words "For men above twenty-five years only" painted outside the door of one comfortable apartment. The Rev. H. Sandford, one of H.M. Inspectors of Schools, while strongly deprecating the admission of Youths to Working Men's Clubs, at a Conference held at Stourbridge last autumn by the South Staffordshire Adult Education Society, recommended, as a desirable alternative, that night schools should add recreation of various kinds to their programme. This is an excellent suggestion, and would, in fact, be equivalent to establishing regular "Youths' Institutes" all over the country. One great objection to the admission of youths to Clubs is that so many of them seem to care for little but the bagatelle-board (and the gymnasium when there is one), varied with occasional "larking" and practical jokes. The due admixture of a certain amount of compulsory teaching, as a condition of enjoying the recreation, would have an excellent effect.

The usual age fixed for admission has been eighteen, but the temptation to falsify their age has been too great to numbers under that age, so that practically the limit has generally been as low as sixteen. But even eighteen is far too young, if the "men above twenty-five" are to be secured as members. Yet imagine the dilemma of managers of Clubs who mourn over the small attendance of adult members, or see them gradually melting away, and yet have facts of the following kind coming under their notice without being able to make provision for the due appropriation of separate rooms to youths and adults. One of the ladies spoken of in a former chapter writes thus :—

> For some months past, on account of the large attendance, a rule has been passed to admit none under twenty-one years of age ; and mothers have often asked me, with tears in their eyes, if some exception could not be made in favour of their sons, so that they might be admitted, and kept out of bad company.

The same earnest entreaties were made to the Committee of the Southwark and other Clubs. A man who had taken a great interest in the Club at Holloway, writes :—

> Speaking to some young men one evening at the Club, I asked them what they thought of it, and in a moment, without thinking of the matter, they said, "Mr. ——, it is a *home* for us !" One of them told me he used to spend every evening at the public-house, but now he spent his evenings at the Club.

And, again, another straw showing which way the tide runs :—

> A youth whom it was necessary to suspend for misconduct in annoying other members, when refused his ticket, said, "Well, I *am* sorry." "What call have you got to be sorry for ?" said a companion. "There's nothing to be sorry about." "Yes, but there is," said the other ; "since I've belonged to the Club I've bought a new shirt, a new pair of stockings, and a new pair of boots."

At the Conference held in Manchester last autumn, the manager of the Great Ancoats Club, while pleading for youths being admitted to these institutions in some way or other, told the meeting that an adult member of the Club had said to him one night, "I say, Anderson, why do you let so many boys come here ? " " Shall I turn your boy out ? " was the prompt reply. " Oh, no," answered the father, rather alarmed at the home-thrust. " For God's sake keep him here as much as you can. His brother goes to a beershop, and plays cards, and never brings home his money." The manager added: " We could have a young Club full every night if we had only got the premises. We have first-rate gymnasts there now. When there was fear that the Club must be closed for want of sufficient funds to meet the heavy rent, several young men said to me, ' We shall all go back to the beershop if you shut up your Club.'" He concluded

by saying, " We could treble our numbers if we had only the
money for larger premises."

It is quite clear then, first, that it is of the greatest importance that youths should have some Institute of their
own, or else rooms to themselves in a Club ; second, that Working
Men's Clubs, as *Men's* Clubs, have suffered immensely from
the youths taking possession of them.   But the question naturally arises, Why did not the grown men come in, at first,
in numbers large enough to subdue or exclude the juvenile
invasion ?   Some working men, when asked this question,
reply, " Because you do not make your Clubs attractive."
There is a deal of truth in that reply, we believe.   Comparatively few of the Clubs even approach the ideal of what was
intended by their first promoters.   The best room is too
often made the reading-room, in weak obliviousness of the
obvious fact that five or six men want to talk and smoke for
one that wants to read in silence.   In equally strange forget-
fulness of the value to tired men of chairs to rest in, too often
only forms are provided, sometimes actually without backs ;
and, as if studiously to prevent that sociability which not
merely hard-worked, little-educated men, but men of all ranks,
specially covet in their hour of rest, long tables are occasionally placed in the Club-rooms, instead of those little round
three-legged deal tables wnich are delightfully adapted to
social grouping.   These may seem trifles.   So is each individual brick that goes to make up a house.   But we get no
house without attending to details.   A working man even
once hinted to us that it was not beneath the dignity
of a Committee to consider the snug and attractive effect of
red curtains judiciously disposed in a Club-room.

But a more serious want felt by working men in these Clubs
has been the want of a *welcome* at them.   (See again " Occasional Paper," No. IX., Appendix.) *They miss the landlord.* The
success of a public-house depends, to a large extent, upon the
character and abilities of that functionary.   In all successful
Clubs, some one or more of the managers, either the steward
or members of the Committee, have exerted themselves, not
merely to keep order, but to make all the members feel welcome and happy.   But in a majority of cases, this, the most
important and most difficult part of the whole business, has
been greatly neglected.   Moreover, at the Clubs, working

men often miss, not only the landlord, but the pot-boy. The first thing a weary operative wants, after getting into a comfortable seat, is to give his orders. It is good to have a bell in the Club-room. " Why," said a cheery artizan to us one day when discussing this point, "I feel twice as much a man when I have given the pot-boy my orders!" They have been *under* orders all day long, and the change of attitude is pleasant, as indicated in the similar remark, given above (p. 105), respecting teachers. Now the refreshment department has not, in general, met these and other idiosyncrasies of working men. All such drawbacks help, in some degree, no doubt, to account for Clubs not having been more popular, at present, and having sometimes failed altogether. Occasionally, indeed, the men have been too much interfered with by the gentlemen who found the money and started the Club, which, of course, would be one of the most fatal mistakes that could be committed; but, on the other hand, sometimes, and we are inclined to believe much more frequently, they have not had sufficient help of various kinds from persons of a higher class. (See, in addition to the Occasional Paper before quoted, the paper entitled " Facts and Fallacies.")

But then the question naturally recurs, Why have not working men themselves made these Clubs more attractive, and supplied the defects which, it is urged, have kept their mates away, and thus allowed the youths to monopolise them? The answer we believe to be mainly this—First, the *élite* of their class—the men who could have taken up this movement and made it a magnificent success if they had liked, in the course of two or three years at longest—are already occupied to the full stretch of their strength and time (often greatly overtasked) in managing their Friendly, Trade, or Co-operative Societies. Secondly, there was a wide-spread suspicion of this movement, at its outset, among the members of Trade Societies all over the kingdom, but especially in London, in consequence of the endeavours made a year or two before the Union began its operations, by some of the great employers of labour during the builders' strike of 1859, to establish Working Men's Institutes, and to make them " Houses of Call." Vast numbers of the skilled operatives of the country feared that the latent object of the Club movement was to break up their Trade organizations ; and although this apprehension was completely dispelled from the minds of their leaders by a meeting held at the office of the Union in June, 1863, it has lingered with most provoking tenacity among the rank and file of the body. Thirdly, there is a common impression that it is merely a "Temperance Dodge," another form of Teetotal agitation. But, fourthly (the chief obstacle, unquestionably), that which has outweighed all the rest put together, has been the attachment of the existing adult generation of working men to the public-house, as a place of sociable resort to which they have become thoroughly accustomed. Connected, of course, with this, is the enormous hindrance arising from their apathy and indifference to their own improvement and well-being. The immense difficulties in the way of getting them to give up the public-house for another meeting-ground, may be best realized by learning the efforts made during the last six or seven years by a few of the leading men in various Friendly and Trade Societies in different parts of the kingdom, especially in London, to get the meetings of their respective societies removed from the public-house to some other locality. In a few instances these efforts have been successful, and, as we mentioned above, among the Odd Fellows and Foresters they are rapidly increasing, but only after years of agitation, carried on in spite of every sort of opposition and opprobrium. (See fifth Annual Report, Appendix.) In a much larger number of cases the agitation has hitherto been unsuccessful. So recently as last, autumn a member of a large Trade Society stated at a meeting of leading representatives of Trade Societies, held at the offices of the Working Men's Club and Institute Union, that, much as he, individually, wished to see his Lodge-meetings held at a Club, he did not dare propose it at present, as he should certainly be "drummed out" if he did. Whereupon a highly skilled and intelligent artizan got up and said he had actually himself suffered that ignominious expulsion a few years before, in consequence of persevering endeavours to remove the meetings of the Trade Society to which he belonged from the tavern where they assembled. Not seldom, we imagine, the secretary and other leading men in these Friendly and Trade Societies have been well plied by the landlord with personal inducements to use all their influence to keep their meetings at his house. The one solitary occasion on which the writer was ever treated with personal and persistent rudeness by working men, was when he attended a meeting of Foresters, by invitation, at a Court held to consider the propriety of purchasing a hall and rooms wherein to hold their meetings, in lieu of the public-house. And although the offensive behaviour (which was confined to two or three) was strongly denounced by the Chairman and others, several members strongly opposed the contemplated investment and removal, and the excitement altogether was remarkable. Equally remarkable, we were informed, was the regret expressed at their meeting the following week by the men in question for their previous behaviour, and the change apparent in the tone and temper of the whole Court was all that could be wished. " It was not the same Court, though all the same men were there," said a member of it with emphasis, when describing the change. But a vote had been taken after many of the best men had left the room wearied and vexed, and by a small majority a decision was passed against removing, which cannot be reversed till another year has elapsed.

Now if there is so much difficulty in persuading the working men to remove their business meetings from places where they know, partly by experience, partly by the reiterated warnings of Mr. Tidd Pratt, that both they and their Societies are suffering damage, we cannot wonder if it is a work of time to persuade them to adjourn their merely sociable gatherings to a Working Men's Club.

But here we are confronted with another " crux," one which the Club promoters, both among the working and upper classes, have been not a little tormented—viz., the great " Beer " question. The original idea of the founders of these Societies was strenuously opposed to allowing any intoxicating drinks whatever on the premises; and out of the whole number established, not above half-a-dozen appear to have introduced beer. Of these, three have ceased to exist; at three others, Leicester, Handsworth, and Birmingham Heath, it has been in daily use as a regular article of refreshment for periods varying from six to twelve months, the quantity allowed to be sold to the same individual in the two latter being limited to one pint each, and unlimited in the former. The writer held various Conferences last autumn with the members and friends of Clubs, as well as with respectable working men unconnected with any Club, and the result (the details will be found in the Report presented to the Committee, see Appendix) was a large amount of evidence in favour of allowing the sale of beer to members, but restricting its consumption to a bar at the entrance, or to the dining-room where there is one, and limiting the quantity to a pint for each member. The main points in the case seem to be on the one hand that the working men who care, or might be brought to care, about Clubs want to get out of the habit of drinking, " treating," and " tossing"— to give up tippling, in short—and for this purpose some of them say it is quite sufficient if they could be relieved from the pressure of the landlord, and from drugged and salted beer*—that the higher tone of the Club and good management would do all the rest. Others, in large numbers, add that it is better not to allow beer in *the rooms* of the Club at all, and to restrict the quantity procurable at the bar. The warmest advocates of beer admit that unless there is a good tone in the Club—careful and thoroughly respectable management with efficient discipline—it would not be safe to introduce it, and that there are Clubs now in good working order, and very useful, where it would be absolutely criminal to introduce fermented liquors. Among the latter would be those in which the youthful element is predominant or even largely mingled, without a sufficient counterpoise of steady, thoughtful, middle-aged men. The advocates for the permission of beer argue, we believe with great truth, that multitudes of grown men will not come to Clubs now because they cannot get there the refreshment they prefer ; and if they stop at a public-house to get it, they like, or are tempted, to remain. On the other hand, against all this it is urged that the pressure of the landlord is not half so powerful an incentive to tippling as the convivial habits of the men ; that Clubs would no longer be a harbour of refuge, or an instrumentality for raising working men to a higher level, but would soon become little better than beershops with a fine name. Some working men, thoroughly conversant with their class, say that it is not so much the inability to get

* Out of thirteen samples of ale and beer procured from London public-houses, and analysed for the Licensing Conference held at Exeter Hall last January, every one had considerable quantities of salt in it.

beer at the Clubs which has kept the great body of working men away from them, as the dislike to " being treated like children " in being forbidden to have any beer there, and their strong repugnance to going to a place which, in consequence of this restriction, is frequently called by their companions " a Teetotal shop."

Whatever may be the truth, however, regarding this question, we suspect it is very closely connected with the fate of the movement in many places. And, after close observation, much thought, and varied discussion, we are satisfied that the rigid rule at first applied to the case of all Clubs must unquestionably be relaxed, and that in a great many cases the Clubs would be largely benefited, the public-houses and beershops materially injured, and the working men as a class immensely improved, if beer could be sold at a bar in the entrance of the Club, in limited quantities, and *never taken into any room except a dining and supper room*, perhaps even then under the same limitation. The extent to which members of Clubs now go in and out in the course of an evening to neighbouring public-houses, the numbers who sit fuddling at those places, because they cannot get a pint in their own Club-house, the increase in value of a public-house or beershop when a Club is opened near it, the number of beershops set up in the neighbourhood of Clubs, with many similar facts, convince us that the total exclusion of beer has been one serious hindrance to the success of Clubs among adult working men. But a hundred facts and arguments equally assure us that as a general rule it can only be safely introduced, at present, where there are all the safeguards above described. Every case, in short, must stand on its own peculiarities, and the question in each must be decided according to its special circumstances.

This subject, and the difficulty in relation to "youths," are closely connected with a point which has been recently raised by the Earl of Lichfield. This nobleman, who, like his brother lord-lieutenant of the neighbouring county, Lord Lyttelton, has been a most valuable friend of the Working Men's Club movement, urges that the plan of admitting any person above a certain age as a member of a Club, on payment of a weekly or quarterly subscription in advance, has not worked well, and that it is highly desirable the elective

principle, as in all gentlemen's Clubs, should now be introduced. The view formerly taken by the original promoters,
and by the Parent Society, was, that the way into the Club
should present as few hindrances as possible, no balloting, or
other ceremony being required for admission to the public-
house. And it is too true that, in a great number of instances, Clubs at present are not sufficiently popular or
attractive to make it at all probable that anything but speedy
extinction would be the result of requiring a ballot. But
wherever, through good management and other causes, there
is a tolerable demand for admission, we believe it would be
exceedingly useful to adopt Lord Lichfield's recommendation.
At first starting, also, when the novelty of the undertaking
would attract, it is highly probable that if election were
required after the first fifty members had joined, and admission
therefore were made a privilege, instead of, as too often at
present, a new comer being regarded as conferring a favour,
there would be a much larger accession of members ; while
the difficulties about age, about the introduction of beer,
bagatelle tables, skittles, *et hoc genus omne*, would be greatly
helped to a satisfactory solution.

A frequent cause of failure among Clubs has been inadequate and inconvenient premises, too high a rent, or a bad
situation. It is quite certain that small premises make the
success of a Club hopeless. " Working men, " observes the
public-spirited founder and supporter of the first and largest
Club at Leeds, Mr. Darnton Lupton, " are gregarious, and
will not go where there is not company." A working man (as
one himself remarked to us) will sometimes walk past half-
a-dozen public-houses because "there are only a few fellows
sitting there," and not turn in till he comes to a taproom or
parlour where there are at least a dozen already assembled.
But large and capital premises require first-rate management
and a great deal of hard work. More than one such Club
has been closed, in the midst of an exceedingly useful career,
simply from sheer inability to meet the heavy rent. In London
the difficulty is felt with overpowering force. The number of
members required to make a Club self-supporting is generally
too large to be comfortably accommodated in the premises.
Several cases, in fact, have occurred in which not large
and heavily-rented Clubs, but more modest experiments, have

suddenly collapsed long before they had had a fair trial. It is very important to observe that this has generally happened because the gentlemen who had previously subscribed to make up the deficient income got tired of doing so before the working men came forward in sufficient numbers to make the Club self-supporting. But as this matter is dwelt upon in "Facts and Fallaties," in the Fifth Annual Report, and in the next chapter, we need not pursue it here. In that chapter we have also urged the importance to the upper classes of society of promoting these Clubs and Institutes, and have glanced at the part which we believe they are to play in the future history of this country. Here, therefore, we conclude our review of the present position of the Working Men's Club and Institute movement in the United Kingdom, and trust that the interest of the subject, compensating for the want of greater attractiveness in the mode of handling it, may induce our readers to continue its consideration a little further.

CHAPTER IV.

WORKING MEN'S CLUBS AND INSTITUTES IN THEIR RE-LATION TO THE UPPER CLASSES AND TO NATIONAL PROGRESS.

In previous chapters of this volume we have dwelt on the nature and objects of Working Men's Clubs and Institutes chiefly in their relation to the class which they are especially intended to benefit. It is, however, of considerable importance that their bearing upon the upper classes, and on our national well-being generally, should also be clearly understood.

That nations as they rise in the scale of civilization lose some of the valuable qualities which distinguished them in their less luxurious and more heroic age—that they have generally been supplied with the means of renewing their national life by younger and hardier peoples, sometimes through commercial intercourse, oftener by being invaded and conquered—are facts well known to the readers of history.

Persia and India overrun by Greece, Greece conquered by Rome, Rome yielding to Goth and German, are among the most familiar of a hundred similar instances. It is needful we should remember that what is true of nations holds good for the different ranks of society in the nations themselves —specially needful for Englishmen to remember this at the present day. A great law of progress, nay, of existence, is here concerned. Always this question comes up again and again, both in the great crises of national life, and in the more gradual transition periods of growth or decay,—Will the older nation, and will the upper classes, welcome or resist the influence of the approaching barbarians, or of the strug- gling lower classes? Will they accept or refuse the benefits that may be conferred on them by the new and vigorous life of their invaders, or inferiors? Will they rejoice in the opportunities offered them of benefiting those invaders or humbler fellow-countrymen? Will they at once educate them, and in turn be taught by them? or will they present merely an armed resistance or disdainful neglect? If the nobler and wiser course be taken, it needs no prophet to assure us that a far richer life and mightier strength is the reward for all parties concerned. If the older nation or the higher class refuse their mission, they are sooner or later inevitably conquered and crushed.

The aristocracy of England in many most important respects did their country good service when it was emerging from barbarism and growing continually into a higher civilization from the tenth to the sixteenth centuries. The great middle classes of this country have played an incalculably useful, often admirable part in its commercial, social, and political history during the seventeenth, eighteenth, and especially during the present century. The question both these classes have to consider is whether they are now continuing to take the same noble lead in defending and developing the life and growth of this nation as did their fathers or forefathers in other days. Are the noblemen of this age exerting themselves as vigorously in defence of their poorer fellow-countrymen from whatever evils oppress them now, as the *Duces, Comites, Jarls*, and great feudal barons were obliged to do when Danes and Normans, Frenchmen, Spaniards, or a hundred other foes of flesh and blood, from within or without, menaced the peace and prosperity of England? In like manner do the younger men of the middle classes feel the inspiration of great ideas connected with commercial, manufacturing, engineering enterprises to the same extent as their predecessors? In a word, do the natural leaders and defenders of the people at the present day recognize and fulfil their duties of guidance and protection, of heroic leadership in any shape, in a degree commensurate with their increased privileges and light as compared with former times? We ask the question not now to discuss it, but to stimulate thought; and, however the last question may be answered, we would ask our readers to inquire in the next place whether there are not signs that the inevitable decay which affects all things human is creeping into the vigour and earnest life of the middle and upper classes of this country—a decay which has gradually overthrown the mightiest nations and the proudest aristocracies, both of rank and of wealth, which the world has seen—a decay that must destroy every nation and all aristocracies, unless they are renovated by new life from younger nations or the humbler, hardier ranks of society. We think there are such signs. An eminent and thoughtful member of our English aristocracy said to us not long ago that while the morality of his class was considerably higher than in former days, he thought their energy was far less. And if we look back to the days of our Plantagenets and Tudors, or even to those of the first Stuarts, and see the part played by our nobility then, in our internal national life, we think we must agree with him. Still more may we have reason to fear that this decadence of energy and of capacity for leadership among the upper classes has commenced when we observe the very different position held by this country in relation to continental politics now compared with what it was in the days of our Henries, in the reigns of Elizabeth, Cromwell, and Anne, or at the close of the great continental war after the battle of Waterloo.

It must be remembered that we are not now saying that the energy of the English nobility was always or generally well directed, nor that they led the people usually in the right direction (though Runnymede and the Spanish Armada are watchwords of .the purest fame) ; we are simply speaking of their consciousness of high functions for leading and governing, and of the energy with which they exercised them. We say that their lives now, with noble exceptions, are aimless and feeble, compared with what they were in former days ; that their energies are expended chiefly in field sports, or on the turf, or else too often in a general policy of resistance to movement of any kind.

With regard to our middle classes, we confess that there seems too much truth in the allegations beginning to be rife against them of a growing tendency to reckless speculation, inordinate greed, and enervating luxury. There have always, of course, been occasional epidemics among merchants and tradesmen when legitimate honest industry and enterprise were swept away by feverish madness and covetousness, but in the present day it would seem as if the fever were becoming chronic, as if the self-indulgent luxuriousness, the indifference to the public weal, to great questions of right and wrong, and the ravening haste to be rich, the worship of wealth, were becoming permanent gangrenes in the commercial life of this nation. While the older men grow more grasping, the younger become more voluptuous, both more selfish. We know all the proofs of an increasingly nobler life among us which might be adduced. We do not for a moment pretend to be able to strike an accurate balance between our present national tendencies to good and to evil. We only assert the *existence* of the evil tendencies, and we say, boldly, that unless some new vital force is introduced into our "body politic," we shall inevitably go the way which other nations, as proud and powerful, have gone before us.

Are not the working classes of this country the element which a wise and merciful Providence now offers to our community for arresting the decay of which we have spoken, and for renovating our national life? The service which Greece rendered to Asia, and Rome to Greece, and Goth to Rome, often in terrible fire-baptisms, amid rapine and blood, to the sound of shrieks and groans, may be rendered to England, to its aristocracy and middle class, to the whole nation—peacefully and to the sound of music—by those hardy sons of toil who build our houses, construct our engines, procure us food, weave and make our garments, furnish us with all the thousand necessaries and luxuries of civilized life.

Only those who have gone with their educated, well-furnished minds and high culture among the working classes, can form an idea of the energy and receptive vigour with which a large proportion of them welcome and profit by this information and culture, if it be imparted to them in a simple, unpretending, popular style—if they feel that it is a friend, not a patron or schoolmaster, who is instructing them. The vast popularity of Penny Readings is an indication of what may be done with regard to our beautiful literature, and the influences of music, in refining and interesting the multitude. Popular *conversaziones* or chat-meetings illustrate how gladly they will enter into the wonders of creation as seen through a microscope ; of art in the shape of stereoscopes, engravings, sculpture ; of science as shown by an electrical machine or air-pump and chemical experiments. Most of what has hitherto been done for the working men in these directions has been of a very loose, desultory character, mere skirmishing raids among them. But the eagerness with which the higher class of London operatives have availed themselves of tickets for the scientific lectures given to them in the Jermyn-street Museum ; especially, also, the regular attendance of artizans at the Working Men's Colleges, London, Ipswich, and Manchester, show an amount of preparedness for more systematic culture which was previously unsuspected. We are, of course, aware that the attendance of working men at Working Men's Colleges has been very far from what was hoped for and desired. Still, enough has been shown of these first-fruits to indicate the mighty harvest awaiting us.

The great multitude of working men come, when they do come, to the study of history, science, literature, art, with fresh, unworn minds and hearts—with a glorious and childlike readiness to wonder, admire, and love — often with that tendency, however, also, to question and probe which is essential to completeness in the character of a scholar. Their minds and hearts are not debilitated by factitious excitements and luxurious self-indulgence, not *blasé*, nor feverish, nor Byronic. The debasing results of surfeited desires, and frivolous hankering after sentimental or systematic gambling excitement, have not yet begun to demoralize their nature or to blunt their powers ; and though betting for drink is far too common, it is widely removed from the extremes of aristocratic " play " and horse-racing. There is, indeed, a terrible amount of stupid apathy and mere animalism in them to be overcome in a great majority of cases. But that is a difficulty as much easier to master than the indifference of the middle and upper classes to systematic culture and a nobler life, as the lighting a boiler fire (ready laid, though somewhat damp, perhaps) and starting a locomotive is more readily accomplished than getting up the steam when the fuel has burnt away and the ashes are all that remain.

For the rekindling of that nobler life among the middle and upper classes, even as for a new appreciation and diffusion of the blessings which art, literature, and science can confer upon a people, we must look to the culture of the working men by the generous and loving instrumentality of the educated classes. A very few illustrations of our meaning must suffice. A gentleman, of great literary culture himself, was observing to us some time since that the study of our magnificent literature was almost an unknown quantity at the present day. Nothing was read but publications of the day, and those too often only of the most ephemeral or even trashy nature. We have heard the same remark and witnessed its truth in many other quarters. But if any gentlemen were exerting themselves to imbue working men with a knowledge and love of English or other literature, leading them by the hand into the wonderful inheritance bequeathed by the genius of bygone ages, the teachers would benefit scarcely less than the taught. So with regard to recovery from the aimless and often unworthy existence, the enervating and frivolous pursuits, the covetous and greedy tendencies, of which we have complained —see how great an interest of the noblest kind would be breathed into a man's life who found that a number of thoughtful, unworn, vigorous intellects welcomed his explanations of great social and political questions, rejoicing to engage with him in friendly wrestlings and earnest argument about Strikes and Lock-outs, Trades' Unions, Co-operation, Currency, Capital, National Education, the Franchise, the Licensing Laws, and a score of other vitally important questions. Nothing can exceed the candour and openness to truth with which working men listen to the views and reasoning of their superiors in knowledge and training, if only they are approached, as we said before, in a brotherly spirit—nothing except, indeed, the gratitude with which they welcome such efforts to enlighten or entertain them.

What we would earnestly ask, then, of those persons who will accept these imperfect hints, is to observe and make extensively known the fact that Working Men's Clubs and Institutes afford the *locus in quo*, the place and opportunity for this interchange of benefits, this communication of culture and knowledge to the less privileged class on the one hand; for finding a noble purpose and dignity in life, a new and blessed spring of power and joy, for the educated classes on the other. Such interchange of good offices cannot go on at the street corners, nor in the public-house, nor in the working man's home, nor in general at the house of the richer man. (Sometimes, however, this last proceeding has taken place with delightful results.) But the Working Men's Club and Institute affords just the meeting-ground required. Some time since a number of working men wanted two or three members of Parliament to meet them for the discussion of certain clauses in a bill before the House. Those M.P.'s were quite willing—glad, we believe—to meet the working men, but we happen to know that they nevertheless remarked, in a tone which showed how naturally they felt the social status of these men was lowered by the fact, and how it placed a gulf between them—" Excellent fellows—but they wanted us to meet them at a pot-house."

The Club and Institute affords persons of every rank and either sex the conditions for usefulness to an unlimited extent. If a gentleman has a microscope or telescope, and wishes to help working men to know something of the wonders of creation in a drop of water, in the dust on a beetle's back, or in the infinite depths of starry space, a Working Men's Club and Institute affords him the opportunity for turning his microscope or telescope to the best possible account. And if a lady has a number of beautiful drawings, and wishes to show them to the working men and their wives, so that their hearts may be gladdened and purified amid their round of drudgery and perhaps low temptations, the Club and Institute equally affords *her* the opportunity. So with regard to instruction in political economy, history, &c.

But we need not do more than indicate the great opportunities for usefulness thus afforded by Working Men's Clubs and Institutes. Alike in the first efforts to establish the Club, and afterwards in managing and maintaining it, in providing entertainments, penny readings, lectures, teachers, speakers and Discussion meetings, and conversation occasionally in the Club Rooms, the help of gentlemen, if it is asked for or welcomed, has been, and will be found invaluable. Working men have remarked to the writer how much they liked to see gentlemen taking part with them, not only in Discussion Meetings, but also in Athletic Sports, Cricket, &c. There is, however, a certain amount of awkwardness, or at all events, shyness, felt in making mutual advances on all such occasions, which is easily and naturally got over by the gentlemen becoming honorary members, or the invited guests, of a Working Men's Club and Institute. Moreover, all these pleasant modes of intercourse, in making both parties better acquainted with each other, would promote united trust and respect, and thus prepare for that mutual good understanding

F

in case of Trade disputes, perhaps for those mutual concessions or explanations, or that successful arbitration, which would give the best chance of fair play for all, and obviate the warlike proceedings of a Strike or Lock-out.

The Working Men's Club and Institute Union made a successful attempt, in the spring and summer of 1865 and 1866, to hold Social Meetings in the Lower Hall, Exeter Hall, for the express purpose of giving working men, and persons of a higher social position, the opportunity of becoming better acquainted with each other, and interchanging their views on subjects of great national interest. The attendance was not, in general, so large as was hoped for, nor was the social element very strongly developed. But a considerable number of remarkably intelligent artizans, and of persons of high rank, learning, and culture came together, week after week (eleven meetings in all were held), and discussed, with great ability and candour, the subjects proposed for consideration—on the whole, much to their mutual satisfaction and benefit. The effect of these meetings, however, was felt far beyond those who attended them. They gave a stimulus to similar gatherings, both in London and many parts of the country, and helped to show how much good might be effected if such *réunions* could be held periodically, in suitable premises, and be properly followed up according to the Society's programme.* (See circular on "Central Hall, &c.," in the Appendix.) What the Central Society has done, and hopes to do far more efficiently, with a Central Hall and Model Club, we hope to see accomplished, in a greater or less degree, by every Club in the kingdom. The bearing of all such interchange of influence upon the elevation and refinement of the working classes, the extent to which it would eradicate class prejudices, and develop in them a sense of citizenship, of common national life, of oneness with the classes above them, the new and nobler links of gratitude by which it would bind them to those upper classes, the preparation it would give them for the wise and faithful exercise of political duties, are fruitful topics, but not lying in our present province to discuss. We must not, however, forget one fact of vital

* The last three Discussions were pretty fully reported, and are very interesting. They have been printed and published in separate papers, by the Union, price 2d.

importance. We all recognize the paramount necessity of giving education to the young. But when not long since we told a working man that a learned and influential friend of education feared he could not comply with our request to help on this movement for Clubs, because it was far more necessary and hopeful to train the young than to improve and educate adults, that working man replied, with deep truth, " It's my belief that if you do not improve and educate the grown men, you'll never be able really to educate their children." And when we consider the power and opportunities of the parents to poison the mind of the children, to neutralize all external good influences, to prevent the child even from getting any real education at all, we cannot wonder that this working man and the friends of Working Men's Clubs urge the value of those societies for promoting national progress not only in the present day, but among those who will constitute the nation when we are in our graves.

The operatives in various trades have agitated within the last few years, successfully, for shorter hours of labour. But is their greater leisure to bring the blessings it might confer, or only a curse? Listen:—

At a meeting held in St. James's, Westminster, under the presidency of Sir John V. Shelley, M.P., to promote the establishment of a Club in that locality, a working man got up and said he hoped it would be formed, and help his mates to make a better use of their leisure than was sometimes the case now. " There's a great cry among us, Mr. Chairman," he continued, " for shorter hours of work, and none cry louder for 'em than I do ; but I tell you what—there's the men in a large workshop over the water, who used to leave work a' Saturdays at four o'clock, and now they've got it down to two. But the only difference I see is, that whereas they used to be seen drunk by six in the evening, now we see them drunk by four o'clock ; and I don't think their shorter hours ha' done 'em much good."

We have always contended that few things would do more to promote a reduction in the hours of labour than Working Men's Clubs and Institutes, if well supported by working men. But then, for the worthy use of these leisure hours, how much depends on the use men of culture are willing to make of the opportunities which members of the Clubs may offer them. It is not difficult to imagine what would have been the effect on the history of mankind had the older nations of the world, each in their turn, applied their knowledge and

F 2

culture to the benefit of the barbarians who gradually came near their borders, making grateful friends of them while they were still in a position of superiority, by using their knowledge, culture, and resources to benefit instead of to repel.

But we must leave that fruitful theme, also, to ask the reader to receive two concluding and practical suggestions.

First. If Working Men's Clubs and Institutes are to be to this nation what we have now described, clearly we must not throw up the movement in disgust or despair, because the working classes have not at once rushed to welcome them as they might welcome a hopeful strike, a new Trade or Friendly Society, a public-house supper, or even a Co-operative Store. The great lesson to be preached now to the gentlemen of England in regard to Working Men's Clubs is—Patience. We would earnestly intreat all whom we could influence to understand that here is a great far-reaching movement, probably destined, under the Divine blessing, to revolutionize our working classes, in one of the best of all possible ways, if only it be wisely upheld and energetically carried on by all, in every rank, who know its value—a movement, therefore, deserving great sacrifices, to be supported reverently, faithfully, and with perseverance. Nothing can be a greater mistake than to suppose because the working classes do not immediately flock to these Clubs, and make them self-supporting, therefore they are not needed, do not meet the working man's wants, and are to be abandoned. People who can contribute money, time, teaching, entertainment, should feel that there is no secular object more deserving of their help than these Clubs and Institutes—that they must give all the help, including money, which may be absolutely needed to nurse the Clubs till they can run alone—that so great a work as they are destined to accomplish cannot be wrought in a day—that the comparatively small number of working men who now see the value of the Clubs are pre-eminently the men who should be helped in their efforts to revolutionize the tastes and habits, to inform the minds and elevate the characters, of the rest of their class. We recently asked a Sheffield alderman, who was contending against any extraneous support being given to these Clubs by the higher classes, how the working men who at present do not believe in Clubs were to be induced to join them, and make

them self-supporting. " I would establish Clubs," replied the
Alderman, " in their midst, and let them see what excellent
things they are ; let them see with their own eyes the superior
advantages offered by the Club above those of the public-
house." " Exactly," we replied, " but for that purpose, until
the men generally were converted to Club life, you would have
to supply the funds from extraneous sources. How long
would you continue to do this ? " " Oh, for six months," was
the reply. " If they didn't choose to see their own interests
by that time, let them take the consequences." " Ah," we
replied, " then we only differ, after all, as to the length of
time for giving help. I should say six years, rather."
Of this there is little doubt—in a great majority of cases at
present the working classes must be helped to keep the
realised concrete Club before their eyes in their respective
localities until they have been won to appreciate it sufficiently
to make it independent of other aid. Certainly it would be
unreasonable to expect that so important a work as this evidently is should be accomplished without great labour and
self-sacrifice ; equally unreasonable to think it could be accomplished by the few leading working men who are not already
absorbed in other enterprises. Let us reflect on what sort of a
business it must be to bring four or five millions of working men
to give up the habitual use of the public-house and beershop
for their social, convivial, and business meetings. When it is
asked, why cannot the men who have established and maintained for many years vast organizations in the shape of
Friendly and Trade Societies, who have formed Co-operative
Societies and Building Associations with such remarkable
success, establish and maintain these Clubs without the help
of gentlemen ? the answer is obvious. In the first place, all
those Societies offer direct pecuniary benefits of various kinds,
and nearly all the Friendly and Trade Societies have had their
head-quarters at the public-house. But, secondly, our readers
can scarcely have forgotten the exposures made two years ago,
on the introduction of Mr. Gladstone's Annuities Bill, of the
unsound condition and bad management of large numbers of
these Benefit Societies ; nor should they be unaware that this
very Co-operative movement, one of the most hopeful in
almost every respect of any initiated for the social well-being
of the working classes, originally appeared to be an utter

failure, lay perfectly dormant for years, as observed in the
Fifth Annual Report (see Appendix),—and then sprung again
into life with the Rochdale Pioneers in 1844. When we
talk of working men being left to bear the whole burden of
Clubs themselves, we should remember the enormous capital
required to maintain the 140,000 public-houses and beershops
which at present serve as Club-houses for the working men.

No, it will not do in this matter, any more than in religion
and politics, to attempt severing class from class, saying that
the hand has no need of the head, or the foot of either. Each
class needs, and is the better for, some mutual service. All
are so bound together (as a certain illustrious friend of the
first Corinthian Christians once reminded them, and the world
generally ever since, too often to little purpose) that if one
member suffers all must feel it, and a benefit conferred upon
one class, even the lowest, reacts favourably on the highest.
If these Clubs are doing, or likely to do, only half they aim
at, let us not stand idly looking on at their struggles or fall,
complaining of the working men for not doing more themselves all at once. Certainly, if any men in this world deserve
help, it is those generous fellows who, earning barely enough
to keep their families, and having but an hour or two's leisure
at the end of a weary day, are, nevertheless, working with
might and main to keep their Clubs in existence. If there
were no other reason for English gentlemen helping English
working men to maintain these centres of social, mental, and
moral improvement, the prospect before us of a large extension
of the franchise might be sufficient to induce persons of property
and leisure to give what help may be required, whether in
building, purchasing, or adapting premises, guaranteeing rent,
procuring furniture, providing books, apparatus, interesting
and entertaining lectures, concerts, &c.

We are glad to notice in this connexion that a leading
Conservative statesman, in putting his name, a year and a-half
ago, to one of the Parent Society's circulars appealing for
funds, adopted and partly suggested the following sentence:—

" There is one other consideration to which we think it
desirable to advert. In the event of any considerable extension of the franchise to the working classes it is impossible to
deny that, on grounds of public policy, their intellectual and
moral improvement would become more than ever important.

But no machinery, no secular agencies of any kind, have hitherto succeeded in reaching the genuine weekly wage men with improving and humanising influences to an extent comparable with these Clubs and Institutes; but the Clubs *have* succeeded in doing so in a degree as exceptional as it is gratifying, and for which every well-wisher to his country, as well as every Christian man and woman belonging to it, should feel profoundly thankful to the Giver of all good." (See again, also, " Facts and Fallacies.")

Secondly, while we would thus invoke the aid of the higher class, we must no less strenuously urge the working men themselves to make this movement fully and ultimately successful by making it their own. We cannot too earnestly appeal to the rest of the working men, the great masses who now stand aloof, and rouse them from their apathy or animalism, while we cannot plead with them too fervently to make these Clubs self-supporting, and independent of money help from other classes. How to do this may not always be easily seen. But as it is a valuable maxim in education to teach from the known to the unknown, so it is not less important in practical life to work from what is already done to what remains to be accomplished. Now the operatives have already shown immense power of organization in their societies for relief in sickness, for maintaining the rate of wages, and for the sale of stores. The men who belong to these societies are the great mass of the operative class, and the managers are their leading representative men. Hence (as we urged, p. 143), every effort should now be made to interest the great Friendly, Trade, and Co-operative organizations of the working classes in this movement, and to appeal to them by every legitimate means in our power to throw into it the same energy and organizing skill, with increased wisdom and knowledge, which they have manifested in those vast corporations. Their leaders are heartily with us, for the most part, already ; but *they* need all the help that can be given them for persuading the rank and file to come after them. They cannot move rapidly in our direction, or they would soon find themselves without many followers ; they have often too little influence with their mates (though that is not peculiar to *their* class) when they first try to lead them to something better and higher than that to which the men have become wedded by custom. Hence they require, and many of them welcome, all the influence that can be exerted by persons in a higher social position, especially by persons eminent for learning, genius, rank, or political standing. And whenever a Lodge meeting of Odd Fellows, a Court of Foresters, and so forth—a meeting of. Trade Society Delegates, or of Co-operative Societies, are willing to hear a short address on these Social Clubs and Institutes—whenever the columns of their publications are open for the diffusion of our views—there is a door opened of the very best and most effectual nature.

Much is now said (and too much cannot be said) about the importance of our artizans improving themselves in their art-workmanship, both for their own dignity and happiness, and lest they be left behind in the competitive race by Continental workmen. Especially it is needful to urge them to avail themselves of the very valuable facilities offered them for that improvement by the Science and Art Department of South Kensington, through the classes organized by Mr. Buckmaster, and the premiums given so liberally to the teachers of those classes. Industrial Exhibitions, Museums, Trade Mutual Improvement Societies (see Report of Conference held at Whittington Club, June, 1864, Appendix), and similar measures, are invaluable for aiding all these purposes. (See also an excellent paper by Mr. Hodgson Pratt, Appendix.) But it is not less needful to remind all who desire to promote this national progress, that we can never hope to find more than a very small percentage of the industrial masses, merely the *élite* of their body, availing themselves systematically of those facilities, until we have immensely diminished the temptations which at present assail them, and help them to obtain, *and to appreciate*, a substitute for the public-house. We must be permitted again to recommend the " Inclined Plane " to the consideration of all friends of the working men. None but those who have lived and worked as these men do, *or who* have lived among them, can form any idea of the obstacles to their intellectual improvement and artistic development presented by their want of thorough early education, by the deadening influence of their daily toil, by the temptations of the public-house, and by the want of facilities for study and relaxation at their homes.

It is indeed impossible, as we are well aware, to urge too strongly on the working men the need and duty of self-reliance and self-help. There must come a time in the case of every Club and Institute, at least in populous neighbourhoods, when, if the artizans or labourers do not make it wholly or chiefly self-supporting, gentlemen cannot be expected to continue their assistance. We simply urge, that for a period varying perhaps from four to seven or eight years, those working men who do desire and work for a Club, should be helped by the class above them to keep it going, and to make it useful, until the rest of their mates are persuaded to frequent it also. But, unquestionably, a time will never come (let us be devoutly thankful that it is so) when the help of the higher classes, in a variety of forms, will not be most valuable and valued in promoting the efficiency of whatever means working men may use for gaining higher culture and the conditions of a nobler life. Emphatically this is true with regard to Working Men's Clubs and Institutes, as we have amply shown. But it is thus that class-prejudices are broken down, and the different ranks of society are knit together in links of mutual regard and respect. The tendency of the movement generally, and of each individual Club, to bring together persons of different rank and degrees of culture, the opportunities the Club affords for removing mutual misunderstandings, and for enabling each party to look at "vexed questions" from each other's point of view, *to enlighten the upper classes in regard to working men and their ways*, is no less important than the facilities it gives for bringing the culture, knowledge, and refinement of those classes to aid in entertaining and instructing the working men. These characteristics of Working Men's Clubs are earnestly dwelt upon as one of their principal merits, and are set forth as one of their most deeply-cherished aims, by the founders and supporters of the Parent Society. As a social and political influence, we can conceive of no higher recommendation.

It is especially on these grounds that Lord Brougham, the Duke of Argyll, and other noblemen and gentlemen, Vice-Presidents of the Society, based their appeal for help to establish a Central Hall and Model Club in London, to be worked by the Council of the Union, and their then Secretary. They urge the incalculable value of having such a common meeting-

ground for working men and those of a higher rank, in the
heart of our great metropolis. But they also urge the help
which such Halls and Clubs might give, both in London and
the country, in healing one of the greatest of our social dis-
eases, one that threatens us even more disastrously in the
future than at present, if it be not removed. We refer to
*the bitter feelings and direct antagonism, too often existing between
employers and employed.* And we would earnestly plead—as it
is there, and in other papers, stoutly maintained—that if the
governing and employing classes of this country will exert
themselves to help our operatives to supplement the deficiencies of their homes and their education, to enjoy the beauties
of Shakespeare and Tennyson, of Mozart and Beethoven, of
painting and sculpture; if they will assist them to learn a little
about the great men who have made England what she is, to
grapple with the mysteries of Political Economy, to study the
laws of Chemistry, Astronomy, and Natural Philosophy, of
Jurisprudence and the progress of Civilization, especially if,
having been thus brought into friendly relations with each
other, the employers and legislators will come occasionally
and hold frank discussions with the workmen, on the working
men's own Club-room floor, on the relations of Capital and
Labour, and the laws that govern us, not only would the
operatives gain a much-needed insight into the position and
difficulties of their employers, as well as learn most important
truths, but those employers themselves would often get useful
hints from their men. And especially the extraordinary ignorance existing among the upper and employing class respecting the institutions and views of the working men, too often
their yet more extraordinary indifference to the temptations
and wants of the working classes, would be greatly and
seasonably diminished by such friendly discussions and intercourse. If happily those governing and capitalist classes will
meet the operatives in this manner, and in a patient friendly
spirit, they will probably find, sooner perhaps than most of
them have expected, that many of their difficulties on the
Labour question, and all their doubts as to the expediency
of welcoming a larger number of these toiling brothers of
theirs to political privileges, will have been entirely laid to
rest for ever. Let them remember that if the working classes
are inferior to themselves in refinement, courtesy, knowledge,

temperance, the position and occupation of these classes, on the other hand, have saved them, to a great extent, from the covetous greed and mammon-worship, from the tendencies to gambling speculation, from the voluptuous self-indulgence, the arrogance, and contemptible struggling for social position, which we have ventured to say are now the bane of the middle and higher classes of England.

It has been said by more than one of the great "seers" of our age, the men who *see* more clearly into the future than their countrymen have generally been willing to believe, that this century cannot terminate without a great "shaking of the nations," without our passing through some such a crisis as marked the fifth, the tenth, and the sixteenth centuries. They say that, for some years past, we have, indeed, been entering upon it. We believe many manifest signs confirm that view. And this at least is certain, that when our great trial-time comes—as come it must sooner or later—whether we shall emerge from it "purified as refined gold," brighter, stronger, and happier than before, or with half our national life and institutions consumed in the fire as "hay, straw, stubble," must depend greatly on the extent to which the more privileged classes of our country speedily stoop to "undo the heavy burdens" and remove the sore temptations which now press so heavily upon the labouring population—on the extent to which they knit that population to themselves by friendly offices of that sympathy *which can only come through knowledge*, and by that brotherly help which dignifies and blesses both the higher and the humbler class.

In a recent novel—in which the author, Mr. H. Kingsley, shows even more fully than in his previous writings the breadth and depth of his genial sympathies with the working classes —there occurs the following capital passage. He has been speaking (as a working man) of one of the personages in the story, a dashing, good-humoured scion of the aristocracy, and then launches forth into the following remarks, describing the whole class as—

. . . men whom those who don't know them sneer at as mere *flaneurs*, but whose suppressed volcanic energy shows itself, to those who care to observe, in that singular, insane, and dangerous amuse-ment, fox-hunting—all of them men with whom falsehood, cowardice, and dishonour are simply nameless impossibilities. We know them better than we did, since the darkening hours of Sebastopol and Delhi, and it was only their own faults that such as I did not know them better before. [But] the halo of glory which was thrown round the heads of these dandies by their magnificent valour from 1854 to 1859, has done the body of them an infinite deal of harm. We can trust you, and will follow you in war, gentlemen ; but in peace, cannot you manage to amalgamate a little more with the middle and lower classes ? Are the old class-distinctions to go on for ever, and leave you dandies, the very men we are ready to take by the hand and make friends of, in a minority, as regards the whole nation, of 1 to 99 ? Can't we see a little more of you, gentlemen, just at this time, when there is no great political difficulty between your class and ours ; if it were only for the reason that no one out of Bedlam supposes that things are always to go on with the same oily smoothness as they are doing just now. I think we understand you, gentlemen. I wish you would take your gloves off sometimes. You have been more courteous to us since the Reform Bill ; but certain ill-conditioned blackguards among us say it is only the courtesy which is engendered of fear, and but ill replaces the old condescending *bonhommie* which we shared with your pointers and your grooms. * * * * is dead, and buried at * * * * : and there happens to be no one alive at present who is able, or cares, to overstate the case of the poor against the rich with quite so much cleverness as he. But at any dark hour another man of similar abilities might come forth and make terrible mischief between us again. You can be earnest and hearty enough about anything of which you see the necessity. Can no one persuade you that the most necessary thing just now is an amalgamation of classes ? You could never get together a *Jeunesse Dorée* without our assistance, and yet you treat us like *sans culottes.—" The Hillyars and the Burtons," Vol. 2, pp.* 209—11.

Would that every Club in the country had such a brave, kindly-spirited gentleman as the writer of that passage to sit on its committee, and take part in its discussions, classes, entertainments, and sports. Would that the gentlemen of England may speedily know how fine a field is open for them. We know well how they will be welcomed by working men, when they enter it in the right spirit ; and we know equally well how much of that genial, generous spirit there is among true English gentlemen. So may God speed their mutual improvement and kindly fellowship !

Therefore, let us here appeal to all who occupy a higher social position than working men—who possess greater advantages of any kind—to use their privileges in promoting this important national movement. Not daunted by the errors nor discouraged by the apathy of the class that so much need our influence, and *whose influence we so greatly need ourselves*, let us steadily labour to establish, and especially to maintain and develop, these Clubs and Institutes. The working men, let us remember, are sure to have them, sooner or later, in the next generation if not in the present. But what an incalculable difference it will make to our upper classes and our national life, whether they obtain them with the co-operation and cordial brotherly help of those who are now their superiors, or without such aid—whether the younger generation of working men grow up in the enjoyment of these Clubs, finding gentlemen already lending them various kinds of generous co-operation, or whether they have nobody to thank, if they get them at all, but themselves.

The aristocracy of this country were once the leaders of the people. Would that that English aristocracy of ours, blending all that is wisest and best with all that is noblest and wealthiest in the land—the aristocracy of intellect and worth, as well as of rank and property—would once again step to the front. In company with the great middle class, who have made our commerce and established our colonies, and given us manufactures, railroads, and steam navigation, let them pour the rich stores of their civilization on the waiting hearts and lives of their toiling brethren. We have said we must not wonder if the working men do not rush forward eagerly to welcome this movement. May we not say that we ought to wonder, with profoundest wonder and sorrow, if in every town and village in the kingdom the gentlemen of England do not use the opportunity now given them (and which once lost cannot be recalled) for raising and benefiting the working classes by means of Working Men's Clubs and Institutes?

CHAPTER V.

HOW CAN CLUBS BE MADE SELF-SUPPORTING?

This is one of the first questions asked by many of the truest friends of the present movement, as well as by those who would be rather glad of an excuse for quietly "shunting" it. Undoubtedly it is a very important one. Working men ought not to be dependent upon charitable contributions for the support of institutions which, by good management and faithful co-operation, they could themselves, in general, very easily maintain without such help. At the same time, we must not forget there is a good deal of mystification, and, sometimes, slightly perverse misapprehension, connected with this subject which needs to be removed. Mr. Smith, the wealthy Baltic merchant, or Mr. Brown, the great manufacturer, turning round his chair to the fire after dinner, observes to his friend, Mr. Jones—

"Capital things these Working Men's Clubs, which are springing up now, here and there. I gave a guinea the other day to one they are getting up in —— Street."

"Yes," replies Mr. Jones, cautiously, "very good things indeed, if the men will support them themselves. But why they should come to you for a guinea I don't clearly see."

"Oh, that's merely to give them a start. The working men can't be expected to find the capital. There's the plant, you know—furniture, books, games, alteration in the premises, and so on. My son put it on that ground," continues Smith, seeing Jones look dubious.

The latter replies with something of calm severity, yet as one deprecating too much rigour in dealing with the benighted "lower orders": "Ah, that's all very well, but they can find capital enough when they like for Trade, Co-operative, and Building Societies; why don't they do it for these Clubs?"

Hereupon—as a "fast" young friend of Mr. Smith's son, who was sipping his port at the table, subsequently observed, *sotto voce*—" the governor seemed stumped."

" Besides," continues Jones, with slightly malignant exulta-
tion, " you'll not find it stop there. They've done you out
of one guinea, and they'll be wanting another by-and-bye.
They'll come whining about not being able to meet their rent,
and declaring that members won't pay up, and fall away in
summer time, and all sorts of mendicant rubbish. No, no;
let the men do the thing themselves, *for* themselves, and *by*
themselves, Sir !—that's the only sound basis to work on. I
don't believe in all this bolstering up and helping folks who
spend at the public-house in a month ten times the amount
they get from us."

Mr. Smith is very much afraid he has been taken in, feels
he has a little fallen in the estimation of Jones as a shrewd
man of business, and answers nervously, " Well, well, it's no
great matter," and changes the subject.

But a few days after, Jones finds the pressure of the times
is beginning to tell even on his well-conducted and respectable
firm. It is clear he will not be able to hold on without temporary assistance, goes to Smith, and explains the state of his
affairs. The case is clear—help may legitimately be given.
Smith is able to give it, or is the friendly medium by which it
is obtained. The recent conversation about Working Men's
Clubs of course never occurs to either of the parties; but
Smith's son has a better memory, and takes an early opportunity of addressing a few after-dinner remarks to his excellent sire, something to the following effect. After a few
soothing introductory observations, he continues—

" Well, now, father, I may be wrong, but it seems to me
what you have just done for Jones is precisely what, in some
shape or other, everybody is called upon to do at one time or
other for somebody else. Didn't you inherit your business
and capital from my grandfather, and haven't you had help at
critical times from different people, from the time you left
school, and before that, or you wouldn't be in the position
you occupy ? "

" Granted. Well ? "

" I mean to say, without going into all the ins and outs of
the matter, that there's nothing unwise in giving help nor
degrading in receiving it, *per se*, for this reason simply,
because it's the law of Providence. What we have to consider, I think, is whether the help is a real benefit to those on

whom it is bestowed; and whether, if we are the receivers, we should be ready to give help, when we can, to others?"

" You talk wisely, James. That is something new. How comes it? Explain."

" Ah, I went to the public meeting the other night, dada, at the Town Hall. It's amazing what a deal of good sense was sported on that occasion."

Further reflection, and perhaps discussion, convinced Mr. Smith that there was a stage in the life of individuals, communities, and enterprises, when help may be legitimately given, which would be injurious at a later period of development— " or embarrassing, papa," as was remarked by Master James Smith, an exceedingly sharp youth in the fifth form at ——— School, when the conversation was resumed round the tea-table. For Mrs. Smith had just observed that when Mr. Smith was in long clothes he had been considerably helped in necessary locomotion by the nurse's arms, but that he had for some time ceased to require such assistance. "And grand-mamma didn't respect you a bit the less for that, papa," interjected Miss Smith, " because she knew you would make such a capital nurse to *us*, as we are all ready to testify."

Clearly, babies can't be self-supporting. A man half smothered in a ditch may need somebody's help to pull him out; or if he be sound asleep in a comfortable bed, he may still be unable to wake himself. Children would not be inclined to pay for their own schooling even if they could afford it; and a man with a broken leg may fairly be carried to a hospital without disgrace (unless he was drunk when the limb was fractured). The cases in which, *inter alia*, help may legitimately, and by the Christian law ought to be given, are—

First. When the recipient cannot or will not help himself at the time, but in consequence of such temporary assistance will probably become both able and willing at a subsequent period; when, in fact, the help tends to make the recipient independent of the need of it—stronger, physically or morally.

Second. When the recipient is willing to give all the help in his own power to those who may legitimately need it.

Third. When it is given to those who ask it for the purpose of helping others to accomplish worthy ends.

If there were no conditions under which it is wise and right to aid our brethren, what would become of brotherly kindness, and how could it have been divinely said, "It is more blessed to give than to receive"?

Tried by every sound test, there is evidently a clear case for helping working men to start these Clubs and Institutes, and in many cases to keep them going *for a time*. As a body, the working classes are not sufficiently awake to the necessity and duty of living a higher life than that which is supported by daily work, and by a pot and a pipe when the work is done. Else, no doubt, they could easily make the Clubs independent of all middle-class help, and at once self-supporting. But they cannot awaken themselves; and those of their own class who long to do it deserve all the assistance in such a task which they require. Some have no appetite for the food which is necessary for them, and you have to create that appetite as well as provide the food. Some of them are half smothered in the slime of intemperance engendered by having no place for social intercourse and recreation but the public-house. Some have not broken limbs, but broken wills, energies, hopes—diseased tastes, starved and stunted or unfurnished minds, perverted principles, undeveloped powers of thought, feeling, action; sometimes they are "perishing for lack of knowledge," and rushing into misguided, perhaps ruinous, courses for want of it. But Working Men's Clubs and Institutes supply a large proportion of the outward conditions required for remedying all these evils, and supplying those wants. Hence people who can give money and time to establish and support them are not only justified in doing so, but are *bound* to do it to the utmost of their ability, and are not to require as a condition of their sympathy that the Club should be self-supporting, until it has had time to grow and gained strength to run alone. Let the middle and upper classes reflect on the vast amount of help they have received from the liberality of past ages in the shape of endowed grammar-schools and Universities, to say nothing of the large endowments of the National Church.

But, on the other hand, all friends of the working men, and especially the working men themselves, are imperatively called upon to see that their Club has the elements of growth in it—that it *tends* towards a state of independency, if it has not yet attained to this desirable condition. Moreover, in many places it is very hard to persuade Mr. Smith and Mr. Jones that they ought to give the requisite help in the early stages of the Club's existence, even though Smith and Jones would be the greatest possible gainers by their poorer neighbours or their workpeople becoming more sober, intelligent, and cheerful. And, lastly, in many localities there are working men, enough, wide awake and well able by themselves to do all that is required, if only the right way is suggested to them. Hence we now propose offering a few suggestions as to the best means of establishing and maintaining Clubs and Institutes without extraneous assistance. It is a matter of primary importance that these Clubs should have some permanent hold on the members, and that the natural but utterly ruinous tendency in many of the said members to pay for a few weeks, and then discontinue doing so for a month or two, should be counteracted in every possible way.

The first and most obvious answer to the question, " How can Clubs be made self-supporting?" clearly is, " By having such a rate of subscription, and getting such a number of members to pay it, as will cover all the expenses." But experience shows that in a large majority of cases this cannot be accomplished in the early days of a Club—say for the first two or three years. It is very important that members should have the option of paying weekly *(though the subscription should always be considered as due for the whole quarter)* ; but if they have this privilege too many lack sufficient zeal, and regard for the just claims of the Club, to pay regularly, especially during the summer months. And even where as many members as the Club rooms can accommodate faithfully pay, the rent is often so high that their contributions are not sufficient to cover the expenditure. Should their numbers be increased, there is no longer sufficient room for them, and members leave because they cannot get a turn at the bagatelle-table, or a seat by the fire, or even comfortable sitting room anywhere. If the subscription is raised, or an entrance-fee demanded, many leave or decline to enter, because they cannot, or think they cannot, afford the additional levy. These last are among the principal causes that led to the temporary suspension of one of the most promising and useful of the London Clubs, St. Martin's, and had something to do with the stoppage of the Scarborough Club.

The second consideration, then, for the members and promoters of these Clubs is to see whether they cannot derive
funds from some extraneous source of income sufficient to
meet the deficit.

In Preston the Club and Institute has managed to pay its
way and be highly successful, by having one of its rooms
open to the public for dinners and refreshments generally.
This room has been much used, especially on market days.
Good management, with an experienced and obliging steward
or stewardess, will generally make this plan answer; but, of
course, it would sometimes require larger premises, and then
the additional rent might swallow up the profits. Occasionally the same room can be open to the public for refreshment, and yet serve the purpose of a Club-room for
the members—exclusively for them, perhaps, after six o'clock
in the evening. But great caution should be used in any
measures that would impair the *Club* feeling, and trespass too
much on the privileged privacy which should distinguish a
Club-house from a public-house.

The sale of refreshments merely to members will seldom,
in the smaller towns and villages, be of much use in making
both ends meet, unless unnecessary expenditure is encouraged, and the sale pushed for "the good of the house," or
of the steward, which, of course, would be introducing one
of the very evils to avoid which the Club is established. But
in larger towns, where there should be many young men
belonging to the Club, and where the members generally might
be further from their homes, this department ought to be very
profitable.

A thoroughly legitimate and very efficient source of revenue
has been derived, in a great many cases, from the proceeds of
Penny Readings, Concerts, Lectures, Exhibitions of Microscopes, and Electrical Machine, Dissolving Views, and other
entertainments, as our friends at Camden Hall and elsewhere
have shown. But, unfortunately, every Club has not, and
cannot get, the use of a large room or hall for these purposes; and when they can, the rent charged sometimes ab-
sorbs the profits. However, no Club should consider itself
properly equipped unless, in one way or another, it does provide such entertainments pretty often—for, independently of
their benefit to the members and the help they ought to bring

to the exchequer, it is a matter of great importance that "the better half" of the family should now and then enjoy the advantages which the Club is intended to bring to their husbands and brothers. Therefore, let it be well understood that some portion of the income of a Club should always be derived, if possible, from weekly or monthly entertainments; and the friends of the working classes should be asked to contribute occasionally, and in turn, sometimes their voices, concertina, or piano; sometimes their microscopes, air-pump, electrical machine, or works of art, stereoscopes, pictures, statuettes, collections of insects, coins, fossils, and so forth; or a magic lanthorn and dissolving views, on rarer occasions; with recitations, readings, and singing on the more frequent and ordinary entertainment evenings.

Industrial Exhibitions have occasionally given most valuable help to the funds of Working Men's Clubs. By such means as these, managers of Clubs may not only add considerably to their funds, but also materially promote one of the main objects for which the Clubs were formed—viz., the moral and social elevation of the working classes. Such a mode of raising money is quite as legitimate, to say the least, as a Bazaar, with which, indeed, it might sometimes be combined.

Other similar modes of raising money, while carrying out the objects of the Club, may suggest themselves to our readers, or may have already been tried. Cricket and Rowing Clubs during the summer help greatly to keep the members together in those fatal dog-days, but, beyond that, cannot be expected to yield much profit to the originating Club and Institute. But excursions to places of antiquarian and historic interest would sometimes be very popular and remunerative. The public might pay one-third or one-half more for their railway tickets (as in Sunday-school excursions) than the Club members, and a good profit might be thus made. The value, however, of rural *fêtes*, picnics, water-parties, cricket matches, athletic sports and contests in summer-time; and musical entertainments, chess and draught matches, conversaziones, &c., in winter-time, is too obvious to need enlarging upon.

While, however, we cannot be too strongly impressed with the need of providing entertainment and instruction in Working Men's Clubs and Institutes, it is equally necessary, in the third place, to remember that many men will be far more interested in measures for promoting the comfort and pecuniary well-being of themselves and their families, than in entertainments or mental excitement of any description. The latter will almost always be welcomed by the younger working men, and be of value to them, not only directly, but also in attaching them to the Club ; but with a considerable number of adults the recreation and mental improvement will often be a subordinate affair, and their connexion with some Provident, Friendly, Co-operative, or similar Society belonging to the Club will be the sheet-anchor to hold them fast. Action of the kind now recommended is both a cause and effect of three distinct benefits to the members, naturally resulting from the Club : first, the becoming interested in other matters than the pot and pipe and mere animal enjoyments, which have too often been the only things many working men have cared about ; second, the saving money and adding to home comforts—especially laying up against a rainy day—ultimately, perhaps, obtaining the advantages of capital as well as of labour ; third, the cherishing that spirit of mutual helpfulness which has been constantly urged as a primary element in the success of these Clubs, and one of their principal objects. But in addition to all this, such commercial societies (so to term them) have a powerful influence in binding the members not only to one another, but also to their Club, and often furnish the strongest attraction for retaining men in membership. The K—— Club is a striking instance in point. The Society had a hard struggle for life, owing to various causes, but early in its career some of its able and zealous managers formed a Provident Loan Society, Coal, Clothing, and Christmas Provident Clubs. These Societies have been very useful to the members, and highly valued. Hence, when the rest of the members of the Club fell away, these continued staunch, and for a long time resisted every proposal to break up the Club, which, they said, would just ruin their Provident Societies. A somewhat similar and important illustration comes to us from the Hull Working Men's Club. The Secretary says in his " Return," kindly furnished to us early in this year—" Our Club now is in the possession of the Co-operative Store, both being on the same premises, and is managed by the committee " (of the Club). Then, in answer to the question, "How far is the

Club self-supporting ? " he writes : " Since we have had it (the Club) in connexion with the Co-operative Store—six months —it has supported itself. *Previously it was losing 1l. weekly."* We cannot insist too strongly on the great mutual benefit which Clubs and Co-operative Stores may confer on each other.

But, *per contra*, a very promising Club has been brought to death's door, mainly, we believe, through the best men connected with it forming a Co-operative Store, and having all their time and energies absorbed in its management, so that the poor Club was deprived of its natural and fittest leaders, fell into incompetent hands, and has gone into a condition from which, we are afraid, no power can rescue it. Let our friends at Hull and elsewhere note this melancholy catastrophe, and take care to secure sufficient *managing power* for both their valuable undertakings. Working men's enterprises so often fail, because of the very limited time at their command. The best men to manage any Society naturally have their hands over full, from the number of important and responsible duties pressed upon them, as a consequence of their having won the confidence of their neighbours.

It is quite certain that independently of the benefit to working men themselves, and their families, from well-conducted Provident Societies of this and similar kinds, a Working Men's Club can only draw a large number of the very men it is most important to attract by having some such benefits of a material character to offer. As, on the one hand, it is of immense value to the Provident Societies that they should meet at the Club instead of at the public-house, it is no less useful to the Club that men who belong to it should find they are the richer for having joined it. This they will undoubtedly be by not being tempted to spend ; but remembering how extremely difficult it is to persuade a man who has been accustomed for years to his pot and pipe at a public-house to exchange the latter for any accommodation elsewhere, as well as to retain him if he does make the experiment, we can well understand the need of offering him some advantages from joining the Club, which, at all events at first, he will appreciate much more heartily than the learning and culture spoken of above. There is a large class of men who would be comparatively indifferent to all the other benefits offered by a Club, but who would give up the tap-room when they saw they would thereby gain a few shillings a month, either in the shape of a dividend, a loan, or an increased sum in sickness, want of employment, old age, or death. Men whom no amount of amusement, still less of information, not the sweetest music, or most thrilling fictions, would draw from their seat at the publican's fireside, have given up the cherished habits of years after joining a Co-operative Store, and have found in the interest (in a twofold sense) arising from having " a share in a shop," in lounging on the counter, watching the sales, talking with *their* shopman, or chatting in the Co-operative " back-parlour " or " reading-room," an attraction strong enough to overcome the temptation of "fuddling " in the old chimney-corner. Other Provident Societies operate in exactly the same way.

In large towns co-operative dining-rooms might be established in connexion with a Club, and be made highly profitable, both to the Club and the shareholders, under good management. There is clearly a wide field for very remunerative enterprise in this matter, as the successful experiments in Glasgow and elsewhere abundantly show.

It is truly remarked by Mr. Plummer, in an article on Working Men's Clubs, in the " Companion to the British Almanack for 1865," p. 99 : " Bad food and bad cookery are two evils which have been productive of much working-class mis-expenditure and disease ; and anything supplying at the cheapest possible rates the blessings of good food and good cookery, deserves to meet with every possible degree of encouragement."

In Southampton we find a Coal Club, formed simultaneously with the re-establishment of one of the original Workmen's Halls, becoming, financially, the mainstay of the Working Men's Club, and bringing in men to join the latter, whose attention and interest would otherwise never have been directed towards it.

The fourth financial point for managers and promoters to consider is, whether, if they labour under this common difficulty or disease, technically known as " impecuniosity," they cannot connect the Club, either at first starting or subsequently, with *some other organization*, which, in one way or other, should be legitimately able to swell its income. This is a very simple matter when it amounts merely to a mutually profitable engagement of the *landlord-and-tenant* nature—*e. gr.*, The committee may let the use of one of its rooms for the weekly or monthly meetings of a Friendly, Trade, Co-operative, or other Working Men's Society. Or probably, better still, a Friendly or Co-operative Society, or a cheap Dining Halls Company, may be able to take premises large enough to accommodate the Club as its tenant. An inquiry was once made of us as to whether the Free Library Act, if applied in a town, could help the establishment of a Club? The answer, of course, was, only by means of either institution becoming landlord or tenant to the other. Very material help might be gained by a Club in all such cases, where there was a friendly disposition on the side of the other institution, by means of which that formidable item of expense, Rent, might be brought into more manageable dimensions.

The scheme for combined action consists then in the Society or Company becoming either tenant or landlord (as suggested above) of premises which can be used for Club purposes after a fixed hour in the evening. We need hardly be at the pains to point out that such a plan is sure to be *mutually* advantageous.

The number of those members of Friendly and Benefit Societies who desire to remove their meetings from the public-house is yearly increasing; and although considerable opposition to this course will often be made, persevering agitation on their part sooner or later opens the eyes of their fellow-members to the great importance of such a step. The chief difficulty is that men long accustomed to the public-house meetings don't like to give up the pleasant social intercourse thereby obtained; but if they find they can have it just as well and much cheaper at a Club and Institute, they will gradually be prevailed on to rent a room there; or if they happen to constitute a large and powerful Society, they may be willing to take a large house and let the Club have the requisite amount of accommodation at a moderate rent. The main point in the case is that the Clubs have not *capital*, and they must often be under the necessity of finding *some other Society that has*, and by which they can be helped in the matter of rent. (See also Chapter IX., on the "Relation of Friendly, Trade, and Similar Societies to Working Men's Clubs.")

The subject becomes much more complicated when we approach the consideration, whether the auxiliary organization can be established, or connected with the Club, for *the express purpose* of augmenting its pecuniary resources—*e. gr.*, Can the promoters or managers of a Club succeed in forming a Limited Liability Company to build a Club-house, and to forego any rent until the Club shall be self-supporting? Or will the men who propose forming the Club take shares in such a company, as at Birmingham-heath, not for the sake of getting a dividend, but of getting a Club?

In large towns, a Cheap Dining-Halls Company might be established by persons who were willing to let the first year's dividends, or such portion as might be required, go towards the furniture, fittings, and rent, of a Club and Institute. A Building Society, or any society formed on Dr. Bowkett's principles, might be established with the same proviso. But the organization which, next to such a company as that of Birmingham-heath, would be most easily set on foot, perhaps, for such an object, would be a Co-operative Store, on account of the strong convictions of the leading working men who head the co-operative movement, in every district, as to the necessity of helping their shareholders to be thoughtful, steady, and well-informed men, and this as much for the commercial success of their enterprise, as for the sake of that mental and moral elevation of their class, which they generally have much at heart. The Industrial and Provident Societies' Act of 1862 was expressly intended, among other useful provisions, to give these societies the power of applying such portion of their profits as the shareholders might think fit to purposes of education, recreation, and so forth. Hence a Co-operative Store, as was suggested at a Monthly Conference of London Secretaries, might be opened with the avowed object of its profits maintaining a Working Men's Club and Institute until the latter was independent of extraneous support. And any Co-operative Society already established, the shareholders of which agreed at a general meeting to avail themselves of the above-mentioned facility, might agree that, say, 10 per cent. of their profits should be given for one year, 5 per cent. for the next, and $2\frac{1}{2}$ for the third, towards the establishment and maintenance of a Club and Institute. In return for such assistance, it might be stipulated that a proportionate number of shareholders should have free tickets of membership in the Club. Thus, if a Co-operative Store were making 200*l.* a-year profit and devoted 5 per cent. to the Club, about thirty shareholders could be made members of the Club, supposing the subscription to the said Club were 1s. 6d. a-quarter or 6s. a-year. In other cases, the Co-operative Society might be able to let the Club have rooms on its own premises at a low rent, or rent free, until the said Club were firmly established and had become self-supporting, as we have noticed above in the case of the Hull Club.

It is necessary, however, to add that, in case the shareholders of the Company or Society assisting the Club take, in return, any benefit of a pecuniary character from the Club, as above described or otherwise, they must take it as private individuals, not in their *corporate* capacity, as this would make their Society liable for the debts of the assisted Institute, by becoming legally a partner in the concern. At Halifax, where a duly-established Working Men's Club failed after a two years' trial, chiefly through being on far too small a scale, the magnificent Co-operative Society have all the Club requisites and accommodation on their premises, now, in perfection. Nearly all the Co-operative Societies in Yorkshire and Lancashire, to their infinite credit, have provided comfortable reading-rooms and libraries on their premises.

There is one way that may occasionally be open to Clubs of lessening their rent, too important to be overlooked, as it would help to solve a question that has already frequently arisen, which was discussed at the Conference held by the Parent Society in May, 1864, and which will be continually more pressing — viz., " Can any co-operation or mutually beneficial relations exist between Mechanics' Institutions and Working Men's Clubs? " We glance at it now, merely to point out that the rooms required by the Club are not, in general, wanted by its members before six P.M., and that they might be used as reading-rooms by the tradesmen and others, in small towns and villages, during the day ; or be let for sewing classes, mothers' meetings, &c. ; on the other hand, the rooms of a Mechanics' Institution, when required chiefly as News and Reading-rooms in the day, might be given up to a Club after six o'clock. Again, where the premises admit of it, the large hall, needful for concerts, lectures, &c.,

might be rented and used by both in common, as at Stourbridge.

The last suggestion we have to offer under this head is one
recently made to us—viz., as to the value of Burial Clubs,
supported, not by regular subscriptions, but by funeral
levies of 6d. or 1s. per member. Where there are already
good Friendly Societies established in the neighbourhood, it
may be impossible or undesirable for the committee of a Club
to form another. But many men already belonging to one
established to provide help in time of sickness, and having no
money to spare for more weekly or monthly payments, would
willingly subscribe a sixpence or even a shilling when a
comrade died, to help the widow and children. This would
not be felt burdensome by those who paid, and the 7l. 10s. or
15l. which a Society of 300 members would thus be able to
give to the bereaved family would be a most seasonable and
benevolent relief. A scheme of this sort would do much to
obtain the support of the wives to the Club in the early days,
when perhaps they were totally ignorant of the other advantages it would confer, or might even be viewing it with
suspicion and dislike. As the members of the Burial Club
whose lives were spared longest would gain least benefit from
it, and after a long time the levy would amount to an insig-
nificant sum, the plan would partake, to a considerable extent,
of the nature of a benevolent fund, and would be proportionately more useful morally than pecuniarily to many who
joined it.

If, however, it were connected with Mr. Gladstone's admirable Life Annuities scheme, it would be placed on a purely
business footing, and while the payments would have to be
considerably larger, and the greater part of them would have
to be made periodically, those members who gained least
benefit from the Burial Fund would be compensated by receiving a Life Annuity after they had attained a given age.

Of course in most of the above cases only members of the
Working Men's Club would be allowed to be members of the
Friendly or Provident Society. Sometimes, however, persons
might be allowed to join the latter, as a means of bringing
them acquainted with the Social Club and its members.

The truth is, that the wants, tastes, and circumstances of
working men are just as various as those of the classes above

them; often much more so, on account of the greater incompleteness of their education and development. Hence a Club
must meet this great variety of taste and want, if it is to
have any considerable number of members. Some must be
attracted by the amusements; others by the social companionship;—some by the reading-room, library, and classes; others
by the Provident and similar Societies;—some will care
chiefly for discussion meetings; others for the "free-and-
easy," or concerts.

But whatever the original inducements to join, able and
zealous managers will always endeavour to bring the members
of a Club to care about its other useful and interesting operations. These are the chief points we have at present to suggest on the very important subject of this chapter. But as
the most important of all is the one first mentioned, we propose suggesting in a future chapter a few more hints for
making the Clubs attractive to working men.

In concluding this most important subject, let us cordially recommend to the best attention of all our readers
the following very interesting account of the rise and
progress of a Club at Buersil, near Rochdale. All honour to
these fourteen cotton operatives who have thus practically
shown what working men can do *if they will!* A Club thus
founded on self-help and self-sacrifice, without resort to the
wealthy and benevolent for a single farthing, has in it all the
elements of most enduring success. We congratulate the
Buersil men on the proud satisfaction they must feel that the
Club and all it contains have been bought by their own hard
labour and heavy sacrifices. A Club so obtained will be
doubly dear to those who have thus made it their own. We
believe this movement will make its way to the hearts of our
people just in proportion as they will make it *their own work.*
Only, we cannot *wait* until this feeling has everywhere grown
up. As yet, the men who will do as these Lancashire lads have
done are too few and far between. Until all England is like
Buersil, we must be content to have Clubs set up by the joint
action of rich and poor. We cannot wait for the Millennium,
and let thousands in the meantime have nothing but the
public-house for their Club. Moreover, though it is a
glorious thing for working men to build up their own Clubs
by such sacrifices as these, we do not want to see working

men refuse such aid from their richer and better-educated brethren as they may receive without any humiliation, and with the greatest advantage to *both*. It is good alike for rich and poor that they should work and pray *together*. Every opportunity of forgetting differences of caste and class in a common work of good should be taken, if our world is to become truly Christian. We are sure that rich and poor have much happiness to derive from working together for the moral, intellectual, and religious elevation of their fellow-citizens. We believe that it is as great a gain to the rich and educated to sit on a Club committee and teach in a Club class as it is to the poor and less instructed to have their brotherly counsel and instruction. We do not want Clubs to be other than self-governed, but a *sprinkling* of men on the committee who have the advantage of the learning, the taste, the self-restraint, and quiet thought that wealth and leisure give, must be an advantage. The opportunity of giving knowledge to others who want it, and of becoming intimately acquainted with their artizan brethren, is a benefit which we hope the rich and educated may never be deprived of.

In one word, Self-Help is a great doctrine, but Mutual Help is a greater ; for it was the lesson bequeathed to us by the Great Brother of us all.

The Editor of the Working Men's Club and Institute Magazine.

Dear Sir,—I promised you somewhat recently that I would send you a sketch of the "origin, progress, and present position of our little Club." I do so in the *hope* and *belief* that others may be benefited thereby, and may be tempted to try to do likewise. At the outset, I must claim the indulgence of your readers for any grammatical errors that may occur, bearing in mind that the writer is himself a working man. I will now proceed to unfold my *tale* as simply and plainly as my abilities will allow. Our Club is known by the name of the "Buersil and Lowerplace Working Men's Club." Its *origin* was as follows : In connexion with the Church Sunday-schools in the neighbourhood there was a number of young men, "teachers," whose misfortune was that they seldom, if ever, saw each other from Sunday to Sunday, and then but during school hours. They felt there was a something short—a connecting link—to bind them together more firmly, to bring them more in contact with each other, and thus cement the good feeling that existed amongst them. It had been often suggested that a news-room would afford them an opportunity of meeting together. But what was to be done? There was no room suitable for the purpose in the neighbourhood. No one was willing to take the lead in such a movement. The clergyman was appealed to, but, kind man though he was, said he could render no assistance, unless the " gentry " of the district would assist him. Thus for a time the matter dropped; but only for a time. On the evening of the 21st of March, 1860, fourteen of the teachers met, on the invitation of one of their number, at his lodgings, to consider a proposition he was desirous of making. It should be borne in mind that the whole of these fourteen persons were, with one exception, *cotton operatives;* that exception being the writer of this sketch, who was at that time serving his apprenticeship in the machine trade. The proposal made was to this effect: The next cottage (an old one) to the one in which they were met was about to become *tenantless*, and it was proposed it should be taken at a weekly rent of one shilling and sixpence. The proposal was adopted, and it was unanimously resolved that a Club should be established, and a Treasurer, Secretary, and Committee was appointed.

*　　*　　*　　*　　*　　*

Having framed our rules, a copy of which I enclose, the next question to be considered was, How were the requisite fittings, &c., to be provided? This proved to be a formidable difficulty; nevertheless it was overcome. Before the meeting dispersed, it was resolved—First, that the house should be taken, one of their number being placed in as tenant; second, a deputation was appointed to wait upon the clergyman, to request him to accept the office of President; thirdly, those present should pay their entrance-fee (one shilling each) according to the rules; fourthly, the total sum so paid (14s.) was ordered to be laid out in the purchasing of wood, to be made into forms by themselves; fifthly, the house was ordered to be cleaned, a person being appointed to attend to it; and, sixthly, it was resolved there should be another meeting on the following Saturday, to report progress, such meeting to be held in the " Club-house." Accordingly, on the following

Saturday afternoon, they again met, but without a seat to sit upon; however, the forms which were only part made were required to do duty. At that meeting it was announced that our clergyman was willing to become President.

We again entered into the question of fittings, &c., and we came to the conclusion " that if the Club was to be a success, we must make it so ourselves." We acted accordingly. One person volunteered at his own expense to purchase a set of fireirons, another brushes, another a couple of chairs, another prints for the walls, another frames for the same, while others subscribed a sum sufficient to purchase cocoa-matting for the newsroom floor.

Thus we began, and continued until we got sufficient for our requirements for the time. It would take, Mr. Editor, more space than you have to spare, were I to enter into all the difficulties that beset our path, and all the little triumphs we achieved; yet there is one other little matter, in connexion with our second meeting, to which I should like to allude.

The premises were not supplied with gas; there was a beer-house almost next door which was. It was felt that to make the Club-rooms look *cheerful* we must have something better than " dips," otherwise, with all our efforts, we could not make the place so attractive as our neighbours. This was a serious matter, involving, as it did, an expenditure of several pounds. It was admitted on all hands what was desirable; but one thing was needful: it was a matter of pounds, shillings, and pence. However, having confidence in the success of our undertaking, we called in the gasfitter, had the rooms lighted to our satisfaction, and advanced amongst us the sum required to discharge the account; the money being advanced until such time as the Club could afford to repay. Shortly afterwards we held our inauguration *Tea Party*, and, by dint of good management, we had a profit remaining which more than repaid the loan. At this time we had about thirty members.

I now come to the second part of my sketch—viz., Progress we have made. Twelve months after the Club was established we had about fifty members; but one thing was notable, that many who joined in the winter months ceased their connexion in the summer. This promised to be a great drawback to the success of the Club, unless some means were

taken to prevent it. The building was so badly ventilated
that it was almost impossible for members to remain in the
rooms during the hot weather. Again and again they argued
that after being in the mill during the day they wanted a little
out-door exercise; various were the objections raised and
many were the remedies proposed. At last the committee
decided upon three things : First, to improve the ventilation
of the rooms; second, that any member ceasing his connexion
with the Club should not be re-admitted unless he gave a
satisfactory reason for so doing; and thirdly, acting upon the
suggestion of their Secretary, they determined upon providing
a play-ground for the summer season. A piece of enclosed
ground was taken for the purpose (from a gentleman who
has since rendered good service to the good cause) at a
nominal rent. We had a large framework erected for swings,
&c., at a cost of 30*l.*, 20*l.* of which we had to obtain on loan,
but have since repaid. We have gradually added amusements as the funds would admit; till now we have one of the
best, if not the best, open-air gymnasiums in the county,
without having asked for or received a single donation towards
the expense of the same. Nay, more than this, we held last
year an athletic festival, by which we were pecuniary losers
to the extent of about 6*l.*; yet the Club gained in two ways
—first by a large addition of members, and secondly by the
addition of about 7*l.* to the funds. It is our rule, in getting
up things of this kind, to make a subscription amongst ourselves and friends towards defraying a portion of the expenses
incurred. While the receipts of the festival last year were
insufficient to cover the expenses, yet the " Members' Special
Fund" not only made up the deficiency, but also added the
amount I have named to the general funds of the Club, in
addition to a quantity of property which had to be purchased
for the occasion. This year our festival has been more successful. Last year it was little known, much less understood;
but this year we came before the public better known and
better understood; and, notwithstanding our expenses have
more than trebled, our receipts have done the same, and we
have only trespassed upon the members' "Special Fund"
(which has been this year much larger than usual) to the
amount of about 2*l.*, the Club benefiting by an increase of
members and the sum of 15*l.*; at the same time we are con-

tinually adding to our stock of properties required for the purpose, besides causing our Club to be better known and appreciated.

Thus our maxim has been, from the first establishment of the Club, *to trust to our own resources, not to others.* This I believe to be the secret of our success. It should not be forgotten that we have had four out of the five and a-half years of our existence to contend against a cotton famine. Many a time our weekly subscriptions have not been sufficient to pay the week's rent and cleaning; yet we still held on; our Club was a meeting-place for our cotton operative members to meet and wile away their time at their educational and sewing classes and amusements. Even at the time I am writing, many are wearing clothing they made themselves at our little Club. Oftentimes have I heard them declare that, had it not been for the Club, they could not have told how to spend their time. To their credit be it said, that, as they came to be employed, they paid up their arrears, in some cases amounting to more than twelve months' subscription at twopence per week. The Club has been, and continues to be, governed by themselves. Knowing their wants and knowing their circumstances, they act accordingly; and while they have much to contend against, they have a bright future before them. Year by year we have steadily increased in the number of members; our annual tea-parties increase in importance (a report of our last you were kind enough to insert in the February number of your Magazine); our annual procession on Whit-Saturday has become one of our village "events," and is always looked forward to with pleasure. I ought not to omit that the young women (all factory girls) of the village school presented to the Club, on the occasion of their first procession, a large and handsome flag, bearing the name of the Club, and the motto, " *Labor omnia vincit.*" There is another feature in connexion with our Club well worth the consideration of your working men readers—viz., our newspapers are almost entirely *given* by the members themselves. Some present one, some another. Those who receive papers from friends at a distance place them upon the tables. These we have from America and other places. One of our old members, who is now in Australia, sends us an illustrated paper every mail. The same

G

rule applies to indoor amusements. By this means we are enabled to devote a large sum to other purposes. We divide the year into two terms—winter and summer. The former commences October 1st and closes March 31st, and the latter the remainder of the year. During the winter we have classes for reading, writing, and arithmetic; debates fortnightly, and lecturets or lectures the same. (Political discussions are forbidden fruit.) These are well attended, and give great satisfaction. I now come to the last part of my subject: Present position. We have on the books 115 members; a library of 350 volumes; the newsroom is supplied with 17 papers, including daily, weekly, and monthly; an excellent gymnasium, which, during the present summer, we have thrown open to the inhabitants generally, on payment of one penny per day. We find that, while it has added much to the pleasure of those who have attended, it promises to be an excellent source of revenue. This position has been, to a great extent, attained by the exertions of the members themselves. At the same time, I cannot but add that we have been much indebted to the kindness of our senior vice-president, who, while he has been anxious the members should manage their own business, has at all times been ready to preside at our public festivals, and to render us assistance as occasion required. We have but one obstacle in our path, and that bids fair to disappear—our present premises are by far too small; we cannot accommodate half our members. Various suggestions have been made to remedy the evil, but have invariably been given up, until a proposition made by the Secretary has been adopted. An architect has been called in; plans made and accepted; a company formed under the Joint-Stock Company's Act, with a capital of 500*l.*, with power to increase. Already 420 shares have been subscribed for, and we are in treaty for a site for the building, in a most eligible situation, and containing about 520 square yards, and, with the revival of the cotton trade, we hope to have our new Club-house ready by Christmas next.

I have already trespassed too much upon your space, and must conclude, with a promise to report progress at some future day.—I am, Sir, yours respectfully,

Buersil, July 4, 1865.   D. SCHOFIELD.

CHAPTER VI.

[The following Chapter is taken from the *Working Men's Club and Institute Magazine* for January, 1865.]

HOW TO MAKE CLUBS SELF-DESTRUCTIVE.

As our Magazine professes to be impartial and catholic in its principles, and as we have already endeavoured to show how Clubs may be made self-supporting, we think it only fair to offer a little encouragement to the other side of the question.

I. *Hints to Promoters.*

To prepare for this catastrophe, begin by showing the men that you do not trust them—that they must be treated like children ; or that, at all events, you mean to do as much for them, and leave as little to themselves, as possible. Avoid having trustees, but get two committees appointed instead— one of gentlemen, the other of working men. Let the gentlemen's committee have the control of all the cash, and let the working men's committee be obliged to ask leave for spending anything. Let there be an appeal from all or any of the decisions of the working men's committee to that of the gentlemen's. Get a supercilious, ungenial manager ; a thoroughly unbusiness-like or intemperate man will do just as well. The purpose can sometimes be answered effectively by having a man and his wife, and allowing the man not to trouble himself at all about the interests of the Club, and by not expecting the wife to concern herself about anything except tea, coffee, and other refreshments. These last had better be of inferior quality, nicely spoiled in making, and rather higher in price than they can be got elsewhere. Admit members under the age of eighteen or twenty. Be very careful that none of the committee ever trouble themselves to go near the Club, or exert any authority while there ; at all events not to do this in turn and with regularity. Let any gentleman interested in the Club carefully abstain from coming near it, or taking any part in the management of entertain-

G 2

ments or classes, under a judicious apprehension of being disliked and distrusted by the members. It must never be considered that the refinement, culture, and education of an upper class man can be of the slightest use to working men, or that the Club is a suitable place for bringing the two classes together for mutually pleasant and profitable relations. If, however, a gentleman can go in a dictatorial spirit, well crammed with suspicions, and can show that he considers the Club *his*, and not *theirs*, the satisfactory result may be sooner produced than probably in any other way. Make no provision for supplying entertainments for the members, and of course avoid having "singing" or "elocution" classes. Should discussion meetings be established, let subjects be proposed which will engender strong personal feeling and give rise to acrimonious remarks, which the chairman must refrain from repressing. Theological topics are admirably adapted for the purpose, on account of the deep interest felt in them. Let a majority refuse altogether the discussion of any subject, otherwise unobjectionable, but particularly desired by a minority.

II *Hints to Members.*

It is important that clerks, tradesmen, and so forth, should, if possible, be induced to join the Club ; not, of course, in order to give help of any kind, but to monopolize the newspapers, bagatelle-board, &c. As this, however, cannot often be accomplished, the members themselves must be encouraged to treat one another in a cold and unfriendly fashion—each taking the best seats, or keeping possession of the most coveted newspapers, magazines, or games—taking care to regard the Club merely as a place where they can get a little amusement and comfort for themselves—carefully pooh-poohing any notion of its being intended as a general good to the working men of the neighbourhood and as an agency for their social elevation. Members must avoid paying their subscription regularly, and must never encourage their fellow-members to do so, or look after them when they have absented themselves—any appearance of interest in one another will not only help to frustrate the desired object, but must be viewed as a mark of bad taste.

If a man can't go to his Club the first two or three nights

in the week, let him be sure to say, "Oh, it's not worth going now this week. I'll wait till next Monday." By this means he will save twopence and set a good example, which, if well followed, will soon close the Club—unless, indeed, the landlord, unfortunately, should agree to deduct from his rent all members' subscription in arrear, which he is very likely to do.

By way of promoting the dissensions above referred to, in connexion with the discussion meeting, it will be very advisable to request that books of a strong sectarian, theological bias, or eminently destructive of received religious opinions, and likely, therefore, to be offensive to some members of the Club, may be introduced into the library; or that newspapers of a similar character be placed on the table. "Each for himself," of course, must be the motto; mutual concessions must be carefully avoided, and nothing like the idea ever be admitted of its ever being a common social platform for men of all sects and parties.

A very useful step will be to introduce frequent dramatic entertainments, with dresses, scenery, and with the female parts performed by female acquaintances of the members. This will be pretty sure to alienate the influential friends and supporters of the Club in the upper ranks, and drive away the slow-going hum-drum working men. Recitations, dialogues, and acting charades without dresses will not be of any use for this purpose, but would tend decidedly the other way. Dancing may also be introduced, with a judiciously frequent succession of "penny hops;" and if without supervision or selection of company, so much the better. Merely proposing these cheerful little amusements will be wise policy; because, if they are resisted, you may probably get up a faction against the ruling powers, and you might, perhaps, worry them into resigning, or, if there are trustees, they will probably refuse permission for these entertainments, and shut up the place, which would be a great relief to all parties concerned, especially to the neighbouring publicans.

In like manner, an agitation might be got up for the introduction of beer into the Club, which, like the other measures, whether successful or not, would delightfully damage the concern, and probably sow the seeds of ultimate disruption. Make a good deal of the cry that "it is not meant to be a Teetotal Club!" that "it is very hard a working man cannot have his beer " wherever he is or whatever he may be doing ; and that, of course, a pewter pot is an inseparable adjunct to a British workman's enjoyment of a sociable evening.

Betting and gambling can be encouraged "on the sly ;" as, of course, anybody has a right to do what he likes with his own. Few measures will be more valuable for the important purposes in view. You must discourage any interest in the mere games themselves ; laugh down the notion of there being any pleasure in the exercise of the skill they may require, and vote the whole thing abominably slow without some trifling stakes. Introduce " cards ;" of course, at first, with an emphatic prohibition against playing for money, which can be gradually and good-humouredly ignored.

If all these measures are frustrated, or fail of their desired effect, get a dozen or two fellows of the roughest character you are acquainted with—thorough-going pot companions— to join the Club for a "lark." Set them to make themselves systematically disagreeable, and to take every opportunity of making each member in particular uncomfortable; and, if possible, of getting up occasionally a general " row." They can take private opportunities of hacking the furniture and games about, cribbing the bagatelle-balls or draughts, and generally of being able to say when they leave, they have had " their —— two-pennorth " out of it, as was recently and elegantly remarked at a large Club.

N.B.—Observe that all these hints to members can only be effectually acted on if the ladies and gentlemen interested in the destruction of the Club will also kindly do their part by attending to the foregoing hints. Anything like that higher tone and ridiculously improving and elevating tendency which would be given by the presence of persons of culture, refinement, and kindly feeling, would probably be a fatal antidote to the best-laid brotherly scheme for disorganization.

All this nonsense about making the Clubs places for something more than mere amusement and gossip must be inexorably snuffed out. A working man's inability to care about anything but smoking, drinking, or playing after his day's work must be fiercely insisted on, and the whole Club and Institute must be kept down as nearly to the level of the beershop as may be practicable.

One other point, but one of great importance, is all we have room for at present. Let the Committees and Secretaries of Clubs be very careful not to lay hold of that "ALPINE ROPE" spoken of in the introduction to the first number of our Magazine. They must carefully abstain from taking in the Magazine, from sending any information to it, and from affiliating with the Union, so that they may avoid getting any useful hints from other parties engaged in this mischievous work, or giving them any in return. By this means, if matters are going wrong, nobody but the Committee, and, by degrees, the members, need know anything about the disease till it is too late to cure it. Like a wounded wild beast, the Club can creep into a hole and die unseen—and as the Central Union and the Club movement generally got no benefit from the Club while living. so it is just possible they may receive some little damage from the fact of its decease. At all events, the chance is worth trying for, and the fact of not affiliating with the Union will, *quoad*, cripple the said Union's usefulness, and that is worth much.

The necessity for all the above trouble in extinguishing the Club may be avoided, however, by sensible precautions when the first proposals for establishing it are mooted. A glance at these must be reserved for a future number. [See next Chapter.]

CHAPTER VII.

[In the pamphlet before referred to, entitled "Hints and Suggestions, &c.," the Parent Society offers some advice as to the measures that may be taken for establishing these Clubs and Institutes. A few more, by reading them backwards, may be gathered from the following paper, originally published in the Society's Magazine for February, 1865.]

HINTS ON THE BEST MEANS FOR PREVENTING THE FORMA-
TION OF WORKING MEN'S CLUBS AND INSTITUTES.

AT the close of the article in our last number, entitled "How to make Clubs Self-Destructive," we observed that "the necessity for all the above trouble in extinguishing the Club might be avoided by judicious obstructions when the first proposals for establishing it are mooted." Let us, therefore, now glance at a few of the said "obstructions," and it may be as well here to state that nearly all the suggestions, both in this chapter and in the last, are happily based on facts which have actually occurred—the few exceptions being, or having been, in a fair way to come under the same category.

Hints to Obstructives.

At the preliminary meeting, to which those gentlemen may have been summoned who are thought likely to aid in the movement, let it be strongly urged that the working man hates being patronized, and that the Clubs, *therefore*, should be entirely self-supporting, or not exist at all. Should this objection be overruled on any of the grounds mentioned in the chapter "How can Clubs be made Self-Supporting?" a good stand may be made on the ground that the Club is not wanted in that particular neighbourhood—though, no doubt, very useful elsewhere; or it can be eloquently maintained that home is the proper place for the working man, and that the Clubs take men away from their homes, carefully ignoring the nature of those homes, and keeping out of sight all the proofs that have been accumulated in the pages of our Occasional Papers and Magazine regarding the absurd notion that the Clubs help to bring men from the public-house *to* their homes, and to make those homes happier in various ways.

If there is a Mechanics' Institute in the town, it may probably be converted into a Malakhoff *piece de resistance,* and the inquiry may indignantly be made why the working men don't avail themselves of the great advantages it is supposed to afford. If they won't go to such a good reading-room, capital lectures, classes, &c., of course they won't avail themselves of such common-place and degrading facilities as talking, smoking, and recreation-rooms. Do not the nobility and gentry of England rush with impetuous eagerness every night, after a hard day's work or play, to classes and lectures, and generally "go in" for hard study? Or if there are a few exceptions among men of a domestic turn, is it not well known that they keep no servants, and that their family sit the whole evening in the kitchen, using it as nursery, parlour, library, and drawing-room, as well as for nice little dinner and music parties?

Should all these and similar arguments prove unavailing, and a number of misguided fanatics be determined to start the Quixotic enterprise, then make the movement as much of " a hole-and-corner " affair as possible, and especially manage to prevent a public meeting being held, as that might give the working men confidence that all was straightforward and "above-board."

As the success of the undertaking will depend mainly, among other important points, on the working men having full confidence in the single-mindedness of the promoters, try and get these gentlemen to connect the Club with some religious organization, or other object exceedingly good in itself, but not likely to be sufficiently appreciated by the individuals they propose to benefit. Working men being proverbially free from suspiciousness, there will be no harm in taking steps that may raise the idea of there being some ulterior object in view. We can never do people any good until they are persuaded that we have some selfish object in view, and working men, of course, are not at all in the habit of supposing that religious people have any sinister object at heart in the schemes they may set on foot for their benefit.

If a public meeting is held, endeavour to give it in some way or other a party or sectarian character, by means of the place at which it is held, the way in which it is announced, or the person invited to be chairman; or a few roughs, previously primed with beer, which the publican will, doubtless, gladly give " free gratis," judiciously placed in different parts of the meeting, will be able either to create a diversion, by means of choral harmonies specially composed for the occasion, or by interrupting the speaker with a few well-chosen questions.

With regard to the speakers, evidently the first qualification is that they should be totally ignorant of the subject. The second, that they should insist upon some extreme views of their own, and get the meeting divided into parties or factions in support thereof or in opposition thereto. One speaker can urge the necessity of uncompromising and exclusive Teetotalism; another can be equally rampant as to the necessity for admitting beer. A strong prejudice may be got up against the movement among the clergy and gentry by insisting that the Club rooms should be opened on a Sunday, or among the working men, by fiercely maintaining that they ought to be entirely closed then.

Points of this and similar character, which can only properly be decided, after a time, by experience and by the subscribers and members themselves, should be pushed prematurely at the public meeting. We have known an influential public meeting end in smoke, and all operations be suspended for a year, mainly owing to one brief, prudent, and well-timed exhortation on a ticklish question, which, but for the purpose in view, should only have been discussed before a deliberative meeting of promoters and members. Contrive, if possible, that the public meeting close without the appointment of a provisional committee for carrying out its objects, by some such speech as, " Oh, that can easily be done by-and-bye; it's getting late now ;" but if the appointment be inevitable, mind and get two or three crotchetty fellows placed upon it—a man of extreme views, and known for his unbusinesslike capacity, appointed as secretary, or some gentleman disliked by the working men, or a working man mistrusted by the employers in the neighbourhood.

When the question of premises has to be discussed, urge the necessity of getting a large building, and raising 2,000*l.* or 3,000*l.*, in order to do the thing " in a way worthy of this important borough ;" at least, if the notion of supposing that the money could possibly be got is sufficiently ridiculous. By diverting the attention of the provisional committee to an impracticable scheme of this nature, a great deal of valuable time will be gained, during which the effect of the public meeting will wear off, zeal be cooled down, and the whole concern probably be shelved for a year or two. On the other hand, premises may be taken in a locality so suitable for the early suffocation of a Club, or which are so small, dark, dirty, and ill-ventilated, that the few members who go will feel like rats in a haunted house, and be speedily reduced to such dismal extremities, that they will ere long devour one another or commit a double suicide—viz., on themselves and the Clubs of which they were the scanty ornaments.

Should you ultimately be unable to prevent a canvass of the neighbourhood for donations, get the donation list headed by leading men with some very small sums ; or you may be able to frustrate the object by proposing the application of the " Free Libraries Act " to the town, and getting all the determined public-house frequenters, close-fisted or unprosperous tradesmen, and public-spirited ratepayers in general, to come up in sufficient numbers to outvote the stupid, misguided artizans, who would gladly see it introduced. Should the proposal to apply the act be rejected, the people of property and employers in the neighbourhood will perhaps be sufficiently exasperated to make this rejection the ground of refusal to do anything to help such a set of low-minded, beer-loving sots as are desiring the establishment of a Working Men's Club and Institute.

But we can only offer hints. The above will be sufficient for wise men ; and we have but little hope that any others read our Magazine. Hence the smallness of the circulation. Go, then, illustrious friends of the working men, where glory waits you—seize every suitable and unsuitable occasion, and nip these pernicious undertakings in the budding hour.

N.B.—Prizes will, probably, ere long be offered for preventing Clubs from being established, or for pleasantly smothering them if they come into existence.

CHAPTER VIII.

HOW TO MAKE CLUBS AND INSTITUTES ATTRACTIVE.

WE have thrown out a few hints in previous chapters as to ways and means for making Clubs self-supporting and self-destructive. But the main point for the former purpose, where the premises are large enough, unquestionably is to make them so attractive that they may always have plenty of members subscribing sufficient, as in gentlemen's Clubs, to enable them to pay their way all the year round. Among the measures requisite for the purpose we have already laid stress on the main *principles* requisite for this end, such as that the working men should feel that the Club is their own, that they are their own masters there, and can be as free and independent as in their own homes ;*

---

* Since writing on this point (which is of course of vital concern) in previous chapters, we have been reminded of a curious fact which occurred several years ago. A public-spirited manufacturer and his son, in Stockport, spent a good deal of money in fitting up reading and news rooms for the enjoyment of their men, but, to their disappointment, found the rooms were so little used that at last they were shut up and the experiment abandoned. About six months afterwards, two of the leading "hands" came to their employer and said, "Measter, will ye gie us the key?" "What key?" asked the gentleman, in surprise. "The key o' thae News-room," replied the men. It was willingly given when their plans were explained. The "hands" formed their own committee, opened and managed the rooms themselves, and the whole affair, which has since greatly developed in various ways, became a useful and prosperous Institute. A precisely similar disappointment has been experienced by the partners in a celebrated engineering establishment in the metropolis, who, in addition to the ordinary provision for reading and recreation, fitted up excellent baths for their men. Besides the hindrance to the use of such advantages, caused by the men's desire to be perfectly free from restraint and surveillance, there is another arising out of their fear of being supposed to be currying favour with their employers ("creeping up their sleeve," in expressive workshop idiom) by using what is thus benevolently provided for them, and sometimes still greater fear of coming under any obligation to them.

that the grown-up men have at least one or two rooms to
themselves into which the youths should have no admission;
that there should be a steward or manager, and if possible a
committee also, who should make the members, especially new
comers, feel that they are *welcome*; that occasional amusements and rational excitement should be provided to supply
the place of the attractions of the public-house; that good and
cheap refreshments should be provided; that Provident and
other economical Societies should be connected with the Club;
that members' wives and daughters should occasionally parti-
cipate in the enjoyments of the Club; and that there should
be a good library both for reading at the Club and for lending
to members.

In addition to these and other recommendations scattered
through this volume, we desire now to add two or three
special suggestions, and also to dwell more emphatically or
at length on some of those already mentioned.

The value of making the accommodation in the principal
conversation, smoking, and reading rooms as comfortable and
cheerful-looking as possible can hardly be over-estimated. In
the letter from Sunderland (quoted page 57), the writer
refers to the apparently trivial, but really important fact, that
in the reading-room everyone was provided with an arm-chair.
Tired men can well appreciate a comfort of this kind. And
yet in too many Clubs we have seen both reading and talking
rooms furnished only with forms, sometimes even without
backs to them. Chairs not only give the needed rest, but
promote that grand desideratum in a Club—viz., sociability.
Small round tables, likewise, in the coffee and smoking-room
are a much more sociable arrangement than those long tables
which are too common. Two or three compartments, also,
divided from the rest of the room, if it be large enough, by
red curtains, give a pleasant aspect to it, and present attractions for cozy "good-fellowship." A bell, by which to summon
the steward or waiter, or other adequate facilities for members
to "give their orders" when they come to the Club, is desirable. It is also well to have a list of prices of every article

---

These fears and jealousies are very sad. But they will vanish as
masters and men both rise to a higher level, and stand to one another,
generally, on the footing of mutual confidence and respect which
ordinarily characterize the relations of an employer and his foreman.

sold hung up in the Club-room. Men are shy of asking prices, and still more of ordering in the dark. At the bottom of the list might be a notice that any person requiring refreshments is requested to ring the bell. If the steward at any time found that from pressure of orders he could not serve the members fast enough, he might be able to engage two or three of the younger members, who, for a trifling remuneration, or for some refreshment, would willingly help him. Anything better than keeping the members long waiting. Then, again, the necessary process of showing one's ticket should be made the occasion rather for the pleasant welcome of a privileged friend than the jealous scrutiny of a possible intruder. It is upon trifles like these now mentioned, that the success of a Club, otherwise well managed, often turns. We have heard the Club at Hull praised in respect of its comfort and attractiveness by a working man at Brighton, and the sociability of the Bradford Club highly spoken of by a London ironfounder.

A very good suggestion was once made to us by an artizan engaged in the Deptford Dockyard (Mr. Cole), that it would often be a great attraction to men if they could have a carpenter's bench, turning-lathe, and other tools at their Club, particularly if there was going to be an Industrial Exhibition in the neighbourhood. Of course men engaged in such occupations during the day would not want them at night. But tailors, shoemakers, compositors, &c., might be very glad of the opportunity to employ themselves for an hour or two in some ingenious labours of a totally different character. In like manner, a joiner might delight in being initiated into the mysteries of an electrial machine, or of chemical combinations; a mason might take an interest in figure drawing and painting, or the various orders of architecture, and in ornamentation according to Ruskin. We must always remember the value of helping men to employ a different set of faculties from those with which they earn their daily bread. It is one of the highest recommendations of a Club that it assists a man to exercise the whole of his intellectual nature, and thereby to become more of a man, less of a mere animal or machine. Culture of every kind is for this reason pre-eminently *humanizing*. Recreation takes a far higher stand when this important function which it performs is duly remembered and honoured.

The daily drudgery by which the bread is earned is often monotonous, deadening in its effects, yet when faithfully performed unspeakably noble. All the more reason for providing agreeable change of occupation and humanizing variety when it is over.

The important question of whether it would not be better that the members of a Club should be elected by ballot, instead of entering by merely paying their subscription, has already been adverted to in Chapter III. But it is worth considering whether the principle of election might not often be better applied by having a Club within a Club—a sort of inner and more select circle, consisting at first of the older members who first joined, and then of those whom they invite or elect to join them. The outline of the plan is given in the following extract from a letter to the Secretary of the Bolton Club; and although they have peculiar facilities for carrying it out, yet as we have insisted on the necessity for the grown-up and married men having at least one or two rooms to themselves in every Club, it would always be possible where this was secured for them to have their select circle and keep it to themselves :—

"150, Strand, June 7, 1867.

"My dear Sir,—I have to thank you for sending me your last Report, which is very interesting, and, on the whole, very satisfactory. Let me beg you and your zealous coadjutors never to be discouraged. The tide is sure to flow in your favour if you can hold on. I have printed the greater part of it in the Appendix to our Annual Report, which will go into several thousand hands, and your Club will thus be helping many others.

"It has occurred to me, considering the great number of rooms you possess, that you might very well adopt, in a modified form, one of the suggestions in our last edition of 'Hints,' &c., recently sent you—viz., that of electing members. Suppose you get a number of the best among your grown-up men to form a sort of select society within the Club, and give them up two good rooms entirely to themselves, with a bagatelle-board in one, and comfortable chairs with little tables in the other? They might call themselves ' The Eclectics,' or ' The Sociables,' and nobody should belong to them or be allowed to come into their rooms until he had been duly proposed one week, and elected by ballot the next; one-third black balls to exclude. You would find a considerable competition, I suspect, among the members of your Club, and ere long among the outside public, to be elected members of this select circle, and those who joined it would stick to it. Of course only quarterly members would be eligible, and probably very few members under twenty-five years would be elected. But this would be a great thing gained—to make men feel it a favour to be allowed to join, instead of (as too often at present) feeling that they are doing you a favour by joining. You need not give 'The Sociables' any news-papers or books, they would go to the ordinary rooms for that.

" Then, again, I think you should always be endeavouring to give greater privileges (not invidiously, but as a natural re-sult) to the quarterly members than to the weeklies, and to the latter than to the penny visitors. Let them all feel this difference, though in a quiet, pleasant, unobtrusive fashion. Then there will be a constant influence at work to make them lengthen their term of subscription.

" Lastly, have you thought of holding an Industrial Ex-hibition? Remember that the Preston Club made 1,000l. by theirs! Of course, I do not for a moment urge constant excite-ment; you will see what I have said about that in our Re-port. It is not by excitement, but by producing a gradual, steady demand among working men for the quiet comforts and advantages of the Club, that permanent prosperity is to be secured. Make the Club more comfortable and attractive than any public-house, and then a certain number of men will come, even without beer. But occasional and reasonable ex-citement, at proper intervals, may bring you money and get you out of debt. Pray let me hear from you from time to time, and believe me, very truly yours,

"HENRY SOLLY."

And let it not be supposed that this would be regarded as an invidious and unbrotherly proceeding by the other frequenters of the Club. English working men specially delight in this kind of select fellowship, while they are at the same time ready to extend it whenever and wherever they feel the ground safe for doing so. The great popularity of the secret orders of Odd-Fellows, Foresters, Druids, and of a large number of lesser confraternities, is some evidence of this statement. We strongly recommend every Club to consider the desirableness of forming an order or society of "Sociables" or " Free Companions" within its borders, and inviting the best and pleasantest of their friends to join it.

Then, again, we are reminded by the mention of Odd-Fellows, &c., that working men—like true-hearted Englishmen, as they are—value " dignities and authorities." They have many orders and degrees of merit in those societies, honour being duly and cordially given according as it is due. And it is very desirable to consider in what way those members of a Club, whether belonging to the inner circle or to the body generally, who have deserved well of their brethren, or who have shown a capacity for special work and important functions, could be placed in suitable posts of honour, and be recognized as belonging to an order of merit. We have alluded to this important subject in the paper " On the Union and Co-operation of Clubs" belonging to the same district, but here we refer more especially to the action of individual Clubs, and to their arrangements for a governing body and officers.

At one of the conferences we attended in the North of England, it was suggested that occasional suppers, to which men might bring their wives, would have a very good effect. We quite believe this. It is a recommendation similar in character to one we would strongly urge—viz., that the Committee should throw open all the rooms in the Club-house for an occasional *conversazione*, say once a-month, when the wives, daughters, and sweethearts should be admitted, and when something amusing or entertainingly-instructive should be provided in each room. There is often much truth in the remark, that until the wives have had some welcome of this kind to the Club they may view it with suspicion ; but once welcomed in this fashion, and receiving an occasional share, however small, in its enjoyments, they become its warm supporters.

There is no doubt that general sociability and " good-fellowship " is one of the principal enjoyments which a Club is intended to supply—which in a certain way a public-house does now give (in most cases) very thoroughly—and which must be supplied by the Club in a variety of ways (none of them debasing), if it is to take the place of the public-house. The Saturday evening "Free and Easy" (under the surveillance of a firm but genial chairman), and sociable little tea-meetings, or suppers, are a great help in promoting the attractiveness, as well as usefulness, of a Club.

The members might each in turn, according to the size of the room be allowed to introduce a friend once or twice to the "Free and Easy," or other entertainments and social meetings, and two or three times, perhaps, on ordinary nights. This would induce many to wish to become members who would otherwise have known nothing about the Club, and would spread its reputation through the workshops or factories of the town. But a privilege of this kind would have to be guarded very carefully, lest it should impair the "Club" feeling of privacy and select companionship. On the *conversazione* nights, if the rooms were not large enough to admit all the members' female friends on every occasion, each member in turn might be allowed two tickets.

Well-managed discussion meetings, or classes with interesting subjects and lively speakers, are always exceedingly popular, as well as extremely useful in an educational point of view. Where it is difficult to establish them for want of enough members willing to take part in them, it might be well to try the plan of appropriating the larger part of the room to those who come to hear but not to speak, and placing chairs and a table in the other part, for the three or four who may be willing to discuss the question, and who might associate two or three others with them as junior counsel. By thus giving greater distinction, responsibility, and dignity to the function of speakers, we may sometimes be able to induce men capable of the effort to make it; and good speakers from other Clubs also may be willing to give up an evening, and to come some distance to lead a debate. Here, also, is an admirable field opened for gentlemen of education, and with popular sympathies, to promote the attractiveness of a Club, and at the same time to advocate what they deem to be important truth. After a few such intellectual contests, with an interested and perhaps applauding audience, a few more members would be induced to come into the arena, until there might be regular sides chosen by the leading speakers, as for a game at cricket. These more public discussions, also, might stimulate members to attempt private practice classes. And once or twice a-year there should be a Discussion or Debate, to which the public generally would be admitted by tickets, distributed by the speakers or committee. Great pains should be taken· in all these discussions, to encourage thoughtful argumentative remarks, and to discourage mere rhetorical flourishes, or *ad captandum* displays. The time allotted to each speaker, on ordinary occasions, should seldom exceed twenty minutes each for the opener and his opponent, and ten minutes for the other speakers, giving an additional ten minutes on the public nights. Brevity involves condensation and thought. Unlimited opportunity invites diffuseness and display. All subjects except Theology should be freely discussed. (See pp. 80-81, and a subsequent chapter, in reference to this exception.)

A Tennis or Fives Court would be very attractive as an out-door game, and might often be secured within a comparatively small space, where no other out-door recreation was possible.

A Natural History or "Field Club," for the summer months, would attract and benefit some members. Occasional exhibitions of collections of insects, &c., floral exhibitions, &c., small prizes being given, would be useful. The microscopic exhibitions of the South Shields Club and Institute have generally been crowded.

Visits to museums, exhibitions of paintings, &c., in small parties of Club members, with some person well qualified to explain and point out objects of interest, would often prove exceedingly agreeable.*

Great care must be exercised, when considering how to make Clubs attractive, to counteract the prevailing tendency of all Institutions for working men to " go upwards "—to be used, that is, by a socially higher class than they were intended for. While the culture of the members is promoted to the utmost, the managers of a Club should always be endeavouring to bring in, at the other end of the Club as it were, a lower class

---

* A few further hints will be found under the head of " Amusement and Education Combined."

than those already benefited by it—of course taking the greatest care not to drive out the existing members by the new admissions. It has been remarked, however, with much truth, that if we get the higher class *of working men*, we shall be sure to get the lower class by degrees. They will follow the fashion after a time. But after all that can be said with regard to making Clubs attractive, no doubt the most powerful element for drawing men into Club fellowship and keeping them as members, is *personal influence* and personal qualities. More may be done by the one, and more depends on the other, than can be matched by nearly all other causes combined. This of course applies especially to the secretary, the committee, and, above all, to the steward. N.B.—An old soldier, if he is sufficiently educated, with pleasant, agreeable manners, cheery as well as firm, often makes a capital steward. As a working man observed once, "they have so many stories to tell," and they know how to make the members welcome, yet keep good order.

There are special modes of action, however, connected with this subject of personal influence that had better be discussed in a separate chapter. But the following correspondence between Mr. B——, honorary treasurer of the F—— Working Men's Club and Institute, and the Secretary to the Union, possibly contains suggestions that may be suitably included in the present chapter :—

" Working Men's Club, F——,
May 10, 1866.

" Dear Sir,—At a recent meeting of our Committee, I was requested to ask your advice, with a view to the amendment of our position. I enclose you what papers I can, to show you our former condition as compared to what we are now. Our members are now only fifty, and they do not all seem to appreciate the value of the Club.

" Of course the subscriptions will not pay expenses, and honorary members tire of supporting an institution for which the working men care so little. We get very few artizans ; there are three builders' establishments, one cabinet-maker, two printers, one coachmaker, and one painter, employing on an average eight or ten hands, of whom we have scarcely one on our books. But perhaps our principal difficulty is, that

the vicar is not with us, and he, of course, influences many
of the men.

" Can you, from these few rough notes, form any idea as
to our best course, and will you kindly advise us, if you can ?

" Apologizing for giving you so much trouble, I am, Sir,
yours faithfully,   " E. B——."

                                           "May 15, 1866.

" My dear Sir,—Having carefully considered your letter,
let me first express earnest sympathy with yourself and the
other friends, both working men and gentlemen, who are
striving to keep up the Working Men's Club in your town.
It was the first we helped to establish, and we are the more
anxious for its fate.

"Secondly, let me draw your attention to your sixth rule,
' That any working man or mechanic (not under sixteen years
of age) may become a member of the Club,' &c. Now, as I
am glad to see by your report that you take in the *Working
Man*, you must have noticed all that has lately been said there
upon the admission of youths to these Clubs. Hence, you
can be at no loss to understand one of the principal causes of
your want of greater success in drawing young men to your
Club. You might get the age for admission raised, as
soon as possible, to twenty-two or twenty-three, so as to have
it, practically, at least up to twenty-one—but twenty-five
would be better still—unless yourself and friends think you
can do more good by turning it completely into a Youths'
Club and Institute. But probably by far the best course would
be to adopt some of the plans mentioned in my papers in the
" *Working Man* " *for providing separate accommodation for the
youths.*

" Thirdly, in working these Clubs, we must always remember that there are two forces required for their successful
management. 1. The energy and interest of the working
men themselves, as the rank and file of the army. 2. The
zeal and co-operation of persons in a higher class as leaders
or helpers, when and where they are wanted. Neither, as a
general rule, has proved to be efficient without the other.

" 1. To secure the interest of working men in a Club, the
first step is usually a public meeting. If you have tried this,

or cannot get speakers likely to rouse the working classes, the next, and far more efficient step in any case, is for those men who do care for the Club to talk about it to those who do not—to do this not merely once or twice, but repeatedly, whenever an opportunity offers, again and again, until at last the right moment comes, and a man's friend or shopmate agrees to join the Club for a time, 'just to see how he likes it.' [It is especially useful to send deputations from the Committee and members of the Club to wait on the members of Friendly and Trade Societies in the town at their monthly Lodge or Court meetings.] Personal influence, in short, is the great secret of success in this Club movement. Nothing can supply its place for any permanent result.

" But wise or injudicious rules and arrangements, of course, may greatly help or mar that influence—*e. gr.*, a rule allowing a member to bring a friend two or three times without payment is of great use ; while penny admissions for a single night are generally mischievous, as destroying the Club feeling, and sense of Club privilege. . . .

" To draw the attention of the operatives of the town to the advantages of your Club, you would probably do well to circulate a few hundreds of the enclosed paper, ' A Few Words to Working Men about Social Clubs and Institutes,' accompanied by a short statement of what advantages your own Club offers, with the rate of subscription, &c.

" If you could get up an exhibition, bazaar, outdoor *fête*, &c.—anything to draw general attention to the Club—it would, of course, be a considerable help. The great difficulty you and all supporters of these Clubs have to contend against is the apathy of the working men, and the clinging love many of them have for the publican's fireside. Whatever will rouse their interest and gain their attention, break in upon their habitual routine, and stupid animal indifference, is of much value.

" But especially the working men who have risen above that low, grovelling condition themselves, must make their comrades understand that at the Club they can be just as much their own masters, just as independent, and free and easy, as at the public-house, subject only to their own rules and good feeling, even as in a public-house they must be subject to the landlord and public opinion. I often think of that man's remark, quoted in our 'Occasional Paper,' No. IX., now enclosed,' Working Men Need and Welcome Help from Gentlemen,' &c., ' We have masters, my lord, all day long, and we don't want 'em at night.'

" 2. The co-operation of gentlemen in securing the success of the Club is fully advocated in the said paper. If you ask men to give up the excitement of tippling and low conversation, you *must* substitute other and better excitement. Persons who can talk in a sociable and interesting way, who can sing, read, and recite, show microscope, telescope, air-pump, describe the human hand and horse's hoof, &c., or bring diagrams, maps, and engravings, may do much to help less educated and privileged folk to enjoy very pleasant evenings without fuddling. In the same way, outdoor games and athletic sports sometimes receive great stimulus from the participation in them to a moderate extent of genial gentle-folks.

" Query.—Have you availed yourselves of all these modes of making your Club flourish? Above all, have you and your fellow self-sacrificing workers tried to make the working men, generally, enter into the spirit of brotherly kindness and unselfish labour for the good of those working with them in the shop or the field? There is no hope nor help for any Club, except so far as the members will care for one another, and not merely for themselves. . . .

" With regard to the unfortunate circumstance of your not having the vicar with you, this is, undoubtedly, much to be regretted, both for the sake of his own usefulness and for that of your Club; but if you and your friends will work on in faith and patience, you will, I trust, be able to show him, six months hence, by actual facts, the great good the Club is doing to his parishioners, and then, we would hope, he may become its cordial friend. I have hitherto had no more valuable and friendly supporters among any class than among the clergy of the Church of England.

" Again, I see by the report of our visitor last autumn, that out of your six rooms you appropriate three to your housekeeper. This is a large deduction from your working power. It is generally considered that one bedroom and a sort of bar-parlour is all that should be reserved exclusively for the housekeeper or steward. A man and his wife without family would find this quite sufficient, because they are occupied in attending to the members during the evening, and can use the Club coffee-room, if they want more space, during the day. By your present arrangements you get no class-rooms, and, as I have often urged in the *Working Man* and elsewhere, a Club cannot long be maintained unless there is something of an educational character connected with it. Even the recreation department cannot be properly kept up without it. For instance, unless there is an elocution class there will probably be a deficiency in new recitations for the weekly sing-song or ' free-and-easy ;' old pieces will be recited or read till the members are tired of them. More than one such entertainment has died out from this cause, thereby seriously injuring the Club. The same applies to a singing-class ; and with regard to the need generally of making the Club more than a mere recreation-shop, and of attaching men to it by higher and stronger ties, let me ask you to refer to the account you will find in the *Working Man* of my visit to Bolton [see pp. 67-68]. A discussion-class or meeting, again, I have always advocated as of immense value, if well managed, and kept free from theological controversy and party bitterness.

" For the summer months, can you not get up a weekly meeting for athletic sports, preparatory to a regular festival, and collect money for prizes ? . . . —I am, dear Sir, very truly yours,

" HENRY SOLLY."

CHAPTER IX.

FURTHER SUGGESTIONS FOR INTERESTING WORKING MEN MORE GENERALLY IN THE MOVEMENT—MUTUAL RELATIONS OF PROVIDENT, FRIENDLY, TRADE, AND CO-OPERATIVE SOCIETIES, WITH WORKING MEN'S CLUBS AND INSTITUTES.

THE object of this and the previous chapter is, we hope, more or less answered by nearly every chapter of the present volume. But it requires a few special remarks.

In the fourth chapter (p. 143) we spoke of the importance of working on organically from what is already done to what remains to be accomplished, and therefore of appealing to the great organizations already existing among working men in behalf of these Clubs and Institutes. From the pamphlet entitled, " Hints and Suggestions," before quoted, we take the following recommendation in regard to the steps to be taken at the outset of the enterprise in any locality :—

" Special application, either by letter, or, better still, by deputations, should be made to the Lodges, Courts, Committees, and other governing bodies of all the Trade, Friendly, Co-operative, Temperance, and Building Societies of working men in the neighbourhood. Their managers and members should be invited to attend the preliminary and other meetings for establishing the Club ; they should be personally canvassed, also, as far as possible, for their support and influence; and their assistance in getting members, both at their business meetings and in their workshops, should be solicited."

The subject is also pressed upon the attention of the friends of the movement in the last Annual Report of the Union, page 8, where it is said that, " There is probably hardly a Working Men's Society in the kingdom, whether Trade, Benefit, Co-operative, &c., however hostile formerly to such a procedure, but would at the present time allow, and in most cases welcome, by at all events a majority of its members, the visit of a deputation from this Society to discuss the subject of Working Men's Clubs. And this mode of agitating the question is in many respects by far the most efficient." (See Appendix.)

But while this course is undoubtedly the right one to pursue, and no measures should be taken either for establishing or reviving a Club without thus endeavouring to interest in it those working men who have already shown their sense of the value of mutual help and of corporate organization, a no less important consideration is the arguments by which they should be asked to see the advantages that Working Men's Clubs would confer in return on their existing Societies.

In reference to Friendly Societies we gave a few facts in Chapter III., illustrating the evils of the present system of holding the meetings of these valuable and praiseworthy societies at public-houses. Quoting from the address issued by the Parent Society to the officers and members of these organizations, we would remark that the importance of removing their meetings to Clubs or private houses of their own is shown by the following facts, stated in a letter from the Registrar of Friendly Societies to the Secretary of the Union. After referring to the case of a Society numbering 120 members, which in the course of three years consumed at their meetings 258 gallons of beer, the Registrar continues : " This is only one instance, out of many, in which a large expenditure takes place in Friendly Societies on account of drink, paid for on compulsion by the members, *because they meet at a public-house.* These charges, and others of a similar character, very often amount to about 5s. in the 1*l.* on the whole amount paid by the members. The meeting at public-houses has also the effect of preventing the establishment of Friendly Societies upon sound principles, as in most populous districts every public-house has one or more Clubs, consisting of sixty, seventy, or perhaps 100 members each ; and as this number is not sufficient to secure the permanency of a Society, however correct the rules and tables may be, it follows, as a matter of course, that in a few years they are dissolved or broken up. But it would have been very different if all the members had formed one Society, and held their meetings in a school-room, or Working Men's Club-room, such as the Working Men's Club and Institute Union desires to establish —besides effecting a great saving in the expense of officers' salaries, as there would be *one* set of officers for the *one*

Friendly Society, instead of several." [At a Benefit Club in the North of England, Mr. Solly recently found that, besides his monthly payment of 1s. 6d., each member was paying 3d. per month to be spent on drink, "for the good of the house" (certainly not for the good of the Club). The number of members being about a hundred, this amounted to 16*l.* 5s. *per annum, or* 25s. *per night, to be spent in drink, by way of rent for the use of a single room once a-month.* This is but one illustration of a very common case.]

Although the Registrar invariably objects to any sum being allowed from the funds of these Societies for beer, it is a well-known fact that, under the name of "Expense Funds," a considerable amount is levied on the members for drink, forming a heavy tax upon them in addition to the regular Club payments. Again, in the Registrar's Report of 1862 to the House of Commons, p. 35, he remarks: "The holding of these Societies at a public-house is also another ground of their failure. . . . In the course of last year the Registrar found that in Herefordshire, since 1793, the number of Societies enrolled and certified was 136; of this number 123 were held at public-houses, and 13 at schools or private rooms. Of those held at public-houses no less than 42 had broken up, but of those held at schools or private rooms only one had been dissolved." Even where no drinking is allowed during business hours, a considerable sum is often spent afterwards, especially by the younger men. These, with other startling facts, point to the melancholy truth, that the very efforts working men make to promote provident habits among themselves, and to lay by for a rainy day, too often are made the means of leading them into wasteful expenditure and even to habits of intemperance; while the thoroughly unsound principles on which Societies meeting at a public-house are generally formed, leave the unfortunate contributors, after many years' hard-earned payments, nothing but an empty box and the remembrance of so many gallons of beer drunk for "the good of the house," to their own injury and loss, and to the Society's ruin.

Mr. Tidd Pratt further remarks that, "When the evils attending the meeting of Friendly Societies in public-houses are pointed out, they are often met by the inquiry, 'If we do not meet in the public-house, where can we meet? We object to a school-room—it is large and cold; no private house will accommodate us. Where can we go to but the tavern?' If the *Working Men's Club and Institute Union* succeeds in founding Working Men's Clubs, the working classes will have a *choice* in the matter; and there is no doubt that a large number will avail themselves of the cheerful and comfortable apartment to be thus obtained, without being compelled to buy drink." The address concludes thus:—

"The Council, therefore, suggest to the consideration of your Society or Lodge officers the desirableness of promoting the establishment of such a Club in your district, if one be not already formed; and, if one has been established, of applying for leave to rent the use of a room in it for the above business purposes. By thus helping to establish or support a Working Men's Club and Institute in your district, they submit that you will promote both the interests of your own Society and the welfare of the working men generally of your neighbourhood."

Of course, many facts similar to the above might be adduced, but our limits will only permit of our mentioning the following circumstance:—

"Not very long ago Mr. Tidd Pratt had to meet the members of a Friendly Society at a public-house in a large town in the West of England. Their subscriptions were 1s. a-month, but several of them who had come to pay their contributions preferred drinking in the tap-room downstairs to coming and paying in their money upstairs. Time wore on, and at last wore out; and ultimately, when Mr. Tidd Pratt was coming away, these sociable, thirsty souls were fined 6d. each, according to their rules, for not paying their month's subscription, while they paid the landlord at the end of the evening *sixpence more than their contributions would have amounted to*, as his share of the benefits gained that night by these very friendly members of a *Benefit* Club. So their account would stand next day (as in hundreds of similar cases) thus: Subscription for a rainy day, still due, 1s.; paid to landlord, 1s. 6d.; fine, 6d.; being a loss of 2s. on the transaction. Had the contributions been received at a Working Men's Club and Institute the balance would have been rather different."—*Working Men's Club Magazine*, p. 91.

With regard to Trade Societies, in the following address

to their members, issued with the consent of the Union in June, 1866, an account will be found of the endeavours made four years ago to remove the apprehensions then existing among the leaders of Trade Societies in regard to the objects of the movement. The address itself endeavours to point out some of the advantages likely to accrue to those societies from the general establishment and efficient support of Working Men's Clubs and Institutes :—

To the Members of the Trade Societies of the United Kingdom.

Working Men's Club and Institute Union,
150, Strand, June, 1866.

Gentlemen,—Believing that Working Men's Clubs and Institutes are essential to the well-being of members of Trades Societies, on the one hand, and that those Clubs would be much the better for the support of Trade Societies, on the other, I beg to submit to your consideration the following remarks (a portion of which I urged upon your attention through the press three years ago). Every year convinces me more strongly of the mutual benefit such societies might confer upon each other.

From the first time that I understood the real nature of Trades Unions, and while I still thought many of their objects unwise, or the methods of aiming at them unjust, I could not help being struck with the magnificent organization to which they had given rise, and at the amount of genuine business power and organic life that was at work to animate all this wonderful mechanism. I saw that both in their ends and in their means they bore a certain analogy to the old Municipal Corporations formed to protect the traders of the middle ages from the pillage and oppression of powerful barons and marauding knights—*i.e.*, they were formed from a sense of common rights and interests, common sympathies and dangers, under the pressure of a necessity for mutual help and protection. I am not hereby countenancing the vulgar error that Capital is the enemy of Labour, for there are but few intelligent men now-a-days who are not aware that precisely the reverse is the case ; for the more capital there is, the greater will be the demand for labour, and the more, therefore, wages must rise ; nor am I by any means so foolish or unjust as to imply that most or many of the employers seek to rob and oppress their workpeople. No analogy holds good in every part ; and I simply refer to the fact that, rightly or wrongly, working men have felt the need of mutual protection to prevent wages being reduced to starvation point, and have consequently banded themselves together in powerful organizations for this purpose.

If other measures as important, or far more so, for promoting this object, have been neglected by working men—if they have sometimes been tyrannical in their proceedings and misguided in their policy—it is quite certain that the merchants and manufacturers who formed their Trade Societies and Guilds two and three hundred years ago were quite as often in the wrong ; and the middle or upper classes of the present day should not be surprised, or harsh in their judgments, if they find the working classes have now to go through the same experience, to learn the right course, and be trained to higher social morality through the same discipline. By the severe lessons of experience, and the penalties of error or of wrong-doing, capitalists have gained many valuable lessons as to their true interests, and have learnt some considerable portion of the lesson which we all have to learn by degrees, that the well-being of each is the interest of all, and the welfare of all most important to the happiness of each. Working men are gradually winning their way to the same results through the same process ; for they, too, have cared for the members of their own class, and have banded themselves together for mutual benefit. And it is when men do thus unite for mutually helpful purposes— whether in the Municipal Corporations, Trading Companies, or Guilds of bygone days, or in the Friendly Societies, Co-operative, Temperance, Building, or Trade Societies of modern times—that they not only get immediate good, mixed of course with more or less alloy, but gradually work their way to far greater good and a better condition generally.

Hence we may believe, heartily, in the value of trade organizations, and at the same time watch and work to get them purified from evil and error, and to make them instruments of greater good.

Now, I have more than once heard members of these Societies complain that good rules have been passed, excellent plans resolved on, and that after a time the first were not acted on, and the second were not carried into effect. The machinery seemed excellent, but somehow it did not work. Matters went from good to bad, and from bad to worse. And after men had been contributing their hardly-earned savings for years, they found their plans breaking down, and their organization breaking up, and when their hair was getting grey they had to begin their trade life all over again, mourning over wasted efforts and money thrown away.

Why is this? Either because the machinery, though good in itself, was badly worked; or because it was defective in principle or construction—perhaps both.

In the first case, the men belonging to the Society, of course, were to blame. Human imperfections of various kinds, mental and moral, spoiled the enterprise. Sometimes there has been a falling off in zeal, sometimes in honesty— here a want of sobriety, there a deficiency of perseverance, good judgment, or business-like management. Weakness, ignorance, or vice were to blame. " Given, first-rate machinery, how to get it worked without sufficient motive power, or power of the right sort?" A tough problem, certainly— not to be solved, I imagine, by any contrivance, however cunning. It can't be done. *Careless, drinking men will ruin the best Trade Society ever formed.* Nor can permanent usefulness be got out of *any* organization, if those who have to work it are selfish men, seeking only their own private interests.

In the second case, greater knowledge and experience, wiser measures at starting, more comprehensive views of the true interests of each and of all, better acquaintance with the great laws that govern the production and distribution of wealth—as scientific a knowledge, in short, of political economy as of engineering or brush-making, tailoring or cabinet-making—would have saved the men who framed the trade regulations and Trades Union machinery from lamentable mistakes, saved the members of the union from disastrous consequences which perhaps affect them mischievously all the rest of their lives.

Hence it seems that we have to raise the average morality

and intelligence of working men, if we are to get the right sort of trade machinery, and to get it worked well when it is formed.

Rather a plain, common-place conclusion this, you will say. Yes, and not one at all worth pressing upon your notice, perhaps, were it not for its relation to the important subject which is now filling the thoughts and raising the hopes of so many thousands of benevolent, true-hearted men and women among all classes at the present day. I mean Working Men's Clubs and Institutes. By help of these Societies, we think there are means now offered to working men for enabling them to raise themselves and their class socially, morally, and politically, such as have never been within their grasp before.

I believe that Working Men's Clubs and Institutes will do more to promote all the wise and legitimate objects for which Trade Societies have been formed, than any other measures for the benefit of the working classes which human wisdom has yet devised. Only in the degree in which their average intelligence and morality are raised can permanent progress be made towards improving their condition. Without that elevation either the best measures will not be thought of by the few, or they will not be accepted by the many; they will be inefficiently carried out, or perhaps treacherously frustrated. The various ways in which Working Men's Clubs and Institutes will promote the welfare of working men are as follows :—

By affording working men places to meet in for transacting the business of their Trade, Co-operative, Friendly, and other Societies, with all the arrangements for Houses of Call, without the temptation or compulsion of drinking—by giving them rooms where they can have a pleasant chat together, rational recreation, mutual improvement, or mere amusement (without having to drink beer by way of paying for their evening's enjoyment)—also by providing opportunities for working men and those of other classes to meet occasionally in discussion classes, and interchange ideas, dispel prejudices, and cultivate kindly sentiments towards each other—by offering the means, through lectures and classes, or the said discussions, to working men of gaining a clearer insight into the laws that govern wages and capital, into the facts of our past history, which have made England what she is, and which explain the varied prosperity or adversity of different classes and sections of the community through the past centuries—by giving an excellent reason for shortening the hours of labour, and taking away the objection that if men left work sooner they would only spend more money in the public-house—by drawing youths at a critical time of life from the streets, casinos, and beershops, into scenes of innocent amusement, improving companionship, or under educational influences—by promoting business habits of management, of self-respect and self-control, of patience under temporary misunderstanding or ingratitude—especially by affording continual demand and occasion for unselfish labours or offerings to promote the general good, thus cherishing public spirit and brotherly feelings—above all, by helping working men to make their own homes happier, to carry home their wages, and educate their children.

Looking at the question simply in regard to Houses of Call, the importance to Trade Societies of having some other place of meeting than the public-house in which to transact their regular business has long been felt by a large number of the intelligent artizans comprising these Societies; for it is a well-known fact, that there is a great deal of hardship, and, at the same time, of temptation to drinking, caused by the present system of the Register of men wanting employment being kept by landlords of public-houses. The names first called off that register are, naturally, though unjustly, not always those first on the list, but too often those of the publican's best customers; and, under any circumstances, men going to the House of Call, either to have their names put down or to inquire the result, must generally spend something "for the good of the house." It is well known how often "the pint brings on the gallon." The foreman, also, or captain of a shop, and the landlord sometimes play into one another's hands in this matter.

The consequence of all this has been, that various attempts have been made by their leading men to get rooms for their business purposes, sometimes at coffee-houses, sometimes at the Secretary's residence, or elsewhere. But these endeavours have not hitherto been generally successful, the rooms having been found either too expensive or unpalatable to the majority

H

of members, and sometimes objectionable on both these grounds.

The true resource for such Societies seems unquestionably to be a Working Men's Club or Institute of the kind I have now referred to, which might provide a place where the Call Book of these Societies could be kept, where their members could attend without being exposed to the evils above alluded to, by renting a room in which to transact their general business, and where they would be free from any interference, so long as nothing was done contrary to morality and law. From the first establishment of this Union, its promoters were very desirous that the proposed Clubs should afford working men an alternative to the public-house for business purposes, as well as a place for social intercourse, recreation, and mental improvement. In accordance with this object, we issued a Circular some time since to the officers and members of Friendly, Provident, and Co-operative Societies; and we now desire to direct your attention to the same important subject, with a view to your establishing or supporting a Social Club and Institute in your neighbourhood.

But if Trade Societies stand so greatly in need of Working Men's Clubs and Institutes, these Societies, on the other hand, valuable as they are, and fast as they are spreading over the country, will not last, and will do comparatively little good while they exist, unless they learn what Trade Societies can teach them, imbibe something of the spirit which Trade Societies can impart to them, and win the general support of Trade Society men. Men will get tired of them if they have gone to them for mere amusement, and in many cases after a time they will begin to sigh for the coarser pleasures of the taproom; or, going upwards instead of downwards, they will want something more earnest, more improving, or more brotherly, than Working Men's Clubs will afford if they are merely places to which men may go for an evening's relaxation. You must breathe into them something of the same organic life, something of the sense of common interests and need of mutual help, of the spirit of corporate union and helpful fellowship, which have formed the secret inner life of your Trade Societies in their best estate—if these Clubs are to last more than a very few years. Their members must feel at least as much in earnest for the promotion of one of the chief objects of the Club—viz., the raising the character and intelligence of their class—as Trades Unions have been in seeking to raise the wages of their particular bodies. There must be as great an interest felt by each member of the Club in seeing that every other member is reaping his full share of happiness and benefit from it, as is felt by each member of a Trades Union in seeing that no brother member is being ground down in his wages, or forced to work beyond a reasonable time.

Then, again, look at the propagandist zeal of many Trade Societies. How zealous they are to draw all the men and youths in their particular trade into their Society—how their souls are vexed at the sight of non-Society men, and of masters employing non-Society men, to the great detriment, as they honestly believe, both of those men and of the trade generally. Let the members of Working Men's Clubs show half as much zeal in bringing outsiders into their Clubs, drawing them from the noisy, spendthrift, coarse, and sometimes disgusting company of the public-house to their quiet, sociable, improving, yet perfectly free-and-easy Club—let them feel but half as much annoyance at seeing their shopmates enticed away to serve tyrannical habits far more oppressive and ruinous than the worst of employers, and the Clubs will prove a greater blessing to our toiling brethren than they or we have yet dared to dream. Learning such lessons as these, and others which time forbids me to dwell upon, from the great trade organizations which, in one way or other—by their wisdom or their folly, by their success or their failure, but always by their earnestness of purpose, mutual helpfulness, and organic action—have done so much to elevate and teach the working classes of this country, the present movement to establish Working Men's Clubs may become, with the help of a higher blessing, full of incalculable far-reaching benefits of every kind. We may go on, step by step, building up a noble structure of social, mental, and moral good for the brave, true-hearted sons of toil, who it is high time should be welcomed to the many social and educational advantages hitherto chiefly confined to the middle and upper classes.

Before concluding, it seems desirable to explain that the question was some time since raised as to whether the Working Men's Club and Institute Union was aiming at objects antagonistic to Trades Societies, and inconsistent, therefore, with that impartial and unsectarian spirit which it had always scrupulously professed. The maintenance of this principle being of the gravest importance, a deputation from the members of the London Trades Council on the one hand, and from the Council of this Union on the other, met in June, 1863. Thomas Hughes, Esq., M.P. (a Vice-President of the Union), was also present. The result is given in a few extracts from a report taken down at the time of the interview.

The Chairman opened the discussion by stating—
" That the Council had unanimously agreed to omit from their publications the paragraph relating to houses of call, finding that it conveyed a totally incorrect impression of their objects."

Mr. Facey, after stating that this removed the chief difficulty, and that he highly esteemed the efforts of the Union to improve the condition and position of the working men, put a question to the Chairman, which that gentleman replied to as follows :—

" That the Union had neither the right nor the power of exercising control over the free discussion of subjects allowed to be brought forward by the Local Committee of any Club."

Mr. Cremer (another of the Trades Deputation) remarked that, " at a former interview between some of the parties now present, a member of the Council and the Secretary had distinctly stated that a Trade Society might, by engaging a room, meet at a Working Men's Club. Now, should a Society meeting at a Club be found on strike, would the Council turn that Society, therefore, into the street ? "

A member of the Council begged the deputation to remember " that the Clubs were not the Clubs of the Council—that the Council neither would nor could exercise either responsible or irresponsible control over them. The designs of the Council were perfectly *bonâ-fide*—there were no ulterior objects."

Mr. Dunning observed that " members of Trades Societies could, it appeared, then, avail themselves (as he hoped they would very largely) of the advantages of Working Men's Clubs ;

but a Trades Society must be quite distinct from a Working Men's Club."

. . . . .

Mr. Ackrill thought "there was clearly nothing to fear from the Council of the Union, the dealing of the Trade Society, in every case, being with the Local Committee. A Trade Society hiring a room, and making no attempt to turn non-Society men out of the Club, would not be interfered with."

. . . . .

Mr. Applegarth remarked that "it appeared to him that when Trade Societies held their meetings at Working Men's Clubs, they would stand in the same relation to the Club as they now did to the publicans. And, therefore, if the Council had the will, they would not have the power to interfere, neither did he think they would desire to do so."

Mr. Odgers asked, "whether they were at liberty to report to the Societies that the Council would not interfere in any action of Trade Societies not illegal or immoral?"

Mr. Solly answered, "Most certainly."

Mr. Odgers expressed himself perfectly satisfied.

Mr. Nieass added that "they were more than satisfied; and thought that, independently of all questions of Trades Societies, the objects of the Society were worthy of cordial support."

. . . . .

Another member of the Council inquired, "if the difficulties in the minds of the delegates had been met by the explanations given?"

Mr. Solly also put the same question with especial reference to the points raised by Mr. Facey.

Mr. Facey and several other delegates answered in the affirmative.

Mr. Allan, Secretary to the Amalgamated Engineers, said "that the previously-entertained suspicions were quite removed. He was very glad he had come, and would give the Union his hearty support."

" Thanks to the Council, for their frank explanations, were then voted, on the motion of Mr. Odgers, seconded by Mr. Cremer, and supported by Mr. Allan."

The Council of the Union, believing that their objects, and

the spirit in which they desire to carry them out, are now becoming generally understood by working men of every trade and section—and wishing to act in harmony with the various existing organizations of the working classes—invite your confidence and co-operation, in common with those of Friendly, Building, Co-operative, and Temperance Societies throughout the kingdom, to carry out the simple but comprehensive and practical plans detailed in their various papers. In making this appeal, the Council do not forget that the question of the good or the harm done by your Societies is one upon which much difference of opinion exists. Upon this question they do not, of course, pronounce any opinion. To do so would be to depart from their strictly impartial and unsectarian platform. They have simply to recognize the fact that you have large organizations, sanctioned and protected by law, existing for purposes believed by their supporters to be right and needful; and we look for your support of these social Clubs and Institutes, not merely on account of the advantages they will bring to working men generally, but also on the ground that any good which your Societies are doing must be enhanced by whatever tends to the general elevation of the class from which their members are drawn; and that any harmful tendencies must be aggravated by arrangements which subject men to the constant pressure of lowering influences. They ask you, therefore, to unite in helping your fellow working men, without sectarian distinctions of any kind, by means of the proposed or existing Clubs and Institutes, to rise above those influences, and to occupy that position in the social scale to which their spirit of mutual helpfulness, as well as their remarkable industry, undoubtedly entitle them.

Make them feel that it is their own cause, and let them make it their own movement. Any advice or help we can give, I need not say, will be gladly rendered. Our publications will be freely sent to any working men desirous of establishing a Club; and we could often put them in communication with other persons, both in their own and the upper class, who would be able and glad to work with them.

If they send me their rules, I will gladly revise them, and if possible attend a preliminary meeting, when asked, without any cost to themselves (though we do not object to travelling expenses being paid when wealthier neighbours subscribe for that and other preliminary outlay), and in every way in our power the members of our Council and myself will thankfully labour with the working men in helping them to help themselves. We cannot, of course, give aid to Trade Societies, as such, in establishing these Clubs, any more than we could help Teetotal or Friendly Societies to do so. But we can help *the individual members* of any Trade Society to form another Society which will give a mighty stimulus and support to every wisely-constituted organization formed to promote the true and enduring welfare " of each and of all."—I remain, Gentlemen, yours very faithfully,

HENRY SOLLY.

In addition to these remarks, we may remind the operative classes that few things would tend more powerfully to enable them to get the best wages and the shortest hours which their respective employers could fairly afford, than their attaining that education, information, sobriety, and courtesy of manner which these Clubs so greatly help to impart. For in proportion as in these respects they rise more nearly to the social level of their employers, they will be treated with that courtesy and respect which would tend powerfully to prevent misunderstandings, and a recourse to the *ultima ratio* of strikes or lock-outs. Their employers will then treat with them for the purchase of their labour on the same terms with which those employers now deal with persons in their own rank of life who have any other commodity to sell, and discuss the rate of wages in the same comparatively courteous spirit which they show towards their foremen, or other leading workmen, whose intelligence and steadiness they have learned to value and respect. Long experience has convinced us that a large proportion of strikes and lock-outs arise from want of a better understanding between masters and men—from mutual suspicions, from unreasonable pride and temper, from want of confidence and of mutual respect. These sad animosities and conflicts do not often take place between the buyers and sellers of ordinary commodities; neither would they between those who have to buy and sell labour and skill if working men were generally as steady, courteous, thoughtful, and well-informed, as the leading men among them are now, and as these Clubs and Institutes would help them generally to become. (Some rather convincing evidence in support of this view may be found in the able pamphlet of Mr. Rupert Kettle, County Court Judge at Wolverhampton, on " Arbitration and Strikes," &c.)

But no less important in 'preventing mischief and in procuring for working men their full share of the fruits of their toil, would be the influence of the Clubs in helping them to save their money, and thus enabling them by co-operation to become capitalists and employers themselves. Let them reflect on the facts mentioned in a previous chapter (pp. 99-103), and on the many similar ones that have come under their own notice, and then ask themselves whether it is not time they should give up the present wasteful and demoralizing system of frequenting public-houses, and accumulate their savings for investment in Co-operative Societies, Industrial Partnerships, Building Societies, &c. By these means they would always be in a position to fall back on their own resources, and embark in business for themselves, if they were unjustly treated, or to accept any wise and friendly offers made by their employers, by other persons of capital, or by prudent men in their own class, to put money into some business concern, and receive a proportionate share of the profits.

Again, let the members of Trade and other societies reflect on the extent to which the Clubs would improve their position when they want to confer with members of Parliament in reference to legislation connected with their various societies, or with any subjects specially affecting them as a class. It would be far easier to procure useful interviews with persons of higher social position, whether in Parliament, or connected with the press, or belonging to the capitalist class, if they could request that interview at their own well-ordered and convenient Club-rooms, where everything testified to their improved habits and higher social standing, than if they could only meet them at a public-house or an employer's yard.

In like manner many a useful discussion could be held at a Club, which employers, members of Parliament, literary, scientific, and other men who greatly influence both the social and pecuniary well-being of working men, would be willing to attend, and where a great deal of light might be mutually thrown on questions that have hitherto been too little under-stood by one party or the other. The way would thus be paved for a good understanding and friendly co-operation in the future, instead of injurious competition or destructive an-tagonism. (See also pp. 136-7.)

An illustration of the way in which working men some-times place themselves, unthinkingly, in a false and rather un-worthy position, occurred not long ago at a public-house supper, held by a branch of a highly-respectable Trade Society, in Pimlico. The landlord's son came into the room in the course of the evening, and announced his intention of " standing a glass of brandy and water all round," which offer was received with vociferous applause ! If those men could become aware of the feelings with which a gentleman would read an account of that kind, they would understand better the reasons for the way in which they are often treated by the middle and upper classes. Ten years hence we trust it will be as impossible for such a thing to happen at a con-vivial meeting of skilled operatives in London as for the pro-prietor of Willis's Rooms to make a similar proposal at any public dinner held there, with a nobleman in the chair. But this change will only come to pass if, in the meantime, they give up the " good fellowship " of the tap-room.

In the same way working men lower themselves, to a de-gree of which they have no conception, in the eyes of gen-tlemen when, touching their hat after performing some slight service or affording a little information, they ask for " some-thing to drink." But this servile custom, we are thankful to notice, is considerably abated within the last few years. To the honour of Lancashire men, we must add that, during a five years' residence in that county, and being in continual communica-tion with working men, we were never once asked, nor did we ever witness any other person being asked, for this contemp-tible compliment.

Having dwelt at some length in the fifth chapter on the way and extent to which Co-operative Societies may do good service to Clubs and Institutes, the following address, which was issued in 1864, may here be submitted to the thoughtful consideration of our readers, especially those of them who belong to any of these valuable organizations:—

ADDRESS TO THE OFFICERS AND MEMBERS OF THE CO-OPERATIVE SOCIETIES OF THE UNITED KINGDOM.

(Reprinted from the *Co-operator.*)

" The Council of the Working Men's Club and Institute Union, recognizing your zealous and widespreading efforts for the elevation of the social position of working men, and believing that your endeavours for that purpose will be greatly aided through the agency of the Working Men's Clubs and Institutes which it is their aim to establish, desire to invite your cordial assistance and co-operation in the establishment and maintenance of such institutions on the principles which are recommended by the Union, as being the best guarantees for success.

" These Clubs provide an inexpensive means of promoting social enjoyment and mutual improvement for all classes of working men ; and must tend to stimulate the progress of every movement calculated to raise and improve their condition. Among other results, they will spread a desire for the development of that great principle of Co-operation—*i.e.*, mutual help—which is as old as civilization, and which has won many of its greatest victories. But none will be more ready than yourselves to admit that, however sound and admirable the principles on which your enterprises are based, those principles can be successfully applied only in proportion to the intelligence, integrity, providence, and brotherly feeling of those who are engaged in the undertaking. At present, owing to the want of a place of resort, other than the public-house, for social intercourse, recreation, or business, the class from which you must draw your shareholders, managers, and customers have less opportunity than could be desired for cultivating those habits which are requisite for successful co-operation, while the influences to which they are often inevitably subjected do not encourage saving and temperance. If they had good Social Clubs of their own, how much of the money now spent at the public-house would be available for paying up their shares, or making ready-money purchases at the stores ! The Council desire, of course, to maintain a position of perfect neutrality with regard to all Societies of working men, whether Co-operative, Building, Trades, Friendly, Provident, or Temperance ; but they desire that members of all these Societies should see how their welfare will be *specially* promoted—but in common with that of all working men—by their co-operation in the formation and maintenance of Social Clubs and Institutes.

" Co-operative Societies are, of all associations of working men, perhaps the best adapted to the formation of these Clubs, and have most to gain from their establishment.

" Working men require to be educated in the principles of business, and to acquire a knowledge of the laws that regulate prices and profits, if they are to manage successfully—or to trust wisely and watch discreetly those who are managing—a Co-operative business. To promote this education and mutual confidence, some such common meeting-ground as these Clubs and Institutes is required. Unreasonable panics, groundless suspicions, and culpable credulity, are alike best prevented by the mental and moral influences. and local arrangements, now proposed to be substituted for those at present existing—viz., the tap-room and street corner.

" The Council, therefore, invite you to assist in applying the great principle which you have embraced so heartily to the social, intellectual, and moral elevation and happiness of the working classes of this country ; and to co-operate, wherever you have the opportunity, in establishing or supporting Working Men's Clubs and Institutes.

" The practical steps for this purpose are : First, to get a meeting of a few of the leading working men in the district, and especially the officers of the various Working Men's Societies ; let them agree upon two or three fundamental rules, and definition of objects, &c., and then appoint a provisional committee. This committee should look out for suitable premises, enrol members, prepare rules to be submitted to the first general meeting of members, draw up statement of objects (to be printed for general circulation), inviting contributions in money, books, &c.; and, lastly, arrange for a public meeting, with the view of interesting the working men generally of the district in the undertaking. It could also put itself at once in communication with the Council of the Union, who would gladly render all the assistance in their power towards gaining local pecuniary help, by giving information or advice, and by helping to get up a public meeting, to which they could generally send a deputation. Where there is a reading-room attached already to a Store or a Mill, it may become the nucleus of a Club ; but it would be far better, in general, to unite with the working men of the neighbourhood to form one for all sections of working men, than attempt to establish an exclusive, and, as it were, sectarian Club, on your own premises. The Club, however, need not at all prevent your having a conversation or a meeting-room at the Store —only the latter should not prevent hearty support being given to the former. If you can have a Working Men's Club and Institute in the neighbourhood, you will not require a *reading*-room at the Co-operative Society ; but a conversation room there might still be very valuable, and would, perhaps, become a feeder to the Club.

" A general explanation of the plans and objects of these Working Men's Clubs and Institutes will be forwarded, and any further information, especially relative to the best means of establishing such a Club, will be readily given by the Secretary of the Working Men's Club and Institute Union, and the Council will at all times be ready to assist with its advice and influence in the formation of such Clubs and Institutions."

Lastly, may we ask those working men who are now exerting themselves so ably and earnestly to improve the pecuniary position of themselves and their class by means of Trade Unions, Co-operative, Friendly, and other Societies, to remember that there are higher ends to be lived for by all of us than increased pecuniary means? If they are wise, they value these only as means to something better than merely a greater share of luxuries, of animal comforts and indulgences, or of worldly consideration. And of this we are certain, that a continually increasing number of the artizans of England feel the infinitely greater value of learning, culture, and refinement above mere ease and animal enjoyment. But what we would also ask them to remember is, that if they would help their companions to seek after those worthier ends, they must point out to them that in proportion as the working classes will now aim at the higher object, will seek and welcome the aid of more educated persons, in the way already urged in former chapters, *they will infallibly gain the lower, but very important, object also.*

If their leaders in their own class, and their friends in the higher class, enable them to become wiser, steadier, more cultivated and refined, *more gentlemanly* in the best sense of the word, they will at the same time—as we urged in that chapter, and as we want these leaders and friends to urge—be enabling them to earn better wages, or a direct share in their employers' profits, and be also giving them the best chance of obtaining shorter hours of labour, by the very same means which help them to use both increased wages and leisure more wisely and nobly.

There is one important question to be considered in connexion with the relation of Trade Unions to Working Men's Clubs, which has been incidentally touched upon in the chapter on " The Neutral Position," &c.—viz., how far a Working Men's Club should encourage or allow a Trade Society to hold its meetings at the Club, particularly when the said Society was engaged in a strike. The matter was so thoroughly discussed at a Conference held by the Central Society, at Newcastle, in 1865, that we cannot do better than give a very brief sketch of the arguments, *pro* and *con.*, then used. The subject was introduced in consequence of one of the rooms of the Club having been let to a Trade Society, which, during its occupancy, had been engaged in a strike; and was put in the following form, " For what purposes may the rooms of a Working Men's Club be let to other parties ?" The first speaker suggested that it ought to be regarded simply as a money question, and that if the Committee of the Club advertised a room to be let to the highest bidder, this would show that it was merely a matter of finance. It was the plan that had been pursued by the Gateshead Temperance Society, and worked well. In reply to a question by the writer, the speaker answered that he did not think their Temperance room would have been let to a Secularist Society. That was a case which would have to be dealt with as exceptional. No general rule would apply in all cases. The delegate from the South Shields Institute said that hitherto they had been exempt there from poor-rates, but if they let their rooms they would have to pay. The delegate from North Shields stated that their large room was let for religious services on a Sunday, and they had met with no difficulty in consequence. The delegate from Jarrow said that their Club let a room to Trade, Provident, Temperance, and other Societies. Their employers, who built the rooms, never complained even of the committee for promoting a strike against themselves for meeting at the Club. They would rather the committee met there than at the public-house. The workmen employed would be more likely to join the Club when they found their Trade Society had the use of a room there. The Honorary Secretary of the Sunderland Club considered that the rooms should be let for any purpose that would promote the objects of the Club—viz., the social, mental, and moral welfare of the members. If more money could be made by letting them for any religious or political purpose·than would be lost by such a course, he would let them. He thought, in such cases, it should be regarded as a financial question. The President of the Newcastle Club said he had often been asked, when canvassing for funds to establish the Club, if it would be used for Trade Society purposes, and always answered that it would not. They might be thought to have broken faith with the public if they were not very careful. The Secretary of this Club said that when they were first asked to allow the use of a room to the men who were agitating for the Saturday half-holiday, they granted it; but on remonstrances being made, the Committee inquired of the writer, and elsewhere, as to the custom in such cases, and then continued to allow the use of the room, but only on payment of rent.

Another speaker observed that "it was better to let the Committee exercise their discretion as to whom the rooms should be let." The writer, in summing up the discussion, observed that if a Trade Society does not meet at a Club, of course it goes to a public-house; but that the great thing is —first, to make the public see that a Club is not at all identified with the objects of any society to which it may let a room; second, that if working men established and properly supported these Clubs themselves, they would be responsible only to themselves for the way in which they let their rooms. He thought that the general rule certainly was, that the rooms might be let for any purpose not illegal or immoral; but there might be exceptions, which must be decided each on its own merits. There was, however, a very great difference between letting a room to any parties merely to transact their business in, and letting it to enable them to propagate their particular views. He could imagine no case (being neither immoral nor illegal) in which the former could be wrong or the latter right, as a question of principle. And he could not doubt that while it was, unquestionably, to be regarded also as a financial question, measures for increasing their income must always be subject to the regulation of principle.

We believe that these views fully meet the difficulty.

A few other suggestions on the subject of this chapter will be found in the following report of a meeting, taken from the *Daily News* of July 4, 1867. The subject of adding lodgings to Club-houses, for men when they first come to a town in search of work, until they can get more permanent accommodation, we regard as of the highest importance. By the present system of coming to the public-house as the house of call, and then having to lodge there, young men often get drawn into mischievous associations from their first entrance into a town, instead of at once getting into a good " set," and under influences as wholesome as pleasant, at a Club :—

" Two meetings have been recently held at the office of the Working Men's Club and Institute Union, 150, Strand, for the purpose of consulting with some of the leading men in the Friendly and Trades Societies of the metropolis, as to the best means of promoting the prosperity and usefulness of Working Men's Clubs and Institutes in London. On the first night, the Rev. H. Solly opened the proceedings by stating that he had found a large amount of sympathy for the Club movement among leading men of the great working class societies, but partly owing to their being so much engaged, and partly to their ignorance of each other's feelings on the subject, they had hitherto done but little to promote the success of these Clubs. Now it was essential to that success, that the Clubs should receive more general support from the great body of intelligent operatives than had yet been given them. But much might be done for this purpose, by bringing together men who had the confidence of the rest, and uniting them in some efficient organization. One reason often given why working men did not support the Clubs in larger numbers, was that they were hampered with too many restrictions, especially as to getting a glass of beer at them.

He (Mr. Solly) believed that many men did not so much care about having beer at Clubs, as that they objected to its exclusion being forced upon them. Both the Council and himself had, however, greatly modified their views on the question of its introduction into Clubs, which, under due regulations, and according to a great amount of evidence, might tend to considerably diminish drinking. He invited all who were present to give their views. Mr. Howell, formerly Secretary to the Bricklayers' Society, considered that Working Men's Clubs had already done a vast deal of good, but they were too formal. Working men wanted to be free and easy after the day's work. He had heard with great regret of the closing of a Club in a very populous London suburb, caused mainly by the clergyman of the parish having kept it 'too tight.' His class hated patronage. The beer, however, was not everything. Gatti's refreshment saloon was crowded every night, though no fermented liquors were sold there. He had found a capital Club at Bradford, in Yorkshire, where the members were very sociable, and at their ease. When the present political agitation was over, and working men were more at liberty, there would be a great amount of interest shown by them in the Club movement. If a Limited Liability Company were formed and established, a good model Club would be sure to pay well. Mr. Guile, Secretary of the Ironfounders' Society, spoke of the great numbers of Societies to which the leading working men have now to attend. These cost money as well as time, and the wives sometimes, especially of the young men, complain, yet no doubt the Clubs are very much wanted. One difficulty is the jealousy felt by members belonging to existing Societies of any new ones rising up. Public meetings would help. In every way the subject must be agitated. A most important matter was to get Club-houses where there would be a few beds for men coming up to London. At present all the houses of call were at public-houses, and they would never be able to make the Club the house of call for a trade so long as the men had to go to 'publics' to sleep. It would be of the greatest value if young men, on first coming to London, could stay at a Club instead of a public-house. Mr. Solly observed that Mr. Allan, Secretary of the Amalgamated Engineers, at a former meeting had urged this point, but complained that Government would not give their

Societies legal protection for investing their funds in building, otherwise they would soon have their own Clubs instead of public-houses. Mr. Guile said that if the Legislature would give their Societies legal protection and require a quarterly publication of their accounts, it would be of great benefit in every way to the whole community. Mr. Cope, Secretary of the Boot Closers' Society, concurred strongly as to the importance of providing a home for young men coming up from the country, and thought that if a central Club could provide a few beds till they got lodgings, it would be of great value. Mr. Shaw, foreman locomotive engineers, London and South Western Railway, described the good effect of moving their Lodge in Leeds from a public-house, and declared his belief that the Clubs would be just the thing that was wanted for all these Trades and Friendly Societies. Mr. Bebbington (porter) thought a Limited Liability Company might be formed to establish such a Central Club as had been proposed. Mr. Guile agreed in this view, if beds were provided —otherwise they never could get rid of the public-houses as houses of call. Mr. Lee (excavator) thought the movement was of the greatest importance. He objected to the introduction of beer into Clubs; but if this would diminish drinking at public-houses he would not oppose it in Clubs. The Clubs would be a great lever, and would raise working men. The Stockport Club had flourished because the men managed it, and the gentlemen came and mixed with them as friends and guests. But the Clubs must be free and easy. Mr. Paterson (cabinet-maker) said the working men were now in a state of transition. The Clubs must be put on a broader basis. It would be of great value if they could have a place where rooms could be had for the head offices of Friendly, Trade, Co-operative, and Building Societies. The money now in the saving banks might be made to bring 10 per cent. instead of $2\frac{3}{4}$ per cent. But the working men must be raised by degrees. It was especially important to get the men who now drank at public-houses to come to the Clubs. Mr. Whateling (shoemaker) thought the suggestion about the lodgings for men on the tramp particularly useful. He recommended sending deputations to the different Trades Societies. Mr. Solly then concluded the proceedings by undertaking to bring the views of the friends present before the

Council, and by thanking them for their attendance that evening. A similar meeting was held on Friday, with much the same results."

The following paragraph from one of the Parent Society's earlier papers corroborates the foregoing remarks. After speaking of the hardships and evils of the present " Houses of Call" system, as mentioned on p. 201, the paper continues thus:—

" . . . But wherever a Working Men's Club exists, this register of persons needing employment, as well as a list of masters seeking for men, might be kept by each Trade Society, and their Lodge meetings held there, instead of at a public-house. Among other great advantages resulting from this change would be the benefit to young men coming up from the country to large towns for work, who of course go straight to a House of Call, which, at present, is almost always at a public-house. They engage a single room for a lodging in the neighbourhood, and if they want society, they will rarely find it where they lodge, but must seek it in the public-house. This will naturally be the one where the register is kept, to which they went on their first arrival, and which is probably frequented by many of their shopmates. But if the register were kept and the Lodge held at a Working Men's Club, and if they carried with them a friendly introduction to the officers and members of that Club, their first start on a new period of life would be made under healthy and improving influences, instead of under those which are too generally injurious in themselves, and leading often to even more mischievous results. A list of respectable lodgings might also be kept at the Club-house."

We conclude this chapter with the following extract from the letter of an hon. secretary to whom we wrote concerning a Club, in the formation and management of which he had taken a leading part. We believe there is a great deal of force in his concluding remarks about the Foresters and Odd Fellows. It is quite possible social Clubs so formed might be much better supported in some places than general Clubs, and that there they should be established on that plan. But, as a general rule, one would much rather see the Clubs open to all working men than limited to those belonging to a particular

Benefit Society or Trade. In this particular case, moreover, we have reason to believe that more regularity and business-like attention to the management of the Club would have made it thoroughly successful; but this does not diminish the importance of viewing the question in the light here mentioned :—

" Dear Mr. Solly,— . . . I extremely regret to say that, practically, the Club is extinct. No Institution was ever more unfortunate in its early life. What with the two strikes, then a dishonest manager, then the necessity of my leaving the Club to those who were not sufficiently in earnest about it, its decline was inevitable. I have convinced myself, however, that another cause was at work to prevent such Club ever being *very* successful here. Our working men are very rough, with the exception of a small minority. The rougher ones have their Unions and Clubs for trade purposes, and they do not mingle with men of a different class, and the more intelligent men are nearly all Foresters or Odd Fellows. We have 500 Foresters in the town, and 100 Odd Fellows. Having joined this body, I see in their Courts the men to whom I looked for support in our Club, and who, I discover, find in Forestry much of that social life which we aimed to provide ; and the discipline of the Court has no mean influence in the education of the members. I cannot but think, in looking at this Club question, that the true idea is that of Forestry—viz., the banding of men together for mutual comfort and support in times of trial, sickness, and for the affording opportunities for the moderate enjoyment of social intercourse. You have so long and well insisted on the necessity of the brotherly element being stimulated and strengthened, that it would be impertinence in me to argue how this is the principle of life, as it were, without which, blood, bones, and sinew are so much dead matter. I long to see the day when the various bodies of Foresters and the like shall dwell in their own Club-houses, and combine all the features of the Institutions you have called into being, and those which now distinguish them from your progeny. . . . Very earnestly wishing your Union every success, with kindest regards to yourself, I remain, yours faithfully," * * *

CHAPTER X.

NEUTRAL POSITION OF WORKING MEN'S CLUBS IN RELIGIOUS, POLITICAL, AND SOCIAL CONTROVERSIES.

The following reply to a letter on a subject ot considerable interest to the managers and members of Clubs is offered as a contribution towards the solution of the very difficult problem, alluded to as the "Religious" question in Chapter III. It was on this question that the first Working Men's Institute in the kingdom—founded by the late lamented Rev. F. W. Robertson, at Brighton—suffered mournful shipwreck; and there is no greater difficulty, in many cases, with which Working Men's Clubs and their promoters have, or will have, to contend.

"———, Jan. 12, 1866.

"Sir,—Will you kindly oblige me by saying if the Club and Institute Union would interpret our first rule ['Rule I.— That this Institution be called the ——— Working Men's Club; the objects of which are to provide instruction and amusement for members, free from sectarianism and party politics.'] as preventing us from receiving any contributions of books or periodicals of a religious tone—say a book of sermons, or any Protestant publication?—I remain, Sir, your obedient servant,

"———, Hon. Sec."

"Working Men's Club and Institute Union,
"150, Strand, London, W.C.,
"Jan. 18, 1866.

"Dear Sir, ... The question in your note is an important one, vitally affecting the very existence of these societies. It is a difficulty, moreover, which has frequently occurred, and naturally will often again arise.

"The general principles which we think should guide the managers and promoters of Clubs in this matter, are as follows: First, since the Club is intended to afford certain social benefits to all working men, without distinction as to their religious or political opinions, holding itself entirely neutral and impartial on all these subjects—as well as on various other controverted questions, such as Teetotalism, Trades Unions, Strikes, &c.—the money contributed by members, whether ordinary or honorary, should not be spent, either in a large or small amount, on books or other publications advocating views on either side of such topics. It would be manifestly unjust to purchase those on one side and not those on the other. But even if both were bought, this would still be a perversion of the objects for which the contributions were given. Nothing like political, religious, or social propagandism and controversy should be allowed in a Club; otherwise, its purely neutral character, its welcome for persons of all sects and parties, would be destroyed. But, secondly, it is quite a different matter when, as in your case, books, &c., of a religious character are offered *as gifts*. The money of the society, in that case, is not being expended for any sectarian purpose, and so far no member could feel aggrieved. But, then, it is plainly necessary that if you accept presents of books or periodicals, newspapers, &c., advocating one view of controverted subjects, you must also receive them if offered when supporting the opposite view; otherwise, you at once take part with the former against the latter, and destroy your neutrality.

"Now, whether it be advisable or not to accept such gifts must depend, I think, very much on local circumstances, and cannot be altogether decided by general principles. If the gift of a volume of sermons is likely to be followed by the presentation of Tom Paine's works, or the presentation of a Protestant newspaper by that of a Roman Catholic journal, the donors of the first *may* consider it better that neither should be given; or if either the religious work or the secularistic publication entering the Club *by itself* were likely to stir up bitter controversy, and convert the peaceful social meeting-ground into an arena of strife, members might feel that the said publication were better withheld. On the contrary, should there be no probability that any of the members would object to the introduction of a particular work or newspaper, and no likelihood of its leading to what could be regarded as retaliation, or to controversy of any kind—if, in short, the publication in question would not be viewed, in all reasonable probability, as a violation of the great fundamental principle of neutrality in such matters—the Club would simply be so much the richer, and, perhaps, the members so much the wiser and better for possessing it.

" Clearly, it is necessary that each such case should stand on its own merits, and be finally determined by local circumstances, under the guidance of the above general principles. For what would be a violation of neutrality in one Club or in one part of the country would not be so regarded in another; and a publication that would only do good in one Club, where a difference of opinion on the subject did not exist, might be the cause of controversies in another that would destroy the society. Moreover, the matter that would be deemed objectionable by some members may be in so small a proportion in a particular publication, or may be so mingled with what all parties view as valuable, that they would gladly bear with the one part for the sake of the other. The managers and members of each society have to exercise a faithful judgment, applying the great principles on which Clubs are formed as far as they will go, and scrupulously testing every proposal by a reference to them; but as faithfully considering whether the *common good* of all the members might not be promoted by any proposed measure which did not interfere with the neutrality of the Club on controverted questions.

" A most important point, I may further be allowed to suggest, is, that every member of a Club who feels strongly on any controverted subject in relation to religion, politics, or social science, should carefully guard against viewing the Club as a convenient platform or fulcrum, whereon to advance his views on those points by direct advocacy, except so far as a discussion class may legitimately, and by common consent, give him a fair opportunity. Unquestionably, a Club would afford a capital machinery for making converts, until the process had broken it up (which would probably be very speedily), even as a razor might excellently serve, for a time, to cut slate pencils. But Clubs are not formed for this purpose, and cannot be used to further it without a perversion of their objects which would be as dishonest as unwise. There are, or

ought to be, suitable agencies for all desirable direct proselytizing, but Clubs are certainly not among the number.
Even in discussion classes, the aim should be mutual improvement and educational enlightenment, rather than propagandism
and proselytizing; and I am strongly of opinion that theological questions had better always be excluded from those
most valuable meetings.

" Herewith I send you two of our publications, containing
passages bearing upon this question, as well as the paper
which you asked for, and I sincerely hope that the views I have
suggested may help to guide your course aright. I cannot
conclude (though I trust it is almost needless to do so, frequently as I have urged the subject in the publications of the
Union) without saying that I am profoundly convinced of the
inestimable benefit these Clubs derive whenever religious influences can be brought to bear upon them to promote the
common good—*not for controversial purposes*, but for the development of men's spiritual nature, cultivating filial reverence
and brotherly feelings, and thus preparing for more specific
religious teaching elsewhere. When this can be done in an
unobtrusive manner, with the full concurrence of the members,
or at all events without exciting opposition, or disturbing the
general harmony, I believe that great good may be accomplished. By these influences I do not necessarily mean direct
religious services, Bible, or prayer-meetings—though I am
thankful to know that even these have been held in more than
one Club by the common agreement of the members, with
unmixed benefit attending them—but I refer more especially
to the influence for good which every sincere Christian must
always exert wherever he goes, and according to the opportunities legitimately offered to him. I have long been convinced that neither Clubs, nor any other societies, founded on
the idea of mutual benefit, can possibly flourish unless they
are managed and worked by persons of high principle, of
single-minded devotedness to duty, and who habitually seek
that help and guidance without which we cannot expect the
Divine blessing on our work.—Believe me, my dear Sir, very
truly yours,   " HENRY SOLLY."

Persons of earnest and conscientious disposition have especial need to accept the foregoing restrictions. A Club offers

great facilities and temptations for pushing one's own convictions on important topics. But, clearly, when a Club is formed simply for social intercourse, mutual improvement, business purposes, and recreation, we have no more right to use it as a means for converting the members to our own views on Politics, Theology, Teetotalism, Trades' Unionism, Secularism, or any other *ism*, than a preacher would have to employ the opportunity given him in the pulpit for promoting the return of a particular candidate to the House of Commons. And although there must not be the slightest attempt to interfere with *the fullest freedom of private conversation in a Club*, repeated or systematic efforts to turn the general conversation of the Club-room into one particular channel, especially for propagandist purposes, would be as unjustifiable (and perhaps even more injurious) as allowing the regular discussion meetings to be made the occasion for sectarian proselytizing of any kind. Great social and political questions should always be frankly discussed at those meetings. To exclude them would be fatal to the usefulness, and probably to the existence of the Club. But there is no such need of allowing theological discussions at them, and there are the strongest possible arguments against doing so.

In the next two chapters we examine the subject a little more in detail.

CHAPTER XI.

OUGHT RELIGIOUS AND POLITICAL DISCUSSIONS TO BE INTRODUCED INTO WORKING MEN'S CLUBS?

OF course, this question simply refers to formal discussions in a class, or formal meeting, not to conversation in the Club room. No inquisitorial surveillance over the talk among members could be permitted; but good taste and feeling will always prevent any member from annoying others by monopolizing that talk, or by speechifying at an unseasonable time.

There is sometimes a difference of opinion, however, as to the propriety of allowing members to introduce either of the above-named topics at regular discussion meetings. Rather strong feeling has sometimes been excited in considering it; and we therefore invite calm and candid attention to the following suggestions:—

In former chapters we have adverted to the general principles that should guide us in all such matters. The Club is to be common ground for persons of all sects and parties; the common good and enjoyment are to be exclusively sought, to the utmost extent compatible with the healthy existence of the Club, on the principles on which it was established.

Now, the educational development of those members who desire it is, undoubtedly, one of the legitimate objects of a Club and Institute. But there can be no branch of that education more important, save one, than that which helps men to deal wisely and faithfully with the duties and rights of citizenship. The discussion of great political questions in a suitable way, and at a seasonable time, is clearly an important function of the members of Working Men's Clubs and Institutes.

Equally certain, however, is it that while the discussion of theological topics is a yet more important branch of complete educational development, it cannot be pursued at a Club without imminent danger of breaking up the society. The subjects involved are so deeply interesting, that the strongest feelings of resentment, indignation, and distress, may easily be excited during a brief debate upon them. Their very sacredness and importance form an insuperable objection to their being discussed in an assembly drawn together from all points of the theological compass, or in a society one of the leading features of which is that no religious distinctions are to be recognized, no sectarian differences to be paraded, and where men of all shades of opinion are to meet and co-operate together for the common good on perfectly unsectarian ground. There are deeper reasons against the discussion of these topics in promiscuous assemblies, but the above, we think, are sufficient, because conclusive.

So strong has been the consciousness among the managers of Clubs that theological discussions would be unsuitable or dangerous, that we are only acquainted with one instance in which they have been permitted. In this case the Club, which was a large and flourishing one, suffered greatly in consequence—first, from the said discussions being allowed, and then from their being stopped. The Club ultimately broke up, and the above circumstances were mentioned as a primary cause of its disorganization. (See pp. 80-81.)

But it may be said, are not all these equally fatal objections to allowing political discussions? We answer, Yes, to the discussion of local party politics—to electioneering discussions —to the discussion, in fact, of any topic, whether social, political, or religious, which would probably rend the Club asunder, or create or cherish party spirit and sectarian animosity among the members. Generally speaking, the question of Total Abstinence, or of the Permissive Bill, could be debated without mischief; but if local circumstances had made either of those subjects an inflammatory battle-cry, the great fundamental principles of these Clubs, dwelt on in the chapters above referred to, would unquestionably prohibit their introduction until a healthier, less irritating, or less factious state of things prevailed. So with regard to politics. Most probably the question of the Extension of the Franchise could be discussed in a Club without any injury to the general good feeling and harmony of the Society; but the fitness of a particular candidate to represent in Parliament the borough or county in which the Club was situated, or of a particular individual to act as churchwarden in the parish, might give rise to very fierce partizan contention, and should by all means be avoided. There is no educational benefit to be gained by such discussions; but wherever there is either educational or practical profit likely to result, without preponderating mischief, by all means let the subject be thoroughly debated.

We were sorry to see that in one of the Working Men's Clubs there was an organization formed during a recent election to promote the return of a certain candidate for the borough; but we are thankful to be at present in ignorance of any similar proceedings elsewhere. We sincerely trust that Clubs will always be honourably preserved during local conflicts of whatever kind from any compromise of their noble unsectarian principles.

CHAPTER XII.

OUGHT DRAMATIC ENTERTAINMENTS AND DANCING TO BE ALLOWED AT WORKING MEN'S CLUBS AND INSTITUTES?

THIS question has, on several occasions, been brought under the consideration of the committees, trustees, and members of these societies. Strong feeling for and against has naturally been manifested, and more than one Club has been dissolved in consequence.

The first point in dealing with the subject is to state clearly and emphatically that in discussing it, the question as to the general or abstract propriety and advantage of theatrical amusements and of dancing must not be introduced. We have nothing to do with that part of the subject. All we have to consider is, whether it is desirable to allow them *as part of the recreations of a Club and Institute*. We may view them as right and good in themselves, and under certain conditions, but not as desirable in Clubs. Or we may regard them as generally pernicious, but exceptionally beneficial in those institutions. In advocating their exclusion or admission there, we pronounce no opinion, then, necessarily, as to their fitness, or the reverse, for other scenes and conditions.

The next point is to inquire what light is thrown upon the question by facts and experience.

At two Clubs in the Western counties dancing was introduced as a weekly entertainment, and led to the dissolution of the Clubs. Persons of improper character resorted to these gatherings, and the respectable working men were gradually driven away. These are the only cases with which we are at present acquainted where dancing was frequently allowed, or made part of the regular programme. Several Clubs have had an occasional ball, at Christmas, *e. gr.*, but that is a totally different matter. We ought to mention that beer was allowed to be drunk at one of the above Clubs; and, we believe, it was brought in on dancing nights at the other, but have not been able to ascertain this positively.

In regard to dramatic entertainments, a large and flourishing Club in a Northern county was broken up entirely in consequence of their being continually given. The downfall of one in the Southern counties was also mainly owing to the same cause; but in the latter case, beer was allowed in the Club, and was considered to be partly responsible for the calamitous result. In a third case, also in the South, dramatic performances have been introduced, but have been prohibited by the gentlemen who stand in the position of trustees. The result was considerable dissatisfaction, and a threatened schism between the members and the aforesaid gentlemen. Ultimately the management of the Club devolved entirely on the working men, and these entertainments were trusted to as a chief source of income. But, as might be expected, the Club could not maintain its ground on such a foundation as this, and ere very long was obliged to close.

These are the only facts with which we are at present acquainted bearing on the discussion.

We next proceed to inquire if there are any general principles that should guide us in the determination of so important a question. And here we must refer to the remarks to be found at p. 35, commencing: "In every enterprise and institution there must be some governing principle, as well as some inspiring idea. . . ."

Let us see how this principle applies to the question under discussion.

The advocates for the introduction of these recreations argue that they will promote the enjoyment of the members, and that dramatic entertainments will also promote their intellectual culture—that the "common consent" of the members, therefore, *ought* to be given. We answer, Not so, if the proposed culture or enjoyment would be offensive to the views or feelings of a considerable number of those who are members of the Club, or even of those who would be but for such amusements. All legitimate measures might be taken to prove the desirableness of introducing any means of innocent enjoyment or culture; but until there was a general agreement on the subject among all the parties who, whether by their numbers, or intelligence, or needful support, or past services, had a right to be heard in the question, clearly the advocates for the entertainments ought to exercise forbearance

and self-denial, even though this involved the entire relin-
quishment of their desires. This may at first seem hard ; but
we must beg those members of a Club who would urge their
plans upon opponents to remember that while there are, no
doubt, many excellent or needful objects to be pursued in this
world, the question is whether a Working Men's Club and
Institute is *the proper organization* for accomplishing them.
We believe both dancing and dramatic entertainments in
themselves to be innocent, rational, and often improving modes
of recreation, *when wisely and properly conducted;* the former, under due regulations, being useful both physically and
as an artistic and refined enjoyment, while dramatic exhibitions
may promote moral and intellectual culture in a very high degree. Children naturally delight both in dancing and (if they
have any imagination) in acting, or in seeing others so engaged. But cheap Dining-rooms, the election of a particular
candidate to the House of Commons, or an Exhibition of fat
cattle and donkeys, may be very desirable objects to carry
out in the estimation of various members of a Club, and yet
the Club would not be exactly the right organization for promoting any one of them.

The reasons against using a Club for these and similar objects might be very various—*e. gr.*, it must not be employed
for party purposes ; neither must it enter on commercial
speculations, having no capital, nor being established for that
object. But they would all be found to group themselves
under two main heads. Either the schemes objected to would
be opposed to the principle of "common consent,"—or to the
purpose for which the Club was founded. It is not enough
to plead that the object is good in itself, if either a considerable number (even though it be a minority) strongly object,
because then you destroy the very life and soul of a Club,
which lies in a common agreement to unite for certain ends ;
or if the object was clearly not contemplated by the founders
of the Club, or does not come within its legitimate province.
In either case, we may be able only to obtain an *approximation*
to a correct decision ; but that is what happens in most human affairs. Sometimes it may be hard to determine whether
a minority is large or important enough to make it right for
the majority to give way ; or whether the proposed undertaking really falls within the true scope of a Club and Insti-

tute's rightful functions. But in many, if not most, cases there would be little difficulty in saying whether either principle would be contravened, if the parties would only bring an *upright, unselfish spirit* to the judgment-seat.

It is certain there can be no Club without common agreement, nor without a strict adherence to fundamental and legitimate objects. Whatever on the one hand tends to irritate and offend—to divide a Club into parties and factions—or on the other aims at effecting purposes which some other, or some special, organization ought to promote, necessarily tends to destroy a Working Men's Club and Institute. "Toys and tools," said a wise man, "get broken by being put to uses for which they were not intended." This should be a guiding maxim for the managers and members of Working Men's Clubs. In the present case, it must be tolerably evident that working *men* are not likely to be passionately desirous of much dancing, or even of frequent theatrical exhibitions.

If a number of said members desire dancing or dramatic entertainments, and believe them to be desirable and improving enjoyments, it is, of course, open to them to form a dancing or dramatic club. Should another set desire to secure the return of a particular candidate to Parliament, they can form an election committee for the purpose. So with a co-operative society, cheap dining-rooms, cattle shows, or any other commercial, æsthetic, or political enterprise. But the Club must be kept to its own purpose, and on its own common social ground. Nay, even if all the members were agreed as to an end which did not come within the legitimate scope of the Club, or which would prevent its fulfilling its rightful functions of being a common social meeting-ground for men of all sects and parties—*e. gr.*, if, all the members being Blues in an election contest, they used the Club as an organization to promote the return of their candidate, and thereby effectually shut the Club against any Yellows—this would equally be a gross violation of the principles on which the Club was formed—a breach of faith towards those who had spent time, money, and strength in establishing a Club which was to be for the social, mental, and moral good of all the working men of the neighbourhood, irrespective of party or creed. But all that we have now said is strictly consistent with the plan, suggested in Chapter V., for an *alliance* between Clubs and some commercial or other organization, with the view of promoting their mutual benefit.

Recitations in dialogue and parts are not only free from all the objections that can be urged against theatrical representations, but are both pleasing and useful in every point of view. It is the dresses, scenery, and performances by females that are in danger of bringing in the destructive and alien elements. But an *occasional* dramatic performance, the parts being performed only by members of the Clubs, with suitable dresses and scenery, might be just as innocent and entertaining, therefore as useful, as a similar performance in any gentleman's home by his family and their friends. It should be a cardinal maxim with the managers of Clubs that occasional excitement is as useful as frequent excitement is mischievous in every point of view.

CHAPTER XIII.

VILLAGE CLUBS.

On this subject we cannot do better than give our readers the following interesting little sketch by the present Vicar of Oldham, the Rev. W. Walters, M.A., read at the Whittington Club Conference, May, 1864, on the question, " In how Small a Community may a Club be Established with a reasonable Hope of Success, either Independently or with a very moderate amount of Nursing ?"—

I cannot answer the question before the Conference better than by describing a Rural Institute which has now been in existence about four years. In the parish of Hanley Castle, Worcestershire, the population of which is about 1,100, a public-house was bought by a resident baronet, and converted into an Institute or Club-house for labourers. The houses are scattered, and not more than 400 or 500 of the parishioners live in the neighbourhood of the Institute. Farm labour is the general employment, but there are several carpenters, bricklayers, &c., for whom the neighbouring town of Malvern furnishes occupation.

The premises are commodious, and well adapted for the purpose. The signboard still swings over the door, but the words " Coach and Horses " have been replaced by the name " Working Man's Institute.

On the ground floor there are three smaller rooms and one larger one, with two kitchens behind. The steward and his wife occupy one of the smaller rooms ; the other two serve for a reading-room and library ; while the larger room is used for lectures, night-school, and band practice. In the yard outside is a double skittle-ground, and the stables have been turned into a two-storied dormitory. This consists of twelve rooms, containing, in all, nineteen beds. One room is reserved for a hospital in case of illness. The beds are let to lodgers at a shilling a-week, which payment entitles them to

I

all the privileges of the Institute, including the use of the bath —a privilege but seldom taken advantage of.

The steward and his wife, recommended by the Army Pensioners' Aid Society, take care of the whole establishment. House, garden, coals, and candles are allowed them, with a weekly payment of sixpence from every lodger, for cooking, &c. A weekly allowance is also made of three shillings, or four and sixpence when the number of lodgers exceeds fifteen, as payment for washing and cleaning.

The members consist of twenty honorary members, who pay ten shillings a-year, and for whose use an agricultural paper, *Bell's Weekly Messenger*, is taken in. The yearly average of ordinary members is sixty, who pay one shilling a-quarter. Monthly members are admitted at fourpence; weekly members at twopence; visitors at one penny each visit.

The balance-sheet of last year shows that 41*l.* 18s. 7d. was paid by lodgers for rent; honorary members contributed 10*l.*; ordinary members 9*l.* These sums, added to the proceeds of lectures and sale of newspapers, made up an income of 67*l.* 10s. The expenses were about 70*l.*; firing being a very large item in the expenditure. The rent paid to the landlord was 10*l.* I should mention that he must have laid out about 200*l.* in the alteration and fitting up of the premises, and our rent is 20*l.*; but from causes hereafter to be mentioned, only half a-year's rent was paid.

I would now enumerate some of the advantages that have been derived from the Institution.

A band, which is an honour to our little village, has steadily practised since the formation of the Institute, and if the members have not learnt a great deal of music, they have acquired a considerable amount of self-respect. Their practice has, on Saturday evenings, attracted listeners, who have smoked their pipes and drunk their coffee with seeming satisfaction.

In summer skittles and cricket, in winter draughts and dominoes, have afforded amusement in an evening to those who had leisure time.

The most successful department has been the night-school, carried on during the winter for two evenings a-week. From seven to eight, boys under seventeen attend; from eight to nine, adults. Last winter, there were twenty-six boys and twenty-seven men on the books, with a united average attendance of thirty-eight. Many have joined the Institute for the sake of the night-school, who would not otherwise have done so ; and although, in the short time to which school is limited, but little instruction can be imparted, still great advantages are thereby gained—viz., the knowledge of character which the parson there acquires, and the acquaintance, I may say friendship, which thus springs up between the teacher and the taught—an acquaintance which, in ministerial work, is productive of most beneficial results.

I pass on to the lodging department. The special object of the dormitories was the relief of the over-crowded cottages. It was hoped that the young men of the village would lodge there. Although this hope was not at the time realized, yet the lodgings answered another purpose. At first a few unsteady young men took up their abode in the Institute, but soon left a place where late hours were not encouraged. Soon after, a large mansion was erected in the neighbourhood, the contract for which was taken by Messrs. Myers ; the Tewkesbury and Malvern Railway was also in course of construction in the outskirts of the parish. Under these circumstances, the Institute became most useful. It saved, to a great extent, the over-crowding of cottages, which so often exists to the very serious detriment of health and morality. The lodgings were generally quite full, up to a year ago, when a man from Lambeth, whose wife and children lay sick of small-pox, left them in alarm, and took work for Messrs. Myers in our village. Before long he sickened of that disorder in the Institute. The natural result was, that the place was for three months shunned by members and lodgers, and our income was materially affected, as before alluded to. No other case occurred, and at the present time there are some fourteen or fifteen lodgers, many of whom are young men belonging to the parish; so that the object for which the lodging department was originally designed is at length in a fair way of being realized.

We have in the country advantages and disadvantages of a totally different character to those with which Institutes and Clubs in towns are concerned.

The agricultural labourer has but little time or money to spend in relaxation. The recreation of the majority is to take off their boots, eat their suppers of vegetables and bacon, smoke their pipes and go to bed, and sleep soundly after some fourteen hours' work. Those of them who are inclined for anything beyond domestic society, go to the public-house to discuss pigs and "taturs" over their cider. But there are many lads in every village who have not yet imbibed a love for drink, and who have no cares to drown at the public. These prefer the roadside to the fireside, and however hard they may have been working, are ready for anything in the shape of amusement. These are the materials for a Rural Club, and it is in their hearts that you must foster a love of the Institute. There is, too, but little to amuse people on winter nights in the country, and therefore lectures, readings, and concerts, are popular with all classes. But, on the other hand, we have great lack of men to act on a committee. Those who can, won't; and those who will, can't; and so the whole management falls into the hands of one man, and is too apt to be looked upon as the hobby of an individual who is responsible for the conduct of the Club, and the rest of the community thus shift the responsibility from their shoulders. Rural Clubs can never be self-supporting. Haymaking and harvest bring down the numbers of members to a very low pitch, and winter, therefore, is the only season when we can look for subscriptions from ordinary members. What we want to arrive at is this: that the Institute or Club should be regarded as a *parochial* institution, a place where Friendly Clubs and Benefit Societies may hold their monthly meetings; where contractors may pay their wages; and where, on a Saturday night, the labourer may come for a little pleasure; where, like a snail, he may put out his horns, and not be ever drawing them in again from restraint or suspicion. When a Club thus, so to speak, gets hold in a village, and you have some energy, perseverance, and sympathy amongst those who are able to help, I believe it may be established in a very small community, with a moderate amount of nursing, and with a reasonable hope of success.

[Persons who are desirous of gaining further information on the subject of Village Clubs, cannot do better than consult an admirable little book by the Rev. J. Whitehead, entitled "Village Sketches," Bosworth and Co., London, price 1s. See also Extracts from letters from Village Clubs at the end of Fifth Annual Report.]

CHAPTER XIV.

In the Report presented by the Council of the Union to the
Annual Meeting held July 6, 1864, the following passage
occurs :—

" The Council would also advert with very great satisfaction to the progress made in establishing Soldiers' Institutes
in various barracks, particularly at Chatham, Aldershott,
and Gibraltar. The influence for good of such Institutes
can scarcely be overrated, and, from all that they hear, the
Council are persuaded that where they are well conducted, and managed partly by the men themselves,
the results will ere long be found to tell powerfully on the
character and discipline as well as on the health of the troops.
But they desire also to call attention to a very important
matter which has been brought under their notice by a judicious and earnest soldiers' friend—viz., the great need for the
establishment of Soldiers' Institutes outside as well as within
the barracks. Soldiers' greatest temptations beset them
during the hours when they are at liberty to go beyond the
barrack-walls, and it is precisely then that places for social
intercourse and amusement, free from temptation, such as
have been successfully established in Gibraltar and Chatham,
would be of incalculable value. One of the last acts of the
late Lord Herbert was to promote measures for effecting this
object."

Hearing that much good had been done in Canada by a
Soldiers' Institute, the Secretary wrote to Major-General
Lord Frederick Paulet on the subject, and his lordship kindly
prepared the following interesting statement in reply. It was
read at the public dinner held by the Parent Society at the
Freemasons' Tavern, May 10, 1866, the Duke of Argyll in
the chair.

*An Account of the " Soldiers' Institute" established in Montreal,
by Major-General Lord Frederick Paulet, C.B. (commanding
Division of Foot Guards in Canada).*

In the winter of 1861-2, when the Trent affair took place,
a large number of troops were despatched to Canada, when
Montreal became unexpectedly the head-quarters of a force
amounting to upwards of 4,000 men, instead of 200, as
formerly.

It soon became apparent that some place of resort and
amusement was necessary to prevent the men from frequenting the numerous spirit-stores and shops that infest Montreal,
where the liquors sold are little short of poisonous.

By my direction, therefore, a committee of officers was
formed with a view to establishing a " Soldiers' Institute."

A house was found adapted to the purpose, and in about
two months was opened to the garrison.

The original funds for the outlay were collected by subscription from the officers. The citizens of the town also
subscribed 120*l.* ; and the Secretary of State for War, on
special application of Lieutenant-General Sir Fenwick Wil-
liams of Kars, granted 250*l.* towards the foundation. It has
always been found that soldiers will esteem an establishment
of this kind more highly if they themselves contribute a
trifling sum ; therefore the subscription of members was
fixed at threepence per month, which included entrance to the
Garrison Library (a small one), situated in the same building.

The Institute consisted at first of a large billiard-room,
writing, and reading-room, and skittle-alley on the basement ;
but from the time it opened the numbers went on increasing
so steadily, that another building was added, affording more
accommodation, by which the billiard-room was separated
from the writing, reading, and *concert-room.* This latter was
much appreciated by the men, who on three evenings in the
week assembled for the purpose of singing, entirely managed
by a committee chosen by themselves, and on no occasion did
I ever hear of any complaint as to drunkenness or disturbance
of any sort. The Institute was managed by a sergeant as
steward, who was responsible to the committee of officers.
There was also a sub-committee composed of soldiers, who
referred any requisitions or complaints to the committee.

The sale of *malt* liquor was unrestricted; and the eatables, such as ham, lobster, cakes, fruit, tea, coffee, &c., were of the best quality, and sold at a profit only sufficient to cover the expenses attending their supply. Up to the time I left the command, in 1863, nothing could exceed the success that attended the scheme, and the number of members had exceeded two thousand.

The extra building was paid for by the receipts; and the subscriptions of officers and others, who had at first assisted, were wholly dispensed with. I have, moreover, reason to know that the good conduct and harmony that existed amongst all arms of the service composing the garrison was in great measure owing to the Institute; and so firmly am I impressed with its merits in any garrison town, that I trust to see, before this year is completed, a large Institute opened to the troops quartered in London, on the same system.

The building is already commenced, and it is part of the plan to set aside one floor, where will be established workshops, for the purpose of enabling the men to ply or learn trades during their leisure hours. Of course the expense of building and purchase of land is enormous; but by the assistance of many who have either served in the Brigade of Guards, or are interested in such movements, a sum of money has been raised, which has been added to by a grant of money from the War-office Estimates, sanctioned and approved of by Earl de Grey and the Marquis of Hartington.

Though this sum will by no means cover the whole expense, yet by its assistance the Institute will probably be opened at the latter end of this year, when, with even moderate success, it is computed that it will be so self-supporting that the debt will be speedily paid off.

I might add that great encouragement has been given to the undertaking by an expression of the wishes of the men composing the two battalions lately in Canada, that a similar Institute should be established in London."

The following letter has also just been received from Lord Paulet in answer to a further inquiry :—

" 26th July, 1867.

" Dear Sir,—The Guards' Institute was opened on the 11th

July, and is now in operation, and successfully. There were 929 subscribers on the day it was opened.—Yours truly,

"FREDERICK PAULET.

"The Rev. H. Solly."

These are very gratifying facts, and it is to be earnestly hoped that the good work may make rapid progress. The position of a soldier in barracks has hitherto been, too often, most deplorable in many points of view. The recent regulations concerning the canteens, whereby, we believe, they are placed under the management of a mixed committee of commissioned and non-commissioned officers, together with the establishment of these capital Institutes, will be of the greatest service in improving the health, morals, and general culture of the troops, as well as in increasing their happiness. The valuable suggestion, also, respecting Soldiers' Institutes outside the barracks in garrison towns must not be lost sight of, though the subject is not free from difficulties.

CHAPTER XV.

YOUTHS' CLUBS AND INSTITUTES.

[THE following paper, by the Rev. Arthur Sweatman, M.A., was read at a meeting of the Social Science Association at Edinburgh, in October, 1863, and was printed in the *Working Men's Club and Institute Magazine* for April, 1865 :—]

The whole question of Evening-Classes and Night-Schools has been lately revived, and public attention has been drawn somewhat prominently to the subject of supplemental education for the working classes. The occasion of this attention to a rather shelved question is no doubt the manifest gap which has appeared in the educational life of the working man.

It is not to be concealed that the training of the school is brought to a very abrupt and premature termination by the necessities which call away our working boys to the earning of their livelihood; and however rigorously the course of teaching may be restricted to those rudiments which will furnish a lad with useful and handy knowledge for the common exigencies of his station, the time is often scant for the laying of even these foundations, and, at the best, their permanence is greatly endangered by the early age at which they must be put to the proof.

Unless a lad so taught find some means of following up his school education co-ordinately with his daily work, there is every prospect of his losing the little learning he had accumulated, and none of his adding to the store. On the other hand, the Mechanics' Institute or Working Men's Club comes to his assistance only after a long interval, in which his knowledge has rusted, and his faculty for study become dull and blunted.

This is the merely educational view of the matter, which has revealed the want of some intermediate agency in the shape of an evening school to supplement the work of the day-school as soon as the office of the latter ceases, and thereby to save it from most probable effacement.

But the general experience of tried schemes for evening instruction seems to have been far from encouraging. The very name of " Night-school" has become suggestive of much unrequited drudgery on the part of the teacher, much wearisomeness and untowardness on the part of the taught, and a general failure of any permanent results in the improvement of the class aimed at.

This acknowledged unsuccess of night-schools, with a few bright exceptions here and there, is perhaps due to an assumption, which is not warranted by experience, that working lads would for the most part desire so to continue the studies of the day-school, and that such supplemental instruction was the great desideratum for meeting the evil.

But it does not prove to be the case that mere teaching, even in subjects of practical usefulness, is either the great want of this class of boys, or to any large extent welcomed by them. To be either useful or welcome, it must be associated with some work of a more social and recreative character ; not only because lads so newly emancipated from the restraints and work of the school-room very naturally shy at anything which seems to threaten a return to the old bonds, but because their day's work fairly entitles them to reasonable recreation at its close, and still more because there are other and more important offices to be done for them than the mere supply of book-learning.

This opens up the social aspect of the question, which seems to be the more important of the two.

The great peril of the system which releases boys at so early an age from the discipline of school, and turns them out loose upon the world imperfectly taught and trained, is, that they are likely to degenerate into a very low condition, mental and moral, and gradually to slip away from all improving and elevating influences. The kind of influence which a Working Men's Club is designed to exercise is just that which it is desirable should be brought to bear upon the boy who has exchanged the slate and copy-book for the desk, the counter, or the tool-bench ; and it is practically found that many boys would find their way into these societies, were not their admission detrimental to the attendance of adult men. For several reasons men do not choose to attend a reading-room or class frequented by boys; and a junior or intermediate institution is thus necessitated, which shall receive youths, until they are of age to avail themselves of the Men's Club.

This is, in the simplest light, the office which those institutions fulfil which have acquired the distinctive title of Youths' Clubs or Institutes. It is the purpose of the present paper to describe the objects and operations of a Youth's Institute, especially illustrating them by a sketch of that established in Islington.

It will be quite understood that any attempt must be hopeless to prescribe a scheme of universal applicability. Local circumstances must greatly guide any plans undertaken for the purpose in question; and besides this, the *class* of lads to be provided for must be clearly defined. For it is plain that even recreations which would be highly appreciated by an intelligent class of town-boys, might offer no inducement to farming-lads in a village, or to a lower grade of boys even in town, and the questions of payment and instruction are equally affected by the same consideration.

The class contemplated by a Youths' Club and Institute is capable of easy definition. It consists of boys and young men between the ages of thirteen and nineteen, who have left an elementary school for some junior situation at a weekly salary or wages, varying from 5s. to 18s. This description creates a distinct, well-defined class within sufficiently wide limits. It embraces the junior clerk in an office or warehouse, the office-boy and errand-boy, the apprentice to a skilled trade, and the son of the small shopkeeper. For the most part, such lads are capable of appreciating a superior kind of recreation to that offered them in the streets—a higher social intercourse, a better style of literature, and a healthier class of amusements, requiring some mental exercise.

They have also their special wants and dangers, which call for such an agency as the Youths' Institute. Their peculiar *wants* are *evening recreation, companionship, an entertaining but healthy literature, useful instruction,* and a *strong guiding influence* to lead *them onward and upward socially and morally ;* their *dangers* are, the long evenings consequent upon early closing, the unrestraint they are allowed at home, the temptations of the streets and of their time of life, and a little money at the bottom of their pockets.

In the case of most of these lads, their own homes afford no supply for these peculiar wants. There is often small accommodation, and less quiet, for writing or study; in the midst of domestic arrangements they may frequently find themselves in the way; the resources of the family in the way of amusements are slender, and out of doors they *must* turn in quest of congenial associates of their own age and tastes.

But all these wants the Youths' Institute is specially designed to supply—recreation, companionship, reading, instruction, and all of a pure and healthy kind.

Its operations may be best explained by an account of an actually existing Institution; and while that at Islington is selected for the purpose, it ought to be stated that the first experiment of the kind was made, with great success, by the Rev. Henry White, of the Chapel Royal, Savoy—first at Dover, in 1857, and afterwards at Charing-cross, in 1860; and that a most flourishing Youths' Club has been carried on for the last five years at Bayswater, by Mr. Charles Baker. Each of these Institutes has possessed its own peculiar features, though planned upon one model.

The Islington Youths' Institute was opened in the first week of October, 1860, at St. George's Hall, Richmond-road, which was engaged for the week evenings only of the seven winter months. This hall was used for reading, recreation, and a weekly lecture; the educational classes being held in a smaller adjacent room. The subscription of members was fixed at 3d. per week.

The success of this first experiment was immediate and marked. 236 boys and youths of various occupations availed themselves of the advantages offered during the season—more than 100 being always in steady membership—and the nightly attendances ranged from 50 to 75.

This success encouraged the Managers to employ the interval before the second winter season in extending and consolidating the scheme. A larger and handsome room was added to the original premises, and furnished for reading and recreation; the old hall being appropriated to the purposes of classes and lectures, and fitted with the necessary desks and forms. A small room was also fitted up for the library and for secretarial purposes; and a class-room added for the use of the Penny Bank, and occasional classes. The Bishop of London became the patron of the Institute, and on the occasion of his visit addressed the members.

Under these improved auspices, the Institute has continued its work to the present time with a steadily increasing success.

The work is chiefly carried on by two Hon. Secretaries, one or both of whom is always present in the reading-room. They are assisted by a staff of gentlemen, who gratuitously conduct the various classes, and in their more mechanical labours by a committee of members, nominated by themselves, who also serve as monitors, and watch over the good order and comfort of the Society.

The conditions of membership are made somewhat stringent by the requirement of a small entrance-fee, and the recommendation of two members ; and the numbers are limited to 160. It is thus made to be regarded as a privilege.

The reading-room is open each evening (Sundays excepted) from half-past six till half-past nine, a short prayer being used at the commencement, and an evening hymn sung at the close. Great pains have been taken to make the room attractive and cheerful, by having it well lighted and warmed, and hung with good pictures.

A large central table, capable of seating about twenty-five readers, is spread with more than three dozen different periodicals, including the daily, illustrated, and local newspapers, the various Boys' Magazines, and the serials of a higher class. Twelve smaller tables, each accommodating three pairs of players, are provided with the games — chess, draughts, solitaire, tactics, and any similar drawing-room amusement that can be found. All the tables are covered with red baize, which adds greatly to the cheerfulness of the room.

This room is unreservedly devoted to recreation. The members are encouraged to the freest and happiest intercourse amongst themselves, and complete confidence towards the managers ; it is sought to cultivate in them courtesy of manners, truthfulness, mutual forbearance, and good temper. No coercion is exercised but what may be needful for the general comfort and propriety. And it is pleasing to state that in this, the characteristic feature of the Institute, the success has been most complete. The reading-room is used with invariable decorum and earnestness; the periodicals and papers find an increasing number of readers; the interest in chess and draughts has become more intense each season, and the Institute can now furnish a large number of skilful players.

At half-past seven, the classes commence; two (sometimes three) being held each evening. They consist of book-keeping, arithmetic, reading, elocution, grammar, writing, dictation, drawing, French, and biblical study. Each member is required to attend at least three of these classes *regularly*, and for encouragement to diligence a large number of prizes are distributed at the close of the season.

On alternate Tuesday evenings *Lectures* of an entertaining or instructive kind are delivered, to which friends are admitted at a small charge.

The *Library* contains at present 800 volumes, chiefly the gifts of friends or grants of societies. It is open for the exchange of books twice a-week, and is used very largely by the members, the issues averaging about 100 volumes weekly.

The Penny Bank receives deposits also twice a-week, and is fairly availed of by the members.

Beyond these regular features of the Youths' Club and Institute, there are various other occasional opportunities, useful or pleasant, which grow out of it, or group themselves around it—summer excursions, by rail or river, with friends and subscribers—gatherings of kindred societies for a distribution of prizes or an outdoor holiday—reciprocal visits from one Institute to another, for friendly rivalry in recitation or to contest a chess tournament—Christmas social meetings and Easter musical entertainments. Such incidents serve to keep up a freshness and spirit about the undertaking, to attach the members to the scheme, and to bind the several Institutes together in a friendly fellowship.

The satisfactory and harmonious tone which pervades the members has been already alluded to. It is in this moral improvement which they have observed resulting from their work that the managers find their chief encouragement. But the success of the scheme is not less apparent upon paper. A few statistics will show how thoroughly St. George's Hall is enjoyed, and its advantages welcomed in the neighbourhood.

The Hall was opened for the present season on Monday evening, 3rd October last. No effort by means of advertisement or otherwise was made to obtain members, but on the first night 95 applicants were enrolled, and by the Friday evening the full number of 160 was completed. From a supernumerary list of applicants the vacancies have been filled up week by week to the present time, until the register shows a total of 245 names entered. The largest number present on any one evening has been 139, and through a most severe winter the attendance has never fallen below 43. The attendances throughout the season show an average of 90 present each night, of 104 for the Monday evenings, and of 140 present during each week. No falling off is being experienced as the season draws to an end.

A few words on finance may be acceptable. The present subscription is 4d. per week; entrance-fee for old members, 6d., for new, 1s. 6d. These payments will amount to about 85l. for the year, of which about 81l. is taken during the seven months when the Institute is open. In the summer, we charge one penny for such members as use the Library, and take about 4l. The Cricket Club is self-supporting. The only other source of regular income is the sale of lecture tickets, producing 3l. or 4l.

Of expenditure, the chief item is for rent, gas, cleaning, and firing—65l. All other permanent expenses, printing class materials, periodicals, postages, &c., are under 20l. So that not the least gratifying feature of a Youth's Club and Institute, well conducted, is that as regards all ordinary expenditure it may be thoroughly *self-supporting*. It is well, too, that the members should feel a consciousness of honest independence; it makes the Institute more really their own property.

The only objects for which it is needful occasionally to ask a little help from personal friends are books for the library, pictures, &c., for the walls, prizes, and an occasional entertainment.

It may be added that during the summer months a Cricket Club is formed among the members, which has proved a source of much healthful enjoyment, and a means of holding them together from one winter season to another.

Such are the means by which Youths' Institutes seek to

supply the gap which has been so long allowed to exist in the
opportunities afforded to the people. A five years' trial
warrants the expectation that they are destined satisfactorily
to answer the vexed question, "What is to be done with our
older boys?" A five years' observation also establishes the
conviction that such boys are open to a good influence, and
ready to submit themselves to it. There is, in the generality
of them, enough of moral good, enough of knowledge and
consciousness of right, instilled in their early training, to pre-
dispose them to welcome and profit by any offer of good in
the stead of evil. It is the absence of any provision for their
harmless recreation, and the refusal to recognize their natural
claim to it, that has driven so many of them into bad ways.

Evil is still to be overcome with good; and splendid
triumphs in the great battle are to be achieved by such
agencies as a Youths' Institute. The idler and lounger, the
good-for-nothing and vicious among our big lads, are to be
redeemed from a lost life, and trained to self-respect and
manliness, frank-heartedness and moral-mindedness, intelligence and industry, to do good and true work in their day
and generation.

The following practical remarks, made at one of the
monthly tea-meetings of the Secretaries of London Clubs,
held at the office of the Union, form a fitting sequel to this
very valuable paper. They will be read with interest, treating
as they do of the rather difficult question—

How to Deal with the Youths,

in relation to those Clubs which they have so uniformly wooed,
and too often won, with a passionate and fatal ardour worthy
of the most dismal and romantic scenes in a modern sensation
novel. The subject was touched upon in Chapter III., but
requires fuller consideration.

The Chairman having inquired the views of each person
present, in turn, as to the age at which they thought persons
might be admitted as members without prejudice to the Club,
six representatives mentioned " eighteen ; " but four of them,
admitting that applicants for admission constantly falsified
their age, urged that measures should be taken to prevent
any coming in who had not actually attained that age, either

by requiring older persons to certify the fact, or by making the nominal age twenty-one. One secretary considered none should be admitted unless they had actually attained the age of twenty-one; another named twenty-two, and another urged twenty-three. Several maintained that none under twenty-five or thirty, even though admitted to the Club, should be allowed to use the bagatelle-room, as, independently of the noise younger men made when playing, it had too often happened that youths came to a Club, learned to play at bagatelle, became passionately fond of it, and then got into the habit of playing at public-houses, for money or beer. It was also recommended by most of those present that no person under twenty-one should be admitted, if at all, without a recommendation, or (as at the Southwark Club) unless two adult members agreed to be answerable for his good behaviour. (This last suggestion carries us back to the renowned institutions of Alfred the Great, and has great virtue in it.) One speaker ably contended that it was really a question of good management, saying that men do not object to the company of *well-behaved* youths, but quite concurred in the exclusion of the latter from the bagatelle-room until their characters were comparatively formed—say, twenty-five years. In judicious management, wisely blending firmness and kindness, would be found, he thought, the solution of all these and similar difficulties. Most, however, agreed that men would not keep company with the youths; but the representatives from Camden Town and St. Bride's considered that grown men did not object to the company of youths as young as sixteen or eighteen. One speaker urged the great importance of not allowing any member under the age of twenty-five to be on the committee; otherwise, as was the case at one time in the Club he belonged to, the youths might get completely the upper hand, and do great mischief. The representative from Chelsea (Mr. Taylor) said they admitted them at the age of eighteen, provided, as long as they were under twenty, some members of the Committee took them under their special charge. At that Club they had twenty-four on their committee, and four of them took it in turn to be there every night; hence such a thing as disorder and noise was quite unknown among them. He maintained that, unless youths are admitted as young as eighteen, " they go to the bad" before they are admitted to the Club. Many youths who used to play bagatelle at beershops in the neighbourhood of this Club never go there now, but play at the Club instead, and without betting or noise. None, however, are allowed to play twice until all who wish it have a chance of playing once. [This Club, however, has since been closed. Some working men of the neighbourhood being asked the reason, said, " it was an excellent thing, but there had been too much patronage and interference." Of course we cannot say how far this representation was correct. Great pains, we know, were taken to make it both useful and pleasant. We fear the want of separate rooms for youths had much to do with the catastrophe.] The representative of another Club urged that there was no possibility of keeping youths out of the bagatelle-room till they had reached any given age. The great point was to let them amuse themselves as they liked; but to be continually taking opportunities of leading them on to care occasionally for something higher and more improving.

We then dwelt on the original and fundamental idea of a Working Men's Club—viz., that of a society of grown men for promoting that social intercourse and pleasant fellowship among themselves which the wealthier classes get at each other's homes, or at their Clubs, but which working men are driven to seek at the public-house. We urged that husbands and fathers of families, men of ripe years and experience, often wished for chat with one another on many subjects of interest, in discussing which they certainly did not desire the company of lads and youths as listeners. Of course, we fully recognized the vast importance of providing a place of resort for the latter, but suggested the various expedients already mentioned; and contended that where youths were admitted indiscriminately to a Club, without any of those precautions, it might be doing a great deal of good in some other way, but it certainly was not answering the purpose for which Working Men's Clubs were and ought to be established. The Secretary of the Southwark Club (Mr. Symons), in a very able speech, then summed up the discussion. He believed that if Clubs could be formed and maintained such as we had described, to which none should be admitted under the age of twenty-five, they would be a very great success, and would meet an extremely urgent want. Perhaps they might be best supported in large towns if each trade had its own Club. At all events, he much wished to see Clubs that would really belong to, and be used by, grown men exclusively. He strongly confirmed, by various illustrations from his own experience, the statements made as to the absurdity of expecting grown-up men to talk familiarly with one another in the presence of youths. What they said would be sure to be misunderstood, or be repeated, perhaps misrepresented. Very likely it would be all over their workshop the next day, or they would hear of it in their families, perhaps in the streets. In every point of view, it was most unpleasant and objectionable to have lads listening to their talk. For these reasons, he would like to see in every Club at least one room where men could be by themselves. But he could not consent to exclude youths altogether. And in the present state of the movement, and of his own Club in particular, he felt that he would rather labour to save those whose characters were not yet formed—who were under the age of twenty-five—than older men; for he had seen the wonderful good done to these young fellows by admitting them to that Club. He would employ, however, various safeguards. He had got power from the Committee to suspend any member guilty of disorderly conduct until the next Committee meeting, and the youths, knowing he had this power, now behaved much better.

(It was mentioned, by-the-bye, in the course of the evening, that the steward of the Holloway Club had the power entrusted to him of turning out any offender for the night, but had never had occasion to exercise it—partly, perhaps, *because* he had the power—partly, no doubt, because of his firm, yet genial, manner with the members.)

Mr. Symons farther mentioned that they had passed a rule making youths only " *associates* " until they attain the age of eighteen, so that they would have no power in managing the Club, or rather mismanaging it, as had formerly been the case. He also suggested that, where there was a great demand for admission on the part of youths, the committee might require them to show a certificate from the secretary that they were in the habit of attending some class or lecture, and of conducting themselves respectably, before giving them a ticket of admission to tho bagatelle-room. This, however, would require a great deal of tact and good management, but in some Clubs he thought it would work well. He wished they were as fortunate as the members of the Chelsea Club in having so many staunch and competent members of committee to take it in turn to attend every evening, and so many popular gentlemen to help work the Club and make it both pleasant and useful. They had only one of this class, their president, Mr. Seaward Tayler, to whom they were under the greatest obligations; but he lived a long way off, and of course could not be very often there.

We must confess that we agree in the doubt expressed above as to whether it is desirable to have a bagatelle-board in it; for experience certainly shows that in several instances youths have learned to play at bagatelle in the Club, have acquired a passion for the same, and have afterwards become systematic players for money at a public-house. Even where that has not happened, it must be confessed that there is generally a great deal of noise connected with the game, and disorderly youths are attracted by it, so that the older members are annoyed and repelled; while, even though no betting or stakes are allowed by the rules, it sometimes happens that lads and youths play for beer, bet, and then adjourn to the public-house after the game to settle their accounts. Of course, no good is without some attendant evil, and the abuse of a good thing is no argument against its use. But it is by no means clear that bagatelle-playing is so decided a benefit for youths as to counterbalance its dangers. Unquestionably it is of the greatest importance, as was well urged by two highly intelligent and respectable working men at the aforesaid London Secretaries' Tea-meetings, that these Clubs should not fall into the error of the old Mechanics' Institutes, and frown upon recreation. Amusements must form *an essential part* of their programme. But it is very different providing bagatelle-tables for grown men, whose characters are comparatively formed, and who would only use them, in general, as gentlemen use their billiard-tables, for an occasional relaxation, and letting youths give themselves up to the game, night after night, perhaps meanwhile acquiring a taste for betting and gambling. If these younkers *would consent to vary* their bagatelle-playing with attendance at classes and lectures, and if a vigilant yet amiable member of the committee, or other official, could guard against betting and rioting among them, the game might be simply a useful and pleasant diversion for them, just as in the drawing-room of a gentleman's home.

But, further, in all cases we would recommend the plan suggested above of admitting youths, if at all, *only as associates*, not as full members, until they have reached a specified age, which we should strongly advise to be fixed at twenty-five years. They would thus obtain no power to interfere with the management of the Club, nor exercise the right of voting, until their age (and, perhaps, previous satisfactory connexion with the Club as associates) gave some guarantee that they would exercise the privileges of full membership judiciously. In all such cases it would be well to require—as is now done in some Clubs, when youths under twenty-one apply for admission—that they should bring a recommendation from two or three of the older members. Obtaining full membership would then be looked forward to as an object of honourable ambition, and would be viewed, perhaps, with something of the old Roman satisfaction felt in putting on the *toga virilis*.

No doubt there are strong reasons for leaving the managing committee some power to admit, in one way or another, youths under twenty-five, or even younger. A father may wish to join a Club chiefly for the sake of encouraging his sons to attend it ; and his presence there, or their own characters, testified to by himself and some other members of the Club, may be sufficient guarantee that they will conduct themselves quietly, and not annoy the older members. And when youths can be brought into a Club without annoying older men, and without learning bad practices there, it is not only a great gain to themselves, but ultimately to the Club, of which they will probably, in time, become staunch and valuable members. Some young men under twenty-five, or even under twenty-one, may be much steadier and pleasanter company for grown-up men than those of older growth. But, equally of course, these cases are exceptional, and we cannot legislate for exceptions. Probably the best solution of the difficulty will be found in the practice of election by ballot recommended elsewhere.

Lastly, on the principle of dealing with facts as we find them, we must not, however, ignore the hapless condition of many existing Clubs, which, before they knew the deadly nature of the mistake, admitted these youthful, innocent-looking allies into the heart of the citadel. Now, the managers of those youth-oppressed Clubs, round which treacherous and deceitful juveniles are clinging, like drowning victims to their would-be preservers, may fairly turn to us and say : " This is all very fine, if we had only known it a year or two ago, and had then adopted the precautions you suggest ; but now two - thirds or three - fourths of our members are under twenty-five. They have driven away all the older men, except those who are content with the quiet reading-room, and lectures, or entertainments. We cannot afford to send them packing, or we could not pay our rent, and should not have thirty members left." Now in answer we might say that, if they cannot have those separate chat and game rooms above proposed ; and that, if the Club was really established for men, and not for youths, the sooner they left off perverting it from its legitimate purpose the better ; that, moreover, as soon as it became known in the neighbourhood that the youths had really been bowed out, the men would gradually return. But there is a middle course in such a case, which was suggested in Chap. III., p. 121. —viz., that adopted at Heywood, and which, in many cases, might be a far better one than making a clean sweep of more than two-thirds of the members of a Club. It secures one room, at all events, in which grown men can always be secure from the presence of lads, where they can have their chat and their pipe in peace, and talk without constraint. This, after all, is the thing of most importance ; and if the older men want to use the bagatelle-board, and cannot afford to have two, they must form their own party and take their turn. At one of the London Clubs they have the great advantage of having a separate entrance and staircase for the youths, as well as separate rooms ; which, in fact, affords the *material* conditions for a Youths' Institute in connexion with a Working Men's Club. Nothing better than an arrangement of this sort could be desired, *if* it be strictly carried out.

CHAPTER XVI.

AMUSEMENT AND EDUCATION COMBINED IN WORKING MEN'S CLUBS.

WHILE it is quite certain that amusement (including in that term social intercourse) is the first thing to be provided for by these Clubs, and that improvement of various kinds (mental, moral, and pecuniary) is the second, it is a point of paramount importance for working men and their friends to see how they can make the second result grow naturally out of the first.

This is not difficult when we once get on the right track. A beneficent Creator has bound together in natural connexion, and in beautiful harmony, things that are pleasant and things that are improving; has made the universe on such a plan that, if we attend to obvious principles, we shall derive immense enjoyment from learning what there is in it, as well as from using our own powers to add to its beauty, its wonders, conveniences, and joys.

One way, however, in which people who know a little have tried to teach it to those who know less, has been used for years at Mechanics' Institutes, and more recently at Working Men's Clubs, in both cases, for the most part, with signal failure. We refer to *Lectures*—but especially to lectures intended to convey knowledge, or to promote improvement. Of course there have been various exceptions. We speak only of the general rule. Lectures, generally, are not well attended. No surer device can be adopted for securing a bad attendance of the members of these Institutions and Clubs than to announce the delivery of " A Lecture," unless some very gifted orator or unusually attractive subject is announced also. " Lecturet," indeed, is a more novel and exciting title, and has been used with good effect. It has been found, however, that the exhibition of diagrams, dissolving views, &c., materially helps to draw or retain an audience. It is a great help, of course, to a tired or uneducated person, to have some illustration to look at, while striving to attend to a verbal description or statement. In the same way, also, experiments in chemistry, or with an electrical machine, air-pump, &c., greatly aid their efforts.

But there is a large class of extremely interesting subjects, on which it is very desirable that working men should get information, but which cannot be illustrated by anything but diagrams and specimens—perhaps not at all. Most literary and historical subjects come under the latter head, and descriptions of the structure and functions of the human body, of animals, of famous cities, fossil remains, &c., under the former. Now an admirable mode of drawing an audience to listen to selections from our noble English literature has been the " Penny Readings," which have achieved such national success, and been productive of such remarkable benefits. That success has been mainly promoted by the introduction of music, and especially of singing, between the readings. The latter alone have sometimes been highly popular; but, as a general rule, the songs have been found needful to win or maintain this popularity, or, at all events, to accomplish the most signal and *repeated* success. Here, then, we have an instance in which no ordinary benefit—viz., an acquaintance with and delight in English literature—has been connected in a perfectly legitimate manner with amusement, so that large numbers of people, who were at once far too uneducated and too wearied to care to come to lectures on English literature, have been both benefited and highly amused by a judicious combination of readings and song.

Now the point we are coming to, guided by these facts, is that we may avail ourselves, to a large extent, of the marvellous power which music possesses to gladden and refine the human heart, for the purpose of procuring an audience to listen with attention to other matter no less interesting, when pleasantly handled, than extracts from poets, humourists, and writers of fiction. Having prepared what would formerly have been called *a lecture*, on " The Hand, the Hoof, and the Wing," founded on Sir Charles Bell's very interesting Bridgewater Treatise, we consulted with the Committee of one of our London Clubs as to the possibility of getting their members to listen to it. We were all agreed that it was very important to offer them something of an instructive or improving character occasionally, by way of variation to the perpetual round of mere amusement previously going on in the Club, and especially at their weekly entertainments; but we were equally agreed that to announce "a lecture" would be to ensure empty benches. Accordingly the Committee, at our suggestion, applied to the obliging Choir of another London Club, and got their consent to come and sing a few songs and give two or three recitations on the occasion of our performance. We got a bill printed, therefore, to the effect that, "At the next Monday evening entertainment," we were to give "a description of the Hand, &c.," "illustrated by diagrams and a few (bony) specimens, interspersed with some songs and recitations by members of the Camden Town Working Men's Club." The plan proved successful. The "entertainment" commenced with two or three songs and a recitation, given in the able and pleasant style with which many of our London Clubbists are familiar; then came the first part of our "description," which consisted mainly of what would, perhaps, have been considered rather dry stuff, if taken by itself (though enlivened occasionally by an anecdote or a joke, if it came handy), but which the previous amusement had sufficiently attracted and braced our audience to swallow contentedly—nay, even cheerfully. About twenty-five minutes of this work was a sufficiently long trial of their patience; but before they were thinking how to get away, we suspended our descriptions of comparative anatomy, and the Chairman again introduced the Choir. Two or three more songs or recitations, and then we concluded our labours with about fifteen minutes' additional description, and ten minutes of exhortation, to make "the many members in one body of their Club work harmoniously and zealously together for the common good."

This experiment having worked so well, we repeated it at three other London Clubs with similar results. A lady (Miss Wallington) kindly gave some of her capital recitations when we went to the Southwark Club, and the members of the other Clubs provided the musical part themselves. We believe that, however comical the thing looks at first, there is no reason why *many* "lectures" should not be divided into two parts, with songs and recitations between, nor why *all* such useful exercises should not be preceded and followed by musical and literary amusement. It has often been urged that the members of Working Men's Clubs must have some other and better excitement offered them if you would withdraw them from the public-house; but if that excitement can occasionally consist of blended amusement and instruction, you are not only doing the members double good at the time, but you are unfolding the higher elements of their nature and character, and making the Club a source of permanent blessing. Penny Readings will always, we trust, maintain their ground, and preserve their present high character; but everything human has a tendency to degenerate, and all human enjoyments require variety. We have heard more than once that these Readings were losing their hold upon the public in particular localities, and required a larger and larger infusion of the comic element (bordering even upon what was coarse) if they were to continue to attract. Much that could be given in the shape of historic and scientific description would be quite as popular and fascinating as extracts from our best authors, if it could be varied, as the "Readings" have been, by music, &c.; and many persons, who would have given a lecture a remarkable wide berth, would come for the sake of the songs, intending patiently to endure the "description," going away surprised and delighted to find, at the end of the evening, how much they have been at once instructed and amused. A striking illustration of the successful working of the above plan was recently afforded at the same Club at which we first tried the experiment last winter. Elihu Burritt had kindly engaged to give a lecture there on the "Charities of London," but when the time came for commencing there were not a dozen people in the hall, nor much prospect of more coming in, though the rest of the Club-rooms were well filled. But, according to arrangement, the piano struck up a lively air; this was followed by a song or two; the hall rapidly filled with members, and Mr. Burritt had a good audience to begin with. Many, we believe, only meant to remain a little while, and then to go back to their games, &c., but, once there, they soon became interested in the lecture, and fascinated by the lecturer's style and manner. Scarcely a person moved till he had finished, and then vehement applause told how successful the attempt had been. Songs concluded the evening, and all felt how good it had been for them to have heard what they did, instead of the whole evening being occupied in their ordinary amusements. In this, as it would be in many other cases, the lecturer did not wish to divide his lecture—which, in fact, would probably have been a mistake in his case; but in general either the subject would admit of the variety, in the middle, of songs and music, or the interest would be sustained throughout to the end. Of course, much depends upon the lecturer being able to say what he has to say in a pleasant, popular way, especially if the subject be a scientific one. But in all cases, however excellent the plan, personal qualities, of course, are a main element of success. Music is, nevertheless, a mighty lever for raising and improving the condition and character of our race, as well as for giving rational enjoyment. Let us apply it in the manifold ways which Working Men's Clubs, among other agencies, abundantly afford.

In the "Occasional Paper No. IX." (Appendix) before referred to, it is remarked that the success of a public-house depends greatly upon the character of the landlord. The paper originally published continued thus: "One main reason is that the first thing most men want in any place or society to which they go for rest or companionship is *to know that they are welcome*. If they are not made to feel this at a Club, either by the steward, the secretary, or a member of the committee, when they first join, and by their own friends or brother members after they have belonged to it for some time, probably they will not go very often. But the next great want is the need of amusement, excitement of some sort or other, a complete change from monotonous toil. Working men get this amusement in a cleverly managed 'public'—not always in the best way; and it is indispensably necessary they should find it at the Club also, but, if possible, in a better way. A few words will indicate why, as is said in the foregoing letter, this is the department in which the help of gentlemen may be so useful. The members of the committee must indeed devote themselves specially to this work of making the Club attractive, but it is much larger than they can generally cope with, unless they get other persons to help them. In the Club it is to be hoped the members will always exclude beer-drinking from the list of their amusements and excitements, but its place must be supplied by something else than merely tea and coffee or ginger-beer. Music and singing, recitations, a discussion class, concert, or other entertainment, are just what is wanted in addition to the ordinary games. But these cannot be provided every night in the week, nor would it be a healthy state of things for any Club, night after night, to be dependent on them. Promoters and managers of Clubs have, perhaps, too much forgotten that the main-stay of a Club, its backbone, should be pleasant, sociable companionship. The best room in the house should be devoted to talking (and smoking, if it be desired), not called, as we have too often seen it, ' *The Reading Room.*' Five men want a chat for one that wants to read. But in order to make men feel as much amused and refreshed there as they do in the taproom, some members or friends of the Club should introduce a little lively, entertaining conversation, whenever there is an opportunity, and not trust to its coming, at first, spontaneously, as it does under the influence of beer and ' good ' (!) fellowship at the ' public.' In Clubs that have been fortunate in getting a large number of pleasant, sociable fellows together, who all know one another, or soon become acquainted, little more in general will be requisite. But where that is not the case, or occasionally even where it is, a gentleman who, in a thoroughly unpresuming manner, with a kindly heart, drops in as a *guest*, not as an overlooker, can often set the talk a-going in a very pleasant, natural way. Perhaps he takes up a newspaper, and having read a paragraph, mentions some anecdote, or personal adventure of his own, bearing upon it, inviting his neighbour to do the same. Or he brings a map, engraving, or diagram, to illustrate events referred to in the newspapers. By the same means he may illustrate his last 'Vacation Ramble ;' or, in default of adventures of his own, he could read an extract from the ' Summer Vacation Rambles ' of some enterprising young barrister or doctor. Another evening he may bring a microscope or stereoscopes; and in one corner of the room, so that nobody need come and look unless they like, he entertains and converses with those who have not found amusement elsewhere. On one occasion a friend brings the skeleton of a bird or of the human hand, and engages those who care to join in an interesting palaver on the structure and uses thereof. Another night a bullock's eye may be dissected, and a highly amusing evening may be the result; decidedly more popular and attractive, as well as more promotive of the main object of the Club—viz., 'good fellowship'—than any amount of mere lecturing. Or a few relations from Hood's or Tennyson's poems may be welcomed, and the germ of an elocution or English literature class be sown. Then some other friend drops in now and then, and plays a game of draughts, or teaches a few members the mysteries of chess. These and a variety of similar amusements, not forced upon the members of a Club, but quietly offered in a simple, friendly way, would make all who have joined in listening or asking questions feel that they have spent a far jollier evening than if they had been fuddling and singing at the Magpie and Stump over the way.

" Our limits forbid further illustrations at present of what is meant in the foregoing letter by asking educated men to help make Working Men's Clubs attractive. The above, however, is quite sufficient to suggest a good deal more. We only beg to state, most explicitly, that all this help is recommended and supposed to be offered *only as supplementary* to what the members may do in that way themselves—never being intruded, and always being given in a thoroughly quiet, unassuming fashion—especially, also, with a view to stimulate the members to do the same sort of thing, according to their ability, among themselves. Where aid is given in this way towards making a Club-room attractive and sociable, we know by long experience that from the Land's End to John o' Groat's it will be right heartily welcomed by working men of every trade, section, and age, with an amount of gratitude and respect proportioned to the brotherly spirit in which it is offered."

CHAPTER XVII.

[The following Paper was read before the Social Science Association at
Edinburgh, in 1863, and is referred to in the one read at York, printed in
the January number of the *Working Men's Club Magazine* (p. 53). We
give a few extracts from it now, with a view rather to enforce the general
principles it advocates, and which cannot be too often urged in these early
formative days of the Club movement, than to press forward at present the
particular plan of an Industrial College. The weak point in all such
schemes for educating and elevating working men is that, in general, as
soon as they get superior culture they seek and obtain employment in
some other walk in life. This operates on the general elevation of their
class much as the desertion of an army by its officers, as fast as they became increasingly qualified to lead their men to victory, would act upon
that body. After referring to the need of the Clubs being far more than
mere antagonists to the beershop, and of their promoting higher objects,
the paper continues thus :—]

"WE must combat the apprehensions of some who would
forbid all political discussions in them, however carefully
guarded from party bitterness and unregulated licence;
against the fears of others who would forbid Trades Societies,
e.g., to hold meetings at them, or at least when their trade
might be on strike ; and against any similar misconceptions
of the broad unsectarian platform on which these Clubs
should stand—of the higher purpose they should subserve, or
of the noble and fruitful development to which they are destined to attain.

" All these petty fears and limitations would only lead to
earnest and benevolent people wasting their energies and
money on enterprises which would be sure to fail. The
working classes are not to be dealt with in this spirit, cannot
be benefited in this narrow-minded way. Such efforts will
but repeat the old story of the child planting its cut flowers
in the garden, and weeping to see them die. Or in some
cases their labours will repeat the older story of sowing good
seed, but where there is no depth of soil. These Working
Men's Clubs must have roots if they are to live and grow, and

sufficient nourishment for those roots to absorb. Friendly, Trade, and Co-operative Societies are all well rooted in the pecuniary interests of the working classes, rooted also in their class feelings, and to some extent in their brotherly sympathies. Well-intentioned people, seeing the evils of intemperance, and deploring the hardship to which working men are exposed by their dependence upon the public-house— anxious, also, to give them a little innocent enjoyment— resolve to get up something as a counter-attraction to the drinking houses, and open a Reading Room, or a Working Men's Club, then wonder and grieve that the working men don't go to it, or gradually forsake it. Now, if our experience is worth anything at all, if we have one message of any importance to deliver, it is this: That you must make the Working Men's Club movement, and must get working men to see that you are making it, a movement for improving the position and character of their whole class, for permanently raising them, socially, mentally, and morally. Nothing short of this will really interest the great mass of the thoughtful, intelligent working men of the United Kingdom, the leaders of their class; and without their hearty co-operation we shall never see these Clubs permanently take root and flourish; they will never become self-supporting; the whole enterprise will be merely a missionary effort, good as far as it goes, but lamentably inadequate and dwarfed. . . . If working men think that it is a scheme merely for petting and amusing them, just to keep them out of mischief, or to draw them into some particular church or chapel, they will have nothing to do with it, or will soon give it up. But if they see it originates in something much nobler and deeper, aims at something far higher and more enduring, be assured, that as they have welcomed and permanently established in their midst vast organizations for promoting their material well-being, so they are ready now to welcome a great organization for assisting their mental and moral elevation. Hence we must dwell on the affirmative, not on the negative side of our work—on its educational as well as on its recreational and temperance aspects; not regard Clubs merely as antagonists of public-houses, of street-corners, of idle hours, or vicious amusements; but throw ourselves, and get working men to throw themselves, heartily into these undertakings, because innocent amusement and rational recreation, music, poetry, literature, science, education of various kinds, art in its manifold forms, all help to make them more human, less animal, help to unfold their higher nature, to purify and develop some of their noblest faculties, to give them education in its truest sense, help to introduce them to their birthright as Englishmen, as citizens, and as men. There can be no question that where these Clubs are judiciously managed, where the leading operatives take them up cordially, and persons of education and refinement *of both sexes* give their cordial support, educational results of no ordinary value will follow, and the Club will do as much to supplement a miserably defective education as a wretchedly narrow home; while mental discipline, increased knowledge, light and truth, no less than harmony, beauty, and joy, will blossom and fructify in the Working Men's Club and Institute, to an extent of which at present we scarcely dare to dream. Let working men see something of these results opening out before them through the instrumentality of this movement, especially let them see how, by giving themselves up to these ennobling influences, instead of to those by which at present they are so often enslaved, they will necessarily rise in the social scale, and approximate in all respects to whatever is superior in the condition of the classes above them, and you need have no doubt of the Clubs taking root amongst them, and ultimately becoming self-supporting.

" It is, perhaps, from this point of view that we can best understand the relation of the Club to the working man's home. None will be greater gainers by the Club than children and wife, if it help the husband, father, son, and brother to become wiser and better-informed, better able to teach, as well as steadier, more provident, more courteous, more human or humane, and help them to rise mentally, socially, morally.

" ' Oh, Sir,' said a poor woman to one of the persons who went round to get members for one of the London Working Men's Clubs which we established last spring, ' if you would only get my husband to join, how happy it would make me !' Perchance, far happier than she knew.

" But we may be told that working men will not appreciate —at all events, will not lay hold of—an abstract idea like this. I may be reminded of what I urged in my paper read at the Dublin Congress, two years ago, concerning the terrible apathy of the great majority of the working classes to any efforts for their mental improvement and moral elevation. I fully admit all this, as fully as ever. Great numbers of the working classes will be deaf to appeals addressed to their need of educational improvement, and indifferent to the abstract idea of social, mental, and moral elevation. Place that idea, then, before them in a concrete form; let it bear a palpable, tangible shape. In one of the papers of the Society which I have the honour of representing officially, we have the following statement: 'Another aim of the Union will be to provide a species of Scholarship or Exhibition to some Working Men's or other College, for deserving youths who have distinguished themselves as students, or by gratuitous services of any kind, in their local Clubs. Possibly, this plan may result in the establishment of a Central Industrial College for working men, in which they could work part of their time at their own trade, and part at the studies of the College, returning after three or four years to an ordinary working man's life with increased power both to perform its duties efficiently and to assist in improving the condition of their fellow-workmen. There are various cases of men working half their time only at a particular trade. Of course, they could only be employed upon jobs not requiring immediate despatch; but in some shops and in several trades employers are glad to have men occasionally who do not require a full week's work throughout the year. The power of appointing to these Scholarships should be shared between the local Society and the Council of the Union, or the Committee of the Club might recommend a certain number from which the Council should select. In like manner, Fellowships, which were originally founded chiefly to promote that which their name imports, might be again established in connexion either with such a College or with local Clubs (perhaps with District Unions), to reward merit, not merely of an intellectual character, and in a way that should promote that brotherly helpfulness and kindly fellowship which it is a chief object of this Union to encourage. Power of appointment might be shared between the District Conferences and the Council of the Union.' If the plan received influential support, I am convinced that there are many large employers of labour who

K

would willingly co-operate in giving facilities to deserving
students for working under them on this half-time system.
Some trades, such as printing, shoemaking, tailoring, or any
other in which working men could establish co-operative
workshops, might be carried on in connexion with the College. Leaving, however, this question, I want now to prove
simply my preamble, and I submit that to induce our hard-
working brethren to aim, and to make them feel *we* are
aiming, at the gradual improvement, education, and lasting
elevation of their whole class, nothing would, probably, be
more efficacious as an external arrangement, than inviting and
assisting them to establish a Central Working Men's Industrial College or University, which should be the culminating
point, as it were, of all these various Working Men's Clubs
and Working Men's Colleges; which should stimulate,
nourish, gather up, and reward the best exertions and results
of the various local affiliated institutions, receiving from them
students, for a limited period, who should work half-time at
their trade and the other half attend classes at the University.
These young men would then return to their respective localities, after two, three, or four years, bringing with them the
culture and the tastes, the knowledge and accomplishments,
which would make them so many centres of refining and
elevating influence in their trade and neighbourhood, while
they would themselves find in the local Club the suitable
sphere and fulcrum for elevating their comrades, for correct-
ing errors, disseminating truths, breaking down various prejudices, and generally for diffusing sound knowledge, as well
as good feeling, on various important subjects among other
classes besides their own.

" The admirable efforts to establish Working Men's Colleges in London, Manchester, Ipswich, Wolverhampton,
Cambridge, and elsewhere, deserve all possible commendation
and support. But it is quite certain, first, that they very
partially succeed in really laying hold of the class they are
intended to benefit; secondly, that the subjects chiefly studied
at them by working men are those which will have a commercial value, and help them to rise in the world. Now,
both these results are, I think, to be regretted; and both, I
believe, arise partly from the necessity for working men at
present coming to study at the College only after a long and

hard day's work. The College which is now advocated would meet these difficulties. It would give a powerful stimulus to the education of working men in those branches of knowledge and of thought which do not necessarily help them to get into a counting-house or a lawyer's office, but which would help them to understand the great laws that regulate wages and capital, the great facts of their country's history, and the glorious works of their country's literature. But, while it would do this, it would also most materially promote the important object I have before referred to. A scheme of this kind would present the whole idea which I have been labouring to develop in a concrete, tangible form to the working classes of this country, and would explain, as well as attract them towards that idea more eloquently and convincingly than a thousand speeches.

" If I were asked what are the means by which I expect the working classes to be roused to take a far deeper interest than most of them do at present in their own mental improvement, such an interest as would lead them to welcome and support an educational establishment of the kind I have been describing, I should answer, Discussion Classes. Every year confirms me in the belief of their value, not only as a means of attracting and retaining thoughtful working men in the Clubs, but still more as a powerful instrumentality for stimulating both them and the younger members to read and reflect. During a protracted discussion on the American War, at a London Club, several young men who previously had scarcely read a line of any history, were engaged, night after night, in the reading-room, studying the History of America; and from the various discussions in which I have taken part with them on questions in English History, English Literature, and especially in matters connected with Political Economy, such as the relations of capital and labour, wages and strikes, I have continually witnessed how their reasoning faculties are thereby developed, their desire for knowledge awakened, the interest and candour with which they listen to arguments opposed to their own opinions, and how great are the opportunities thus afforded for men of higher culture to impart to them valuable information and sounder views, at the very moment when their interest and attention are fully roused. Education at such a time is pre-eminently 'striking while the iron is hot.' [And, as we have urged in Chapter IV., p. 146, the more educated classes would learn not a little themselves from the working men at these discussion meetings.]

" But, leaving this as a mere hint, on which time will not permit me to enlarge, allow me, in conclusion, to observe that it will perhaps be said, 'Are you not aiming at a great social revolution among the working classes? and are you not repeating the old miserable mistake of attempting to revolutionize men's characters by mere outward arrangements, to bring large masses of men within the pale of high social and moral civilization by machinery?' We believe it *is* a great social revolution at which we are aiming. We plead guilty to the charge, humbly, but most gratefully. We believe it is high time we should all unite in bringing about that revolution. It has been only too long delayed. But we should be weak and blind indeed if we thought it was to be effected merely by opening Club-houses, or even by adding to them classes, lectures, and Colleges. From the very outset of this movement, from the day when the admirable man who is the founder of Working Men's Colleges declared that those institutions must be based upon the great principle of human brotherhood, from the day when we accepted that conclusion, and resolved that these Clubs should be, not merely *places* to which men might go, but *Societies* to which they should belong, we think we have had our foot upon the Rock, and the heart of our movement animated, however feebly, by the immortal Spirit of Mutual Helpfulness and Brotherly Love. We have faith in this Spirit, and believe that it will contribute the power and secure the blessing requisite for complete and permanent success."

CHAPTER XVIII.

DISTRICT UNIONS OF CLUBS; AND CO-OPERATION BETWEEN INDIVIDUAL CLUBS.

THE union of a large number of Local Societies would be of service to each individual Society, by affording the stimulus derived from the fact of co-operation for a common object, and by placing it in a better position to meet any difficulties which may occur than could be secured by isolated efforts. Advice or mediation if required, and the benefit of experience drawn from similar Societies in union, would always be at the service of affiliated Clubs, if an active secretary could be found to devote a few hours every week to the operations of each District Union. But, of course, both he and the committee of such Union would scrupulously abstain from any interference with the local management of the Clubs, unless legitimately invited to give advice or friendly arbitration.

It is worth notice that an important benefit resulting from the establishment of Clubs will be the wider sphere of usefulness thus opened to the members. Those working men who, like our great poet, are " bent to serve their Maker and their ‹ fellow-men," will find in their Club a ready field for noble and self-denying effort. Opportunities will be thus afforded them not only for self-culture, but also for promoting the social, moral, and religious well-being of their associates, and much benevolent impulse, which is at present fruitless, will there find ample scope for its development in action. The equitable adjustment of the various problems involved in the government of these Societies will call into exercise the administrative powers of working men. But an important development of this benefit would result from the formation of District Unions in the appointment of representatives to District Conferences and Festivals, and the still larger field thus opened to those members who, by faithful service, had won the respect and consideration of the Local Societies ; it being always of primary importance for any community that there should be ample facilities for its ablest and worthiest members being recognized and employed. As *Degrees* are given by Universities for merit in intellectual proficiency, and honours granted for military, naval, and civic services to the State ; and as it is no less expedient than right to distinguish other kinds of merit and service, especially among the working classes at the present day, so the above simple and informal distinctions (rendered more or less permanent and public by registered lists) will promote an important object in addition to the direct benefit to be obtained by the proposed Conferences. This object is obtained in some Friendly Societies by the " Dispensation Board,' which forms an honourable record of those who have worthily filled offices of responsibility and distinction in the Society. The opportunities, moreover, which these representatives will enjoy of intercourse and co-operation with men of superior education and wider experience, will form of themselves a valuable training for the worthy discharge of all their social duties. It may be hoped that the increase in this class of working men throughout the country may afford an impetus to the establishment in large towns of Colleges similar to those in London and Ipswich, and, perhaps, to the establishment of the Central Industrial College spoken of in the previous chapter.

But the more immediate and practical benefits that would accrue from District Organizations are stated in the following address from the Council of the Central Society issued to the Committees of Working Men's Clubs and Institutes, on the " Advantages and Means of District Co-operation between Working Men's Clubs and Institutes ":—

" The Council of the Union, being aware that considerable benefit may be derived by the various Clubs in a district uniting to promote each other's usefulness and prosperity, in a brotherly spirit, and on the Christian principle of mutual sympathy, beg to offer the following suggestions to the managers and friends of those Societies:—

" 1st. While some Clubs are flourishing, others, within a comparatively short distance, are languishing, or even dying out, probably for want of some advice, stimulus, or assistance of various kinds, which could easily be afforded by other

Clubs, if they were acquainted with their neighbours' needs, or were invited to co-operate with them.

" 2nd. The usefulness and vigour of Clubs that *are* prospering might often be greatly promoted by occasional concerted action with other Clubs in the same district.

" 3rd. Hence it becomes important that all the Societies in a given district should be able to communicate with a common centre (either a committee or district secretary), for the purpose of giving and obtaining information and advice, and for arranging plans of mutual usefulness.

" Those plans have been carried out with great benefit in several cases already, and may be described in general terms as follows :—

" If funds can be obtained, either by forming a special District Union, and soliciting annual subscriptions, or by uniting the Clubs to some existing Association, a visiting agent should be engaged to spend his evenings in visiting the Clubs, learning their plans, wants, and capabilities, and duly reporting the information so gained to a district committee or secretary. [This plan was successfully carried out for more than twelve months in the metropolitan districts, a visiting agent being employed by the Working Men's Club and Institute Union.] But if this should not be practicable, the Secretary of the District Committee, if one be established, should endeavour to procure the same information by letter, and various means of inquiry.

" In either case, the next step should be to propose to the Committees of Clubs situated conveniently for the purpose—

" I. An interchange of friendly visits—

" 1st. For chess, draught, or bagatelle matches, in winter ; cricket and football in summer.

" 2nd. For entertainments—music, singing, recitation, &c. —the singing and elocution classes of one Club giving their services for an evening's enjoyment to the members of another Club, and at another time having the compliment returned. Or the visit might be simply an informal friendly tea-meeting for social intercourse, with any amusements provided by the entertainers.

" 3rd. For discussions on topics previously announced.

" 4th. For trials of strength and skill in athletic sports.

" II. Meetings once or twice a-year of all the Clubs in the

district, for rural *fêtes*, picnics, musical, artistic, or literary performances, for which, as well as for athletic sports, prizes might be given.

" III. Meetings of two or three Clubs for special professional entertainments, concerts, or lectures, in a hall conveniently situated for the purpose, when the expense might be too great for a single Club to bear. Expenses and profits in this case might be equally shared, or the profits given to a poor and languishing Club, to revive it. Similar arrangements might also be made for joint classes in a central spot, in cases where candidates for such classes in the individual Clubs were not sufficiently numerous to procure a teacher.

" IV. Circulating libraries might be established for the district, or Clubs might interchange a portion of their stock of books on loan for a specified time. This might be done, also, with any scientific apparatus, collections of geological specimens, of insects, botanical collections, &c.

" V. Lecturers, and persons who give musical or other entertainments, &c., might be engaged through the District Committee for a number of Clubs in succession, whose managers might desire such an arrangement. This would materially facilitate such engagements, and in case of professional lecturers would considerably reduce the cost.

" VI. The Clubs in the district might be invited to purchase jointly a good set of dissolving views, an oxy-hydrogen microscope, a powerful telescope, electrical machine, air-pump, &c., which should circulate among them in turn.

" VII. Plans might be arranged by which a member of one Club going to work for a time in the neighbourhood of another might receive a friendly welcome, and be allowed Club privileges for a specified time without payment, so long as he was a *bond-fide* member, by payment, of the first Club. An exchange, also, of the privileges of membership with neighbouring Mechanics' or Literary Institutions, perhaps at reduced rates, might in some cases be effected.

" VIII. Exhibitions of paintings, statuary, and other objects of interest, contributed on loan by members of Clubs and their friends, might sometimes be arranged, either by their jointly engaging a Central Hall for the purpose, or by having the exhibition at the rooms of each Club in rotation. Industrial Exhibitions might be organized in a similar manner. [A lady connected with the Union has kindly offered the loan of her valuable collection of water-colour drawings, &c., in the event of one or more Metropolitan Clubs arranging for such Local Club Exhibitions.]

"If these and similar plans of co-operation are energetically carried out in that brotherly spirit which is the life of Working Men's Clubs, and of the whole movement, great benefits will be conferred on all their members; and a blessing may be looked for on those who give, as well as on those who receive, these advantages."

In addition to the District Festivals mentioned in the foregoing address, probably at sufficient intervals a national gathering, similar to those of the Welsh Eisteddfods, might be advantageously held. At all these assemblies there should be musical and artistic performances of various kinds, and prizes given, instead of the mere eating and drinking, which at present constitutes the chief object of many festive assemblies, or the only amusement provided at the annual gathering of most Friendly and Trade Societies. The occasion might also be taken for conferring any other honours which the District or Central Union might desire to bestow. Athletic sports would often form a part of the programme. District exhibitions also of objects of interest connected with the geological, botanical, antiquarian, and other characteristic features of the district, would in due time grow out of this association of Working Men's Societies, and furnish during many intervening months or years additional interest for country walks or class-room labours.

It will be seen that, while isolated Clubs must be comparatively powerless in obtaining for this movement generally that wide recognition and hearty co-operation on which its success so greatly depends, the Clubs, united in District Unions and so with the Central Society, will insure an effective advocacy of their claims to public attention, and each individual Club will gain in its own locality more support, more influence, and more members, as the cause, through a powerful organized representation, grows into public favour and national importance.

It is very essential that a means of constant intercommunication should be open to the Secretaries or Managers of various Clubs, for the purpose of giving and receiving information in cases of difficulty relating either to the management or development of the Local Clubs. This can be best secured through the agency of such District co-operation with the Central Society, who can either solve the difficulty at once, from the results of their experience in similar cases, or advise reference to other Clubs which have passed successfully through the same embarrassment. Many a Club might be saved from injury or even dissolution by timely communication of its difficulties to a District Union Committee or to the Central Society.

In conclusion, as Working Men's Friendly Societies and Trades Unions are organized to promote the pecuniary well-being of their members, so these Unions of Working Men's Clubs, equally with the Clubs themselves, should be organized to promote the mental and moral welfare of the members, as well as indirectly thus to aid their social improvement. And, as we see that those Friendly Societies and Trades Unions have done much to educate working men, and to raise them from a state of stupid improvidence and indifference, or of mere animal existence, even when badly managed or aiming at hurtful ends, so we may be well assured of the immense benefit that may accrue to working men from judicious and friendly organization for worthy and elevating purposes. It is always of great value for the cultivation of men's intellectual and moral nature to unite them in organized arrangements, so long as their individual life and character are duly respected. But if both the means and the ends of such organic life are of a wise and noble character, leading up, as all things wise and noble must do, to the highest ends for which men are created, and receiving—as all such enterprizes do—the blessing of our Father in heaven, there are no limits to the beneficent results which may gradually be obtained.

APPENDIX.

PAGE 191, &c.

WORKING MEN WANT, AND WELCOME, HELP FROM GENTLE-MEN IN CONDUCTING CLUBS.

[Published as an "Occasional Paper," No. IX., by the Union, in Feb., 1866.]

THE following letters (being rejected by the *Times*) originally appeared in the *Daily News*, and the Council of the Union, cordially endorsing the views expressed in them, desire now to give them a wider circulation :—

TO THE EDITOR OF THE DAILY NEWS.

Sir,—Allow me to ask the favour of your inserting the accompanying letter, as it appears to me to deal with a very important subject in a clear and forcible manner.—I am, Sir, yours obediently,

Hagley, Dec. 13.   LYTTELTON.

" Working Men's Club and Institute Union, 150, Strand, W.C., Dec. 6, 1865.

" Dear Lord Lyttelton,—Knowing the deep interest you take in the promotion of these Working Men's Clubs, I write to ask your kind attention to some facts bearing upon your speech recently delivered at Bilston, and subsequently commented on in a leader in the *Times*.

" An earnest and hard-working clergyman, rector of a densely-peopled parish, two years ago helped a number of working men to establish a Club. He raised the requisite funds, got them capital premises, and gave them as good a start as could be desired. But his hopes have been grievously disappointed. In some respects the Club, no doubt, has been mismanaged, but in a letter to me concerning it this gentle-man says that 'the difficulty arises from the unconquerable apathy of the men themselves.' There is too much truth in this. But is it the main difficulty? Let us consider.

"Now, there are about 190 Clubs and Institutes [at present about 280 or 300] in the kingdom, with about 50,000 members, many of them doing a vast amount of good. At least three people, young or old, are probably more or less the happier and better for their father, son, or brother belonging to a Working Men's Club, and we may, therefore, safely estimate the number of persons benefited by these most useful institutions at about 200,000. Yet far too many of them are in a languishing state; and I regret to say I have now before me a list of seventeen that have been shut up during the last two years. Admission of youths, bad situation and premises, or high rents, have had much to do with most of these failures, but the great overpowering mischief in every case has been the want of a few capable and devoted men to take sustained interest in the Club, and work it efficiently. Every other hindrance (except, indeed, utterly inadequate premises in a bad locality) may be overcome, but nothing will compensate for the want of good management. Wretchedly disheartening, indeed, is that ' apathy' among the men whom the best of their own class and ourselves are trying to help; but it is not 'unconquerable' when the right men grapple with it, as every Club can prove which has been efficiently 'worked.' The fact is, we have all of us, in every rank, got to learn that *these Clubs are nothing more* (or less) *than great opportunities.* ' For the working men?' Yes, but not for them only. What I have earnestly desired to press upon your lordship's attention, as you truly said at Bilston, is, that these hard-working brothers of ours want the help of men in the classes socially above them; and I repeat what you then referred to—viz., that of all the Clubs which have been formed in the country I only know of one that has been established and has flourished without such help, including in that word much more than money aid.

"The reasons for this would fill a pamphlet. You are aware that I have given many of them in the publications of our Union, and read them before meetings of the Social Science Association. But what I want now is to bring the fact again strongly before you in order that your deserved influence in this movement may be used to make it known and felt widely. For, indeed, the need is urgent. I have pressed it on the attention of the clergyman above referred to, and reminded him that out of his large and cultivated congregation not a single gentleman has ever taken the slightest interest in the Club that he established. Possibly some would be willing to do so, but fear lest they be unwelcome intruders. I know a Club that was actually ruined because the one gentleman who had every reason for interesting himself in its affairs, and who, if he had gone among the men occasionally, would have been right cordially welcomed, stood entirely aloof lest he should seem to be unduly interfering in its management. Therefore I appeal to you to help in making English gentlemen understand there is probably not a Club in the country where they would not be welcomed if they offer friendly services in a brotherly spirit, and scarcely a Club in their own neighbourhood whose usefulness and vigour they might not greatly promote. Of course the most obvious and primary way of being useful is by serving on the committee if invited to do so. Want of time to attend properly to the business of the Club, or want of business habits, or bickerings and jealousies, are among the most frequent causes of mismanagement, and a pleasant-tempered gentleman may often render invaluable service on a Working Men's Club committee. [See also 'Facts and Fallacies, &c.,' on this point, p. 4.] But I mean a great deal more than this. Let me explain, very briefly, by referring to a sentence in the *Times'* leader [*Times*, November 14, 1865] on your speech at Bilston—viz., 'Nobody, be he rich or poor, will ever carry anything from an institution of this sort [to wit, a Club] which he has not carried there.' Now I would submit that this depends a good deal upon whom he meets at it. Certainly there is deep truth in those words so far as they may refer to the fact that we can none of us receive any good except in proportion to our capacity and disposition for receiving it. But is there not another and equally important fact—viz., that men may carry away from their Club a large amount of good which they did not bring with them, if they have met there men better and wiser than themselves? Mr. Thomas Hughes, M.P., was in the habit for some time of meeting every Wednesday evening as many of the students of the Working Men's College in Great Ormond-street as liked to come into the coffee-room for tea and chat. It requires no effort to believe, as we are told, that the men who met him felt themselves considerably the richer and happier for having done so. Gentlemen combining the qualities needful for making working men enjoy and profit greatly by their presence for an hour or two occasionally in a Club are happily not scarce in this country, though they may not be aware of their own qualifications. It is not a formal lecture that is often wanted. Pleasant, genial talk, giving information if it is asked for, but not obtruding it, with the aid, perhaps, occasionally of a microscope, or a map, a diagram, an engraving, or a book of travels, frank interchange of views in formal discussion, or mere free-and-easy chat, possibly partaking with the members in a game of chess or draughts, cricket or skittles, and athletic sports—this is the sort of thing that English gentlemen are needed to give wherever they find it would now and then be welcomed in Working Men's Clubs. The rights of the working men in their own institutions cannot be too sacredly respected. No working men will go near a Club if it isn't their own. 'We have masters all day long,' said a working man at one of our Conferences, 'and we don't want 'em at night.' But gentlemen coming to the Clubs occasionally as guests in an unassuming friendly fashion supply just the element without which the great majority of Clubs either cannot flourish or with which they will quadruple their usefulness. Your lordship must be aware how greatly the success of a public-house depends on the character of its landlord. Working Men's Clubs depend for their success, first, on their committee; secondly, on their steward; but, thirdly, on their receiving the genial, refining, amusing, and instructive co-operation of educated men, just enough raised above the rest of the members to become naturally and legitimately their leaders in the sphere of social enjoyment and intellectual progress. Not twenty per cent. of the working classes at present frequent and consistently support these Clubs. 'Make them more attractive,' they say, 'and you will find them crowded.' Exactly. But that is just where the help of the classes above the working men is needed—including in that category all who have had the means of gaining larger culture and broader views than most of the weekly-wage class, whether they be university men or tradesmen, clerks, overlookers, or professional men. If a tithe of the number of educated, self-denying persons who have thrown themselves into the work of Sunday-school teaching and similar noble agencies would now devote themselves in the right spirit to making these Clubs really attractive and useful to the working classes of the kingdom, by using all the numberless means open to them, this movement would become one of the very greatest blessings the industrial classes have ever received. Without that help it will not, cannot, altogether fail of doing immense good—but it will in many places temporarily collapse as rapidly as it has risen, and only revive again ten or twenty years hence, when a large number of the present generation of toiling workers will have passed beyond our reach to help or to hinder them.

"I beg to remain, my dear lord, with many thanks for all the valuable help you have given us, very truly yours,

"HENRY SOLLY.

"London, December 6."

PAGE 157.

PROVIDENT OR "FRIENDS OF LABOUR" LOAN SOCIETIES.

[Reprinted from the " Working Men's Club and Institute Magazine," No. 10.]

IN answer to numerous inquiries respecting the objects and working of "Friends of Labour" Loan Societies, I most respectfully make the following observations and suggestions, at Mr. Solly's request:—

Their name originated from the object for which they were established; and to carry out their original object with integrity great care should be taken to make them what they are called, "The Friends of Labour."

The great and all-absorbing question with many thoughtful working men has been for some years past, how to procure for the labourer the greatest proportion of the proceeds of his labour. In the pursuit of this study they have become impressed with the important fact that (in the present state of society, at least) labour, unaided by capital and skill, is all but valueless. To obtain the latter of these two important aids, Working Men's Clubs, Industrial Associations, Museums and Schools of Art, and properly-organized Exhibitions, are everywhere being promoted, but the former being the more attractive, and its value more easily appreciable, associations for its attainment, to the number of some thousands, have been long in operation, either in the form of Provident, Building, Land, or Loan Societies, and of this latter kind upwards of 2,000 have been established, under the denomination of "Friends of Labour."

There are, and ever have been, innumerable instances of men to whom the loan of a few pounds, and even in some cases shillings, would have been the means of stemming the tide of adversity, pay out the broker installed by an unfeeling landlord after a long illness or other serious affliction, replace their stock in trade, provide some necessary implements or materials for the performance of their daily occupation, equip a son for sea, provide a premium for an apprentice, or a capital for some young and enterprising workman. An article on Loan Societies in *Chambers's Information for the People* thus describes their constitution: "The institution called a Loan Society contemplates the same benefits to be conferred on a humbler portion of the trading class than those who resort to banks. By making small advances to such persons, it enables them to make little ventures in business, which they could not otherwise have attempted, and often sends them forward upon a career which leads to their permanent advancement in life. One might at first sight dread the effects of such anticipations of income; but, practically, the loan system, when rightly conducted, works well, and is productive of much good."

One of the greatest objections hitherto made was their being held at public-houses. An investment of 6d. weekly produced in twelve months, in an ordinary society, a gross gain of about 1s. 8d., in connexion with which were fifty-two visits to the society's *public-house* office, the lowest amount generally spent being 2d. each visit, and in the great majority of cases much more—2d. × 52 = 8s. 8d., being the expense of realising 1s. 8d. This, however, is entirely obviated by holding them at Workmen's Clubs.

The societies originally contemplated by the act were

formed for the most part of benevolent or affluent persons, who invested their money for the purpose of assisting deserving members of the industrious classes. The founders of the " Friends of Labour Association," whilst thoroughly appreciating the generosity and good feeling of the promoters and managers of these and similar institutions, believe it would far more conduce to the general well-being and future elevation of their fellow workmen, if they could be induced, and in some cases assisted, to help themselves and one another. With this view, they decided to establish a fund to lend in sums of from 10s. to 15*l.*, to those who required it, and who, by their rules, might be eligible to receive it. To entitle a man to a loan of 1*l.*, he must have subscribed 6d. per week for at least thirteen weeks, and so on in proportion—the fact of his subscribing regularly for a certain length of time being considered an evidence of character sufficient to justify the expectation of punctual repayments—not, as many have supposed, that the member's stock was to be the security for the amount lent.

The loans are granted to applicants in rotation, very few being ever refused. Persons are seldom admitted as members without good reference; except at some public-houses where the landlord starts a society for " the good of the house," recommending as *good* members every one he can draw together, the more intemperate the better for him, though these, of course, are far from being friends of labour, though falsely so denominated. Members can, therefore, safely calculate on getting loans whenever they require them.

Interest at the rate of 13 per cent. per annum is charged for the use of money lent, which, after paying all reasonable expenses, leaves about 5 per cent. dividend for the investors. Many societies profess to give much more, which is apparently effected by the members paying officers and other expenses out of their pockets once a-quarter, which enables all the profits to be credited to their account, a proceeding which often causes serious disputes, and is, at least, very unbusiness-like.

No person is allowed a second loan until the first has been regularly repaid.

In the event of any borrower wilfully neglecting to repay his loan, especially if it appears that a fraud is intended, the act provides that summary proceedings *may* be taken for the recovery of balance then unpaid, together with costs. (See 26 and 27 Vic., c. 56.) But in enforcing this power it should, and I believe generally is, borne in mind that the society is not a friend of capital, but of labour. This should be more especially considered when any one suggests the infliction of fines or other penalties for any neglect or irregularity in the repayment of loans. In the first place, if a man is poor, or in more than ordinary difficulties, it is manifestly in direct violation of the great fundamental principle of the society to in any way inflict a fine or other penalty on the man you profess to befriend. The realizing of large dividends is the business of the friend of capital.

It is, moreover, distinctly stated in the act under which they are enrolled, that it shall not be lawful for the rules of any such society to impose any fine or other penalty for any irregularity in the repayment of any loan other than by the immediate payment of the balance of the loan then unpaid.

In a useful pamphlet on reciprocal loans and the advantages of combination, by Dr. Bowkett, of Poplar, that truly earnest friend of the industrious classes, he explains how 100 men contributing 6d. per week to a common fund can borrow (and without interest) 20*l.* each, repaying the same at the extraordinarily low rate of 2s. 6d. per week, every one being accommodated in the short period of six years, and his contributions returned in about nine years from the commencement of the society. If this plan were adopted in Labour Loan Societies, workmen might soon become their own employers.

W. O. POCKLINGTON,

Metropolitan Visiting Agent (for the Union).

150, Strand, June, 1865.

PAGE 117.

CLUBS IN IRELAND.

SINCE the remarks on this subject were made on the above page, we have heard that Mrs. Crampton, widow of the late Judge Crampton, has succeeded, by dint of great and praiseworthy exertions, in procuring funds with which she has erected an excellent Working Men's Club and Institute at Bray, in Ireland. She still requires 100*l.* to complete her beneficent work, and we earnestly hope she may soon see this, the Pioneer Club of our Sister Isle, opened under the happiest auspices, and worthily valued by many of her countrymen.

PAGE 15.

WORKING MEN'S COLLEGES.

SHORTLY after the meetings referred to in page 15, the writer put the matter in the form of a pamphlet for general circulation, from which the following passages are taken :—

Working Men's Colleges: A Few Thoughts about Them.

What is a Working Men's College?

A society or corporation for systematic education, mutual improvement, and recreation, in which the benefit of working men is especially aimed at.

Why should such a Society be called a College?

Because that is a name many hundred years old in this country, and expresses better than any other a brotherhood or fellowship of grown-up persons united together for the mental and moral improvement of each and all.

Why should such Colleges be established?

Because the means hitherto adopted for carrying on the education and rational recreation of the working classes have been insufficient for that purpose.

What is the constitution and government of these Colleges?

That depends on the views of those who form the College. But the simplest plan is to have a council, consisting of the voluntary teachers and of certain persons in addition, elected annually by the rest of the Society.

This council should arrange for the classes, lectures, meetings, rational amusements, and all other plans necessary for carrying into effect the objects of the College.

There should be some small annual subscription (perhaps 2s. 6d.), payment of which, and signature of the rules, would constitute any person above a fixed age a member of the Society, with a small payment in addition for attendance on each class.

All persons forming such a College should have some voice in arranging its constitution, and in appointing the members of the council by which it is to be governed. [It would not be at all desirable, however, that the students of a " College " as distinguished from the members of a " Club " should have any share in its government until they had obtained some distinction, or passed some specified examination.]

[These suggestions were followed by extracts reprinted from the *Lancaster Guardian* of the 12th and 19th of May, 1860.]

" The subject of educational classes for adults was brought before the public of Lancaster, at the last *soirée* of the Mechanics' Institute, and on that occasion, a resolution was adopted which declared that amongst the best means to secure ' the profitable employment of the leisure hours of apprentices and artizans,' was ' especially the formation of adult classes in history, literature, political economy, and sciences generally, which persons of education are earnestly invited to assist in conducting.' This resolution evidently pointed to the institution of a similar organization to the Working Men's Colleges which have been established in some of the large centres of population, but it was conceived that some forms of entertainment might be grafted upon this organization to supply the wants of those who had been rescued by Temperance Societies from degrading habits. Perhaps we cannot do better here than submit some extracts from a correspondence which has passed between the Rev. H. Solly, of this town, and the Rev. F. D. Maurice, M.A., the zealous and noble-minded promoter of these Colleges."

" Mr. Solly writes as follows:—

" ' There are several gentlemen here interested in the education of the working classes, and who are desirous of doing something next winter to promote it more efficiently by having adult classes taught the subjects taken up by your Working Men's College. On the other hand, there are a number interested in the Temperance movement, and who are asking the question that comes now from all parts of the country, ' How are we to provide rational amusement and improving occupation of an evening for the persons whom we persuade to give up the public-house?' The Mayor has undertaken to have a meeting for conference, probably this day week, between these parties, because I feel persuaded that the two objects should be pursued by means of the *same* organization, although the men whom we want to benefit are in a very different intellectual and even moral condition. I am almost sure that the true organization for the purpose is the one you and your fellow - workers have so admirably inaugurated in London. But it is only within a very recent period that it has occurred to me that a Working Men's College was the society by which reclaimed drunkards might be suitably entertained and educated (and by which, even, drunkards might be reclaimed). I had always thought of the College merely as an institution for promoting the education of the more intelligent, skilled, and steady artizans. But you have invariably based it upon the idea of Brotherhood, and maintained that we must revert to the original fundamental conception of the College as a Society, a fellowship for mutual help in the great purpose of life—viz., education—education of the whole man, physical, intellectual, moral, and spiritual. And if this be the true idea, as I am sure it is, certainly it cannot be beneath, or wide of, the function of a Working Men's College to seek to bring within its influence the more unfortunate members of the working class, and to use such agencies as shall be suited for their less advanced or perverted condition, thus bringing them on by degrees to appreciate the opportunities of higher culture. Will you tell me if I am right in thinking, therefore, that a Working Men's College might legitimately—*i.e.*, according to its true conception, and the views of those earnest men who in various parts of the country are promoting these Colleges—have time and rooms devoted to rational amusements, chess, draughts, &c., readings of poetry and fiction, cheap concerts, recitations, &c., by way of attracting and occupying those who have hitherto spent much of their leisure time in the public-house, always of course with a view of leading them in due times and seasons to higher and more improving occupations? If this is not a work which the College can take up, then some more popular organization must be sought for; and this work will be divorced from that with which I think it should naturally be allied—viz., the education of the higher nature of man. It

will remain a function merely of Temperance Societies, which
from their narrow basis and limited aims are not competent to
perform it in a way that shall lead on to something higher and
better. Temperance Societies do not secure the co-operation
of multitudes of educated and benevolent people who would,
nevertheless, in a suitable organization work most efficiently,
both for temperance *and* education. I believe they are doing
vast good, and I have long worked with them; but for several
years past it has been evident that they needed supplementing
by some more educational agency. One of the best and
noblest things about them is the spirit of hearty brotherhood
in which they originated, and which, in turn, they have
cherished—brotherhood, not merely with the worthy and respectable, but with the degraded and fallen. The question is,
' Does the brotherly spirit of a Working Men's College go as
low as that?' You have said with deep truth that Mechanics'
Institutions have failed for want of that spirit. They have
been merely places to which certain individuals went to learn
certain lessons, or hear certain lectures, and read books or
newspapers. But if Working Men's Colleges, while aiming
to impart the highest education working men can receive, and
so taking up the functions of Mechanics' Institutions, can be
so instinct with the spirit of Christian brotherhood as to fulfil
also the functions of Temperance Societies—not by administer-
ing the pledge (although I know the immense value of the
pledge as a separate instrumentality), but by the higher and
more permanent influences of an educational fellowship in the
deepest sense of both these words—then there can be no
need of any other organization. The same card of membership which admits the sober, skilled artizan to his French or
algebra class, and the University graduate to his tutor's
chair, will also admit the bricklayer to a cheap concert, to his
newspaper and cup of coffee, or a discussion class, and will
draw the schoolmaster or busy professional man to give readings
from Shakespeare or Dickens to collegians fatigued with, or
unprepared for, severer studies. . . . If you could send
me a few lines which I might read to the meeting, saying
whether, in your opinion, I am proposing a legitimate development of the principle of the College, one that would help to
give it a wider support and more popular influence, or a dangerous and unhealthy perversion both of the principle and

aims of those who have originated these Colleges, I think it would be very useful, and I should feel deeply obliged. In the latter case we would seek for some other mode of accomplishing our object.' "

" Mr. Maurice, in his reply, said : ' I cannot see the least reason why you should not establish a College of which it shall be a main object to secure amusement and occupation for those who will otherwise frequent public-houses. The more various the methods and organization of Colleges are, provided the principle of fellowship for a moral end is kept in sight, the more is the principle likely to be recognized. The least attempt on our part, or any one's part, to prescribe a formula for Colleges, or to make ourselves into a pattern College, would be bad for us as well as for those whom we controlled. I believe there is no ambition of the kind amongst us. We shall be glad to help any who will receive our help, but we will not bind them, even if they wished to be bound. I should think you must be immeasurably better judges of what is wanted for Lancaster than we in London can be. Experience appears to show that there is a danger of Colleges or Institutes for amusements sinking into mere Concert Clubs, or Dancing Clubs. But against that you will of course be on your guard.' "

" At the Conference last week there were present the Committees of the Mechanics' Institute and Temperance Society, and others interested in the scheme under consideration. The Council Chamber was very well filled.

" The Mayor opened the proceedings, and then called upon the Rev. H. Solly, who, at considerable length, unfolded his views upon the subject. After referring to the Mechanics' Institution and the Temperance Society, he spoke of the interest which had been excited in the minds of many friends of the working men by the London Working Men's College, from the first meeting at Mr. Maurice's house, at which he had been present ; and then referred to the Working Men's Colleges which had since been established in Halifax, Manchester, Wolverhampton, Oxford, Cambridge, Boston, &c. But these excellent institutions had not succeeded in bringing working men together to the extent that was desired, and one reason he believed to be that they had not sufficiently aimed at attracting the large class who now frequent the

public-house. One of H.M. Inspectors of Schools, who had
taken a lively interest in the Working Men's College at Manchester, had recently expressed to him the same view, and
authorized him to give it as his (Mr. Morell's) conviction that
these Colleges "have not gone low enough." They had just
been compelled, he said, at Manchester, to close one of those
institutions, or rather to amalgamate it with the other, for
want of sufficient attendance. Having some doubt whether
the originators of Working Men's Colleges would consider
such a variation from their own programme as was now contemplated in the light of a development or a perversion of
their views, he had written to Mr. Maurice, who had replied
in the terms above cited. Mr. Solly therefore thought the
Temperance Society on the one hand, and the Mechanics' Institute on the other, might co-operate and form a College in
which they could combine some modes of amusement with
advanced classes, not by amalgamating the two societies, but
by friendly co-operation. He also referred to the importance
of the corporate principle, out of which all true civilization
had sprung, and upon which it was based, and he ventured
to say that working men sometimes betrayed a truer instinct
in going to a public-house for the sake of fellowship than in
simply joining classes for self-culture. In conclusion, Mr.
Solly reminded the meeting that the Temperance agitation
had begun in Preston twenty-five years ago, and he should be
glad indeed if some such development of this grand reform on
the one hand, and of the educational movement on the other,
as the one which they now sought after, should also originate
in a Lancashire town."

[At the second meeting above referred to, there were
between 600 and 700 working men present, who received Mr.
Solly's views with great heartiness, and a provisional committee was formed to which all the factories and workshops
in the town were invited to send delegates. The arguments
and views offered by that gentleman were substantially the
same as those embodied in the various subsequent papers. A
considerable number of delegates were sent, and the ultimate
result was the formation of the "Lancaster Working Men's
Mutual Improvement and Recreation Society.]

The following extracts from Mr. Maurice's noble lectures on "Learning and Working," delivered previously

to the establishment of the Working Men's College in London
in 1854, were then given in the pamphlet, and will help to
explain the objects aimed at :—
"It is unquestionably a great and blessed thing for any
learner to feel that he is not merely to get a certain portion of
information, but that he belongs to a body "—a society for the
promotion of learning. . . . "We may ask rough-handed
men who are already members of a factory [or workshop] to
become members of a College, and it is our fault if we do not
make them understand that we mean a real fellowship of
mutual learning and teaching—of actual joint workers. . . .
The words University and College point to a corporate life, not
to mere instruction. We wish to do what our fathers did,
when they provided Colleges for England as it was in those
days. . . . They educated Englishmen, to whatever class they
might belong. They matriculated [initiated] them into
societies regularly organized, that they might know they were
connected with that which is permanent, not merely with
that which is artificial and transitory—with what is human and
divine, not merely with producing and exchanging."—(*Learning and Working, pp.* 183-7. Macmillan, 1855.)
[The pamphlet concluded as follows :—]
"In further support of the foregoing remarks, we may observe the value of cordial union in a permanent society as applied to the promotion of other objects than education and
amusement — the Co-operative Societies at Rochdale and
Leeds, for instance, and the various Benefit Clubs all over the
country. Then, again, how little strength or power for permanent usefulness would be found in Christian Churches, if
the members of them merely came together once a-week to
join in worship and to listen to a sermon. But when they
form a Christian brotherhood, a true fellowship for the promotion of each other's welfare and of the great objects for
which their Church exists, they gain that wonderful power
which the genius of Wesley foresaw when he formed his
organized Societies.
"Mutual Improvement Societies are excellent things in their
way, but they do not provide that systematic teaching and
those regular classes which are needful for the real education
of working men. Moreover, it is not merely mutual teaching
which is required by them. Some working men in every

town, many in some towns, are prepared and anxious for more advanced and systematic teaching than they could afford one another; and which it is hoped persons of education would be found willing to impart, if students could be found thankful to receive it. There is the more reason to hope for this, because nothing so improves and deepens a man's own knowledge of any subject as the benevolent effort to impart that knowledge to others. Only by teaching others can we complete our own education.

" Female classes should of course be formed in connexion with these Colleges, where practicable, as they have been in cases where efficient female superintendence and tuition could be obtained.

" The advantages then to be gained by a Working Men's College over Mechanics' Institutions are *the permanent organization of learners and teachers in a brotherly fellowship for education and recreation*, attracting the humblest working man by rational amusement and instruction given in a form that he can enjoy, and inviting the more educated artizan by affording the higher culture which he requires ; while at the same time all are expected to give as well as to receive. The advantages of such an organization over Mutual Improvement Societies and Recreation Societies are the systematic and continuous instruction (and the certificates which may be given that such education has been received), as well as the provision for rational recreation, all which can be afforded in their most efficient forms only when persons of different classes and attainments unite together in friendly co-operation for these important purposes.

" Societies established merely for promoting what in itself is a most important object—viz., rational recreation, fail from not being connected with higher objects, and from not being able, therefore, to develop the brotherly and corporate principle.

" In an organization intended for the benefit of persons of all sects, and of no sect at all, it is obvious that there must be no specific form of belief put forward as the basis of the Society; but inasmuch as there can be no true brotherhood without the recognition of a common Fatherhood, and no permanent efficient organization for a moral purpose without the virtual confession of a Divine order on which all human associations should be grounded, it is believed that a Working Men's

College, without presuming to intrude upon the belief or non-belief of any person, must be essentially religious alike in its foundation, constitution, and practical working.

" Lastly, if such organizations as are now spoken of should be established throughout the country under the common name of Working Men's Colleges (which seems probable), they will derive considerable support from the common sympathies which will unite them as Colleges in the same corporate and brotherly spirit which should inspire the individual members of each College. Certificates of proficiency might be granted after annual examinations, which would have a distinctive value in various ways. Recommendations and introductions, afforded by one College, would be a ready passport to a welcome and position in another, as well as in society at large. Ultimately perhaps all the Colleges might be embraced in the higher organization of a University."

[The following interesting and able letter from one of Mr. Maurice's earliest and most efficient coadjutors, a Cambridge graduate (who afterwards joined the Council of the Working Men's Club and Institute Union) was subsequently received.]

44, Lansdown-crescent, Cheltenham, Sept. 1, 1860.

Dear Mr. Solly,— . . . I think as time goes on you will be more and more confirmed in your opinion that the name " Working Men's College " is of importance. I shall be very sorry to hear that you have been unable to give this title to your institution. None else, I am sure, so well embodies the purpose and principles which are actuating you. The word " College " has the great merit of being at once old and new. It represents the principle of union which has been at the bottom of all social progress, and at the same time challenges people's attention by the new aspect and application given to the principle. The other titles suggested seem to me objectionable on special grounds. For instance, " Working Men's Mutual Improvement Society." If a name says as much as that, it surely ought to say more—something to imply that the improvement is to be mutual not only as between one man and another of the same class, *but as between men of different classes*. Of the two, this is surely the most important kind of mutuality. It is no affectation to say that in our College at least the teachers know that the work does them as much good as it does the students. This recognition of the mutual responsibilities of various classes, separated as they have hitherto been by mere accidents of occupation and position, is the very most important business of a College. Then, again, the double title, " Mechanics' Institute *and* Working Men's Club," involves either a redundance or something like a contradiction. If the first half of the title be taken literally, it is included in the second. But custom and experience have made the words " Mechanics' Institute " mean something very different from what the originators of the Institutes intended ; and to recover or retain the essence of the *thing* they aimed at, we are almost obliged to take another *name* to mark this difference. The good done by the Institutes has been immense. The promoters of Working Men's Colleges have been the first to acknowledge this. Where they have failed, or come short of their original aims, it has been, we believe, from a want of a sufficient recognition of the great principle of human fellowship, which must be the ground of all healthy and vigorous action. We are never tired of reiterating this, because we know that the more men get to believe in it, the readier they will be to acknowledge the mutual responsibilities of various classes, and the equal right of all to whatever intellectual advantages they can get. Of this principle we mean the word " College " to be a symbol ; and no one can doubt that to have a purpose clearly symbolized in a word is a great aid towards working the purpose out. Your Institute seems to be made of materials out of which may be formed a Working Men's College more truly deserving of the name than any now existing. Its numbers are great, and it must necessarily be of greater moment to the town, as filling a larger place in comparison to the population, than any of the Colleges set up in the larger cities.—Wishing you every success, believe me to be yours very sincerely,

R. B. LITCHFIELD.

The Rev. H. Solly, Lancaster.

PAGE 125.

"DRUMMED OUT" OF A TRADE SOCIETY.

Since the foregoing page was written we have heard from the artizan there referred to that quite recently no less than three Upholsterers' Trade Societies in London were being removed from public-houses. Courage !

PAGE 144.

A FEW WORDS TO THE MEMBERS OF WORKING MEN'S CLUBS
IN NORTH, EAST, AND NORTH-EAST LONDON, ON SUBUR-
BAN MUSEUMS OF SCIENCE AND ART.

FRIENDS,—On the 6th May last, a meeting was held at the South Kensington Museum, at the summons of Lord Granville, the President of the Committee of Council on Education, to consider how the temporary iron building of that museum might be made use of for the establishment of one or more Suburban Museums of Science and Art.

Lord Granville stated at this meeting that the time having come for replacing the iron building in which the South Kensington Collections had been placed by an erection of a more permanent character, the Department of Science and Art had thought that these materials* might be distributed among some three or more of the London districts, with the view of enabling the inhabitants to establish local museums like the one at South Kensington. He thought that such institutions should be multiplied so as to afford enjoyment and instruction to all classes—more widely than could be obtained from one single institution. The Committee of Council on Education had therefore invited the representatives of the London districts and others interested in this object to attend the meeting, with the view of ascertaining what the different districts would do and what they wished done ; whether sites would be offered ; what money would be raised, and, gene-

* The building is 226 feet long by 126 feet wide, made up of three parallel ranges. It originally cost 12,000l.

rally, what steps would be taken to turn the Government offer to account.

The meeting was well attended, and the great importance of the establishment of district museums for the benefit of the working classes was urged by representatives of the southern, eastern, north-eastern, and north-western districts. The Rev. Newman Hall, among others, stated that it was impossible to contend against the demoralizing and debasing tendencies of the public-house, unless there was something of this character to attract the great mass of the working population in their hours of leisure, more especially in the evenings. Mr. Benjamin Lucraft, cabinet-maker, as representative of a meeting of operatives at Hoxton, showed how urgently necessary it became, when our markets were open to the whole world, that the working men of England should have the opportunities of improving their taste which foreign operatives possessed; that at present for want of such local museums, they were competing with those workmen at a disadvantage, and that a single museum at the extreme south-west of London could not supply what was required. Lord Granville, in concluding the proceedings, expressed his entire concurrence in these views, and stated that a period of six months would be given to the inhabitants of the London districts to mature their plans and submit definite proposals to the Department of Science and Art. At the end of that time the Department would consider in what manner the present building should be distributed among the respective claimants, according to the plans submitted by them.

Now, I have been asked by some working men of the north-east of London to lay this brief statement before the members of Working Men's Clubs and Institutes in that district. They think that the operatives of every district ought to be up and doing in this matter, and they wish that their district should do what it can. Some time ago a " North-East Working-Class Museum Committee " was formed, for the purpose of bringing this important question before the people of that part of the town, but the members of this committee have not had the means or time to organize public meetings, and consequently but little progress has been made. It has therefore been suggested that there should be a combined conference of the members of Working Men's Clubs in the north-east of London to meet a deputation from the committee just named. The Essex-road Club being considered conveniently central for such a meeting, I was requested to write to the Secretary of that institution, to ask the favour of their lending their hall for the proposed meeting. They have very kindly and promptly granted the application, and the proposed meeting will therefore be held at the Essex-road Club, 1, Tufnell-place, Islington, on Wednesday evening, November 8, at eight o'clock.

If I am asked why the members of Working Men's Clubs and Institutes should more than others be asked to enter into this movement for the establishment of local museums, I would reply as follows : The object in view is one which deeply concerns the interest of the skilled operatives of this country. They form a body too numerous and scattered to be addressed *en masse ;* and to influence them, therefore, in any question of this kind, access must be had to those bodies and fraternities which, more or less, represent them. Now, Trades and Benefit Societies are formed for special objects, which are altogether different from that now before us. But in the Working Men's Clubs and Institutes I think we have an organization peculiarly fit to deal with such questions. These societies represent an effort on the part of the working classes for the amelioration of their moral, intellectual, and social condition. They have been set on foot by the " representative men " of their order, for the purpose of enabling themselves and their brethren to find the means of amusement, refreshment, social intercourse, and organization for Trades or Provident business, without being obliged to resort to public-houses for these objects. I think the members of these Clubs and Institutes will take all the more interest in them, if they can make them the basis of movements like the one which forms the subject of this circular. The working classes want a machinery by which they can combine for purposes of general interest not connected with any party ; and it seems to me that this machinery is to be found in the Clubs. If the members can thus find work to do for their class, these institutions will assume a new value in their eyes ; and who so fit to take the lead in any movement affecting the general welfare as the men who have had the determined courage to break down the old public-house life and adopt the Clubs instead ?

In the next place I may be asked—Why should *working men* be called upon to take an active part in this movement for the establishment of museums of science and art in the London districts? That question was well answered by the Rev. Newman Hall and Mr. Lucraft, at the meeting which I have referred to at the beginning of this paper. It was well answered, too, by Mr. Layard, at the *conversazione* in the Agricultural Hall, on the 20th September last, to which the members of the London Clubs were invited specially to hear the member for Southwark on this subject. Let me try, in the compass of a few lines, to state why the working men should take up this question. It appears to me that those in authority are much more likely to do what is wanted, and to to be supported in what they do by the House of Commons, if the working classes make their voice heard. Otherwise, people will say that the working class take no interest in the matter, and either nothing will be done, or something different from what is wanted. This establishment of local museums of art is required by the interests of the skilled operatives of the country, and therefore they should take a share in the work, that it may be done in the right way.

The work is one of no small consequence. Under the system of free-trade and open markets which is gradually being adopted by all nations, a great industrial competition is opened for the manufacturers and workmen of Europe. The countries which can combine most skill, taste, and industry will win in this race. The wonderful progress we have made since the Exhibition of 1851 shows what we *might* do if our people had the advantages which the people of the Continent possess in the shape of Museums of Art.

The favourable report made upon our art-manufactures in 1862 by the French Commissioners, and the increased demand for them in the foreign markets, as mentioned by Mr. Layard, afford striking proofs of what we can do. But those who have asked me to draw up this circular mentioned some equally striking facts which tell just the other way, showing that in many Fine-Art Trades, foreign competition has, quite recently, driven home-productions out of the market. What else could be expected? Though the South Kensington Museum and its Schools, with the Schools of Art which have been established all over the kingdom, have done wonders for

the national taste, our workmen are still at an enormous disadvantage as compared with foreign workmen. The latter
have had access to beautiful objects of art in museums and
public places for generations past. They have been *nursed*
upon art and taste. Our people have only *now* had these
advantages placed within their reach, and on a very small
scale. To place them on a level with their foreign competi-
tors, they ought to have Museums of Art multiplied, not only
in London, but in all our great manufacturing towns. To
the great mass of the workmen in London, South Kensington
is a closed building. They must have museums within easy
reach for them to visit every week, and open in the evening
as well as in the day-time. It will not be difficult to make a
beginning in each of the great manufacturing districts of
London. The proposed break-up of the Iron Buildings at
South Kensington affords the opportunity. When the
museum has been once begun, duplicates from the Government museums, from the private museums of men of wealth,
and from manufactories, will soon find their way to the new
institutions. In time, lectures and classes will be established
in connexion with these collections, in order that there may be
systematic instruction in art.

There will be a secondary result attained which is of no
mean importance. Of all people in the world none more
require the means of access to the innocent and elevating
enjoyment to be derived from works of beauty, than the hard-
worked dwellers in our crowded, gloomy English towns.
Far more do they require it than their brethren in the gay
cities of the South, where earth, air, and sky alike teem with
beauty and exhilarate the heart. To the absence of the means
of such enjoyment as would be afforded by such museums we
may ascribe much of the intemperance, which is so great a
source of misery and crime. Music-halls and public-houses
will not be resorted to as they are now, with a fatal effect
upon the habits and character of our people, when they have
something better to go to in their hours of leisure. Give
them rational and elevating means of enjoyment, and those
that are unworthy and degrading will, in a great measure, be
abandoned.

In the above remarks I hope I have given the members of
Clubs and operatives generally some good reasons for attend-

L

ing the proposed meeting at the Essex-road Club, on Wednesday, the 8th November.—Yours faithfully,

HODGSON PRATT,

A Member of the Council of the W. M. C. and I. Union,
and Chairman of its Executive Committee.

[A committee was formed to carry out the important objects
above stated, and an enthusiastic public meeting was subsequently held; but the whole enterprise fell through at last for
want of its receiving the support of men with sufficient leisure
and public spirit to carry it on.]

PAGES 145-6.

CENTRAL WORKING MEN'S HALL AND CLUB, IN CONNEXION
WITH THE WORKING MEN'S CLUB AND INSTITUTE UNION.

*Appeal from Lord Brougham (President), the Duke of Argyll,
the Earl of Lichfield, Lord Lyttelton, Hon. W. Cowper, M.P.,
A. H. Layard, Esq., M.P. (Vice-Presidents).*

150, Strand, June, 1866.

THE President, Vice-Presidents, and Council of this Society
have long felt convinced that the important objects which they
have in view would be materially promoted by the establishment in the metropolis of a Central Working Men's Hall and
Club, and by the possession of more suitable premises for their
own immediate work. In fact, it has become evident that,
otherwise, this remarkably interesting social movement will be
seriously checked and stunted. Several influential meetings
of the Council have strongly recommended steps to be taken
at once for accomplishing the object, and it was specially
advocated at the recent Public Dinner of the Society by the
Chairman and other speakers.

A place where all persons interested in Working Men's
Clubs and Institutes might interchange, occasionally or in
periodical meetings, information, experience, and advice, is
much wanted; the present premises of the Union having

proved far too small and inconvenient, not only for that purpose, but also for its ordinary work.

Rooms have had to be hired several times, at a considerable expense, and even then have failed to answer the purpose.

The advantages resulting from the buildings possessed by the Royal Institution, the Society of Arts, the Sunday-school Union, &c., afford some indication of the benefit that would accrue to the regular income of this Society (which at present is utterly inadequate to its work), as well as the help that would be given to the movement generally, by its possessing suitable head-quarters. New premises of some kind being essential, it is most desirable that these should be combined with other important objects.

Central Working Men's Club.

One of the most important of those objects unquestionably is to establish a Central Working Men's Club, which should effect not only all the beneficial purposes of such institutions in the highest possible degree, but which should thereby serve as an example or model of what Working Men's Clubs and Institutes in many respects are intended to be, the important purposes they are meant to serve, and the good they may accomplish, especially for the younger men who may seek education.

Mr. Solly has communicated to the Council his strong conviction of the duty of transferring to the management and development of such a Club and Institute a considerable portion of the time he has hitherto devoted to the ordinary work of the Society, feeling convinced that this alone *would enable him to show in a practical manner the real value of Clubs to the highest welfare of the working classes*, and form a key-stone to the work in which he has long been engaged. The Council know that several of the leading operatives of most mark and talent among their class would gladly take the opportunity of uniting with him and others in working out this interesting experiment.

Central Working Men's Hall.

One of the greatest recommendations of Working Men's Clubs and Institutes is the opportunity they afford the *members of different ranks of the community* for becoming better acquainted with each other's aims and convictions, and more united in feeling.

A great step would be taken in that direction if a *Central Hall* were established in the metropolis in connexion with the proposed Central Club. The Hall and Club together would form a common meeting-ground, where members of Working Men's Clubs and representative men of all classes and interests —those who study our social problems, and those who experience their working practically—might meet for conferences both by lectures and in discussion meetings, on those great social and political questions which concern all good citizens alike. Employers and employed might meet there on neutral ground to arrange their differences ; and men eminent in various walks of life could there impart to working men the knowledge and tastes which their greater opportunities had enabled them to acquire. We believe the benefit in such cases would be *mutual.*

Permit us to request your perusal of Mr. Solly's letter, and of further details, with several interesting extracts bearing upon this subject, to be found below.

The Council would be glad either to build or to purchase suitable premises. A site and also buildings have been already offered them, well adapted to the object, *but these will soon be disposed of unless applied for at once.* In either case, they estimate, from carefully-prepared calculations, that a sum of about *Twelve Thousand Pounds* will be requisite to accomplish the object satisfactorily, and it is felt that it would be easier to raise this sum, once for all, than to collect permanent *annual subscriptions* for the rental of premises. The Council would, however, be glad to receive donations in the shape of three or four yearly instalments, if more convenient to the donors. As to the expense of maintenance and current charges, they feel convinced, so great is the want of Halls for public meetings, that an income might be obtained from letting, such as would more than cover the expense of maintenance, &c.

We have only to observe, in conclusion, that although the undertaking now proposed is not only in perfect harmony with the general objects of the Union, but is pre-eminently calculated to promote them, the funds raised in connexion with this scheme will be kept quite distinct from its general funds.

If, however, it should be thought expedient at any future time to amalgamate the two funds, this could be agreed to at a meeting to which all contributors would be summoned. On behalf, therefore, of the Vice-Presidents and Council, we respectfully and earnestly solicit your kind assistance by a donation towards the fund for purchasing or building suitable premises for the objects in view.

H. BROUGHAM, *President.*

ARGYLL; LICHFIELD; LYTTELTON; } *Vice-*
WILLIAM COWPER; A. H. LAYARD, } *Presidents.*

Letter from the Rev. H. Solly (referred to above).

"To the Council of the Working Men's Club and Institute Union.

"Gentlemen,—Referring to what has already passed between us in regard to the need of a Central Working Men's Hall and Club, permit me now to repeat my strong conviction that it is essential to the success of the great movement you are guiding that we should be speedily put in possession of the necessary premises. I see no possibility of the satisfactory prosecution of our work, nor, indeed, of my continuing to prosecute it in connexion with the Union, unless we not only obtain such premises, but obtain them before the opportunities now offered us shall have passed away.

"In endeavouring to rouse the working classes to form and support these Social Clubs and Institutes, my object, as you are well aware, was not merely to help them to obtain amusement and places of meeting free from temptation, but to help them, in various ways, to live a higher and more manly life; to obtain for them that larger culture to which many among them are now aspiring, and to make both their work and their play nobler. In the quotations I send from Mr. Gladstone and Mr. Grote, and in Miss Swanwick's and Mr. Neill's letters, you will find eloquently expressed the views I have long entertained as to the need of bringing those influences to bear upon the working classes of this country, which such a Hall and Club in London alone could supply. It is true that, alike in Greece and in Italy, we have seen how impotent the highest art and the noblest poetry are to preserve a nation from the deepest corruption. I know well that far Higher influences than these are requisite to save from destruction, or to unfold in its perfection, the life of a nation. But I am equally convinced that Christianity demands the loyal service of Art and Poetry, as well as of Science, Commerce, and Inventive Genius, for the full establishment of her kingdom, and for the overthrow of all the powers of Evil which resist her sway. The purposes of God require for their accomplishment the employment of *all* the beneficent agencies He has graciously privileged us to use.

" By the co-operation—which I have reason to believe would be willingly given—of persons eminent in different ranks of society and in various departments of culture and information; by the help of experience gained from our being at the centre of the movement, as well as by my own exertions, I am convinced we might have an institution which would be a signal blessing, not only to those who belonged to it, but indirectly to the whole of the working classes of the kingdom. Those who gave such help would be even greater gainers than those who received it.

" If any doubt exists as to the desire of the leading artizans of London for interesting information, I may refer to the remarkable demand among them for tickets to attend the scientific lectures delivered to the working classes at the Hall in Jermyn-street during the winter months, under the arrangements of the Department of Science and Art. Surely it cannot be less inportant to offer them first-class instruction in History, Literature, and Political Economy than in Material Science; while undoubtedly these subjects would be regarded by them as even yet more interesting. And although the Council, without similar assistance from Government, could not hope to engage the regular professional services of such eminent men as have given courses of scientific lectures in Jermyn-street, there is little doubt that men of the highest eminence in various departments would willingly afford occasional assistance towards bringing the knowledge, genius, and culture of the more privileged classes of this community to benefit the toiling hand-workers of the metropolis.

" The Social Meetings held last year, and renewed this spring, under the auspices of our Society, although falling far short of what might be accomplished with more suitable accommodation and uniform arrangements, sufficiently indicated how valuable such meetings in our own premises would be. *Conversaziones* and other interesting entertainments, to which working men could bring their wives and daughters, could also be held there; and recreation of a higher kind than is generally within their reach might be made available for the working classes generally. Meetings, also, could be held there for the reading of essays written in competition for prizes offered by the Council, or by other friends, for Chess and Draught Matches, and for periodical exhibitions of works of art, art-workmanship, &c.

" In regard to the value of such a Club to the general work of the Union, I may also mention that those persons who are interested in our movement are constantly resorting to the office of the Union in London, for the purpose of learning the best mode of making these Clubs successful, and of being directed to what are considered the best of the London Clubs, that they might see their practical operations. Nothing would so effectually give such persons a thorough knowledge of the best way of accomplishing their object as the sight of a "Model" Club at actual work, and which would especially show how these institutions are to be maintained in efficient working order. Working men coming up from the country would find there a temporary home, and pleasant fellowship, of a most valuable character.

" I entirely concur in the remark made in one of the following extracts as to the importance of not leaving this undertaking until the London working men shall take it in hand, themselves alone, without the sympathy and co-operation of persons socially and educationally above them. That would be a result almost as much to be regretted as the opposite error of our attempting to establish a Working Men's Club and Institute without prevailing on working men to take a leading part in its management. But let me be allowed to add one word of a personal character, and to say how earnestly I desire that this enterprise may also not be deferred, through any unnecessary delay, until I myself shall be prevented from devoting to it any remaining years or strength reserved for me. Should I succeed in procuring, by *any* instrumentality (though I trust it may be in connexion with this Society), the means of working such a Central Club and Hall, I should spare no time and effort to make it as fruitful of blessings to the working classes as their warmest and wisest friends could desire.—I am, Gentlemen, yours very faithfully,

"HENRY SOLLY."

___

Letter to Mr. Solly by a member of the Council, Miss Swanwick, the Translator of "Æschylus"—a lady who has laboured for years in practical efforts to accomplish what she here recommends.

1, High Wickham, Hastings, May 7.

Dear Mr. Solly,—* * * * From my country retreat I have followed with interest the proceedings of our Society. I am particularly pleased to see that the conferences in Exeter Hall have been renewed, and am sorry that I am not able, as last year, to be present. Though absent in person, I am with you in spirit, and I cannot resist troubling you with a few suggestions with reference to the proposed Hall, an object in which I have always felt a very warm interest. I was, however, decidedly opposed to taking any permanent building last year, because it appeared to me that the objects to be attained were not then distinctly realized, and that it would be a cause of regret to have encumbered the Society with the possession of unsuitable premises. Now the time seems to me to have arrived for carrying out the project on a truly noble scale, and when in my solitude I realize the grand national ends to which it may be made subservient, I cannot but hope that steps may be taken at once towards its realization.

It seems to be universally recognized that some agency is wanted to counteract the tendencies of our modern civilization to separate society into distinct, and, too often, antagonistic classes—a result fatal to the highest interests of the community —and that for this object some common meeting-ground should be provided for the free interchange of thought between those endowed with leisure and educational culture, and those trained chiefly in the school of toil.

It is obvious that this object cannot be attained, except to a very limited extent, by the establishment of Clubs alone ; some supplementary agency is needed to afford an opportunity of occasional personal communion between the members of West End Clubs and members of Working Men's Clubs, and where by a kindly interchange of thought, and by association in common objects, they may learn to cherish feelings of reciprocal consideration and regard. The want alluded to is not altogether met by the Social Meetings in Exeter Hall, which, valuable as they are, are necessarily of a temporary character, embracing only the one element of *discussion*, but affording no opportunity for combined action. The proposed Hall would, I believe, not only meet the case, but be subservient also to many other important objects, besides being a grand school of social and political science, where, through the medium of lectures and discussions, all classes alike might derive instruction and improvement, an object peculiarly important when we consider the political tendencies of the age. It might also be made a fine school of *art*, thus supplementing our Schools of Design, the objects of which are almost purely technical. This object might be obtained by occasional exhibitions of first-class works of Art, accompanied, when suitable, by exposition from those really competent to instruct in such matters, pointing out the principles which underlie all art, and illustrating the connexion which obtains between the several members of the sisterhood— poetry, music, painting, &c. Much might thus be done to elevate the taste of the working classes, and to bring into closer union the spheres of utility and beauty—an object the realization of which, we have the highest authority for saying, is of extreme importance on grounds of commercial policy, as well as of moral improvement.

I will not dwell upon the numerous other purposes, *national* and *international*, to which the Hall might be made subservient, and the importance of which can hardly be overestimated. * * * * When I remember the munificence displayed by Mr. Peabody, in ameliorating the physical condition of the London poor, I cannot but think that many of our noblemen, endowed with wealth and large hearts, would gladly come forward to realize a scheme which would be an immense boon to the more intelligent among the working classes. When Halls are regarded simply as pecuniary speculations, the proprietors imagine themselves constrained to adapt their entertainments to suit the taste of all classes, and thus good music and poetry are often associated with much that is of a low and injurious character. The want of Halls for various social purposes is, I believe, so much felt by working men, that, with their growing wealth and intelligence, if no steps are taken to supply the deficiency, they will probably, ere many years are over, combine and erect them for themselves. Not only would they thus lose the immense advantage of association with men of higher culture than their own, whose co-operation, save in exceptional cases, they would not be able to command, but accomplishing their objects without the assistance of men of higher social position, a proud feeling of isolation would be generated, and the gulf between the upper and lower classes of society, which is already to be deprecated, and which the proposed Hall would tend to bridge over, would be irretrievably widened and deepened. * * * *

The grand, underlying idea which gives significance to the undertaking is the illustration which it will afford that the English aristocracy and gentry recognize and accept their high and legitimate function as leaders of the people, not only in arms, but in everything which tends to elevate and refine the national character and taste. Viewed under this aspect, it may be regarded as the inauguration of the reign of love and mutual help between the different classes of society.

Should Halls, on the proposed principle, as supplementary to Clubs, be erected not only in London, but in other large towns, a step would thus be taken towards the formation of permanent galleries of modern art, in which local talent and even the first-class artists of the day, in whatever material they may work— oil, water-colour, or marble—should be adequately represented. Such permanent galleries (whether connected with the Halls in question or not) could not fail to exert a beneficial influence on Art; they would tend to impart a more national character to it, and thus counteract the trade element which is beginning to invade its province.

Occasional loan exhibitions of the works not only of ancient but of modern painters, which it would be in the power of the aristocratic and wealthy members of the Society to command, would be a great boon to the working men, especially in a situation very generally accessible.

I had no intention, when I took up my pen, of writing this long communication. In solitude, however, we are apt to indulge in dreams; if mine is an idle one, I can only apologize for having trespassed so long upon your time, and with best hopes and wishes, I am, very sincerely yours,

A. SWANWICK.

In the admirable address given by the Right. Hon. W. E. Gladstone, M.P., at Burslem, October 26, 1862, the following passage, referred to above, forms a striking comment on the proposed undertaking:—

"Of imagination, fancy, taste, of the highest cultivation in all its forms, this great nation has abundance ; of industry, skill, perseverance, mechanical contrivance, it has a yet larger stock, which overflows our narrow bounds and floods the world. The one great want is to bring these two groups of qualities harmoniously together."—*Wedgwood.*

In referring to this passage in Mr. Gladstone's address in the introduction to her translation of "Æschylus, &c.," Miss Swanwick continues thus :—

"I believe that in poetry will be found one of the missing links through whose agency this alliance between the spheres of beauty and utility is to be consummated. Milton speaks of 'the glorious, the magnificent uses which may be made of poetry, both in divine and human things ;' while Shelley characterized it as 'a fountain for ever *flowing with wisdom* and delight.'

"It becomes, therefore, a question of deep national interest to consider by what agencies these renovating and purifying influences may be diffused and brought home to the heart of this great nation. From Greece, the fountain of all instruction in matters of art, we may, perhaps, take a hint as to one large and important department of national education.

"In this connexion I am tempted to quote a passage from Grote's 'History of Greece,' where, after alluding to the abundance in all the productions of the tragic muse at Athens, he proceeds :—

" ' All this abundance found its way to the minds of the great body of the citizens, not excepting even the poorest. So powerful a body of poetic influence has probably never been brought to act upon the emotions of any other population; and when we consider the extraordinary beauty of these immortal compositions which first stamped tragedy as a separate department of poetry, which gave to it a dignity never since reached, we shall be satisfied that the tastes, the sentiments, and the intellectual standard of the Athenian multitude must have been sensibly improved and exalted by such lessons. The reception of such pleasures through the eye and the ear, as well as amidst a sympathizing crowd, was a fact of no small importance in the mental history of Athens. It contributed to exalt their imagination, like the grand edifices and ornaments added during the same period to their Acropolis.' "—*Grote's History of Greece.*

Extract from Letter to Mr. Solly, referring to Mr. Gladstone's Address, by W. M. Neill, Esq., one of the Vice-Presidents and best friends of the Society.

* * * " The erection of your Central Hall would be one practical response to this eloquent call—one important step in this work in which it falls to you to take a leading part—the elevation of the mental and moral nature of working men. None will deny that this work is vast enough to call forth your energy—that it is, indeed, the pressing want of the day—the only means, perhaps, by which England, with her small extent of territory, and necessarily limited population, can be kept at the head of the nations. How was it, let me ask, that ancient Greece with her handful of people filled so large a space in the world's history, if not by the cultivation, physical, mental, moral, and especially æsthetic, not of the upper class alone, but of the mass of her citizens. Is it not a reproach to England that we should be so far behind heathen, and I may add Catholic countries, in this respect ? . . ."

PAGE 110.

THE WHITTINGTON CLUB CONFERENCE.

The discussion at the conference in question arose out of a paper written by Mrs. Bayly, on " The Moral Aspects of Workmen's Halls and Clubs." Mr. Varley urged the necessity of exerting Christian influences in them if they were to be successful. Mr. Turley, of the Soho Club, thereupon protested against their being used as a means of proselytizing; and Sir Frederick Grey, President of the St. Martin's Club, having been alluded to, observed that "he quite agreed with the last speaker, that anything of the kind would be fatal to the existence of Clubs. No one would think, he hoped, that he was excluding religion, or throwing difficulties in the way of the working classes becoming religious, by what he said; but in his opinion the Club was not the place for the carrying out of religious objects. They were formed for other purposes. That they would minister indirectly to the moral and religious welfare of the people, he could not doubt; but he could as little doubt, indeed he was completely satisfied, that if religion were avowedly introduced, it would do mischief."

The CHAIRMAN (Lord Lyttelton) then made the following excellent observations: "He said that there was evidently some confusion, and he wished to draw attention to a manifest distinction between what a Club could and should do as a Club, and what the individual members might do. That the members should have decided religious convictions was most desirable; and the very fact of their being actuated by such convictions could not be without some effect; but to call that proselytizing would be absurd. If it was proselytizing, no one could help it. By his life and conduct, every such person was inevitably proselytizing to a certain extent. It was, however, a fundamental point in Working Men's Clubs, and, indeed, in all Clubs, that religious uniformity was excluded from consideration in connexion with membership and management, and he would point out that they must exclude either certain subjects or certain persons. For his own part, he rejoiced to see persons of the same religious opinions banded together to carry out their views; but he also rejoiced that men could meet and work together irrespective of religious differences. He desired to see both, and he saw no objection to either in its proper place. No one would imagine, he supposed, that if the promoters of benevolent enterprises were not actuated by religious or high moral motives, their work would be better done, or more successful for that fact.

". . . Mr. SOLLY said that while all felt the importance of not obtruding religion and teetotalism on a Club, all, doubtless, would wish that the higher good might be obtained. If the members of any Club wished to have a Bible-class or a tee-total meeting, by paying rent for a room in it they abstained from compromising the Club as such, and at the same time afforded an opportunity to all the members to attend to such subjects.

" The Earl of LICHFIELD said that the discussion had taken him by surprise. He could appeal to every document pub-lished by the Union, and ask whether anything had ever been said which, fairly construed, could be regarded as indicating a wish to promulgate or to discuss any particular religious views, or even Teetotalism. Everything that had been said or printed by the Union showed that such a course was as far as possible from their intention. . . . He approved of Mr. Solly's suggestion, that by there being a room in the Club hired for the purpose, certain topics could be discussed which it was desirable should be discussed, but which the Club, as a Club, could not touch. Perhaps a resolution re-commending the plan might be adopted. . . . It was ulti-mately agreed that Mr. Solly's suggestion would do good ser-vice without being embodied in a definite resolution."

At the same conference, a valuable paper on

" *Trades Institutes*,"

by Mr. Pocklington, was read, after the reading of which Mr. SOLLY drew attention to the fact that this plan was one of the first with which he was acquainted for bringing masters and men together in friendly and useful relations within one Institute. A somewhat similar plan had been brought before him a few weeks ago by some of the masters and journeymen bakers of the metropolis. But Mr. Pocklington's idea was more com-plete, and embraced a higher range of objects. He (Mr. Solly) was inclined to believe that in trades requiring special scientific instruction—such as the dyers, also in trades *sui generis*, such as the bakers—there was clearly a need, at all events room, for a special Trades Institute, in addition to an ordinary Working Men's Club and Institute.

" Mr. CONOLLY decidedly objected to the plan, which he thought would interfere with legitimate Trades Societies. He believed the time had not yet come when the masters and men could meet in this way.

" The Earl of LICHFIELD expressed his opinion that the idea was exceedingly interesting, and deserved full consideration.

" Mr. BAINBRIDGE stated that, several years ago, in his trade (the upholsterers) they had formed a Trades' Institute with very beneficial results. It embraced most of the objects referred to by Mr. Pocklington, but did not include any plan for the meeting of masters and journeymen.

" Mr. POCKLINGTON replied to Mr. Conolly's objections, and specially dwelt upon the value of the Conciliation Councils, referred to in his paper, as a means of preventing strikes and lock-outs. These Councils had been found to be of great value on the Continent."

We strongly recommend a careful perusal of the whole Report of the Conference, from which the foregoing extracts are taken. It may be had at the Office of the Society, 150, Strand, price 6d.

PAGE 119.
SUPPORT GIVEN BY THE PRESS.

IN speaking of the rapid extension of the movement, special acknowledgment should be made of the hearty and invaluable support given to it by most of the London and Provincial newspaper press, representing all shades of political and religious opinions.

The value of the help thus given has been simply incalculable; and that a movement of this nature should, for the most part, have been thus warmly promoted, is no slight testimony to the high character of our national press.

Just as we are going to press, we hear from Hobart Town that another Club has recently been opened there.

PAGE 75.
ST. JAMES AND SOHO CLUB.

SINCE the foregoing account was written, we have heard that this Club has just been enabled, by the kind assistance of Mr. Hoare, to obtain far better premises than their present, and which seem in every respect admirably adapted for their requirements. They hope to move into them in the course of two or three months, so that about Christmas-time they will probably be delighted to receive visitors in their new abode, and will show, we trust, what a Working Men's Club and Institute ought to be. They will then be found at the corner of Richmond-street, Rupert-street, Haymarket.

PAGE 117.

STATISTICS AND RESULTS.

The number of Working Men's Clubs and Institutes of the existence of which the Council are at present aware, is *two hundred and sixty-two.* But as they are frequently hearing accidentally of the establishment or existence of Clubs previously unknown to them, these figures must be taken only as an approximation to the truth. Judging by experience, the number actually now in operation would be about *two hundred and eighty, or three hundred.*

According to Returns received from 115 Clubs, the number of members varies from 1,312 and 1,000 down to 27, giving an average of 171 members to each Club. This is an increase on last year, when the average was 152 for each Club. If the same average be taken for those Clubs that have not sent in returns (and some of the Scotch Clubs, which are among the latter, have very high numbers), we have a total of about 44,058 men belonging to the Clubs whose existence is known to the Council.

Of the 115 Clubs sending Returns, *sixty-nine* report themselves as *self-supporting,* or very nearly so ; and of these *fifty-three* are entirely self-supporting. This is a much larger proportion than that of last year. If there is the same proportion among those that have not sent in returns, we should have a total of about 162 Clubs self-supporting, or very nearly so, at the present time.

In these 115 Clubs sending Returns there have been one hundred and fifty-two Educational *classes* in operation during the past winter. These, however, are to be regarded as a subsidiary, though very important, element in the operations of the Clubs.

Thirty Clubs report that *Provident Societies* of various kinds have either been formed by their members, or hold their meetings at the Club. Nearly all state that they have had various *Lectures and Entertainments* during the six winter months, amounting to 250 Lectures and 1,096 Entertainments for the 115 Clubs; or probably 622 Lectures and 2,761 Entertainments for the whole number of Clubs and Institutes during the last winter. The number of books in the various libraries of the Clubs amounts to 51,436. The *Games*, &c., provided include Chess, Draughts, Dominoes, Tactics, Bagatelle, Skittles, Bowls, Boxing Gloves, Gymnastics, Quoits, Cricket, Football, &c.

Extracts from Letters and " Returns."

The following are a very few extracts from letters and " Returns," received from various Clubs, affording a sample of their condition, and of the amount of good that is being done by these Institutions. They might be considerably multiplied, did space permit. As frequent inquiries are made respecting the success of Working Men's Clubs in villages and very small towns, it is well to mention that the first eight extracts all relate to Clubs in such localities ; the rest are from towns varying in population from 5,000 up to 500,000 :—

"Many thanks for the 'Hints and Suggestions.' I find them to tally exactly with our experience. . . . As to our Club, I can only say in a few words that it has undoubtedly decreased the amount of drunkenness to the rate of 50 per cent. Several of our members, now the most regular attendants, were particularly notorious as drunkards. Secondly. It has kept hold of youths of eighteen, whom we should have lost sight of after leaving the night school. Thirdly. It is a good refuge for the single men in the village, who have no fireside of their own by which to smoke their pipes, as if we had no Club, they must go to the public-house."—*Extracted from Kingham Letter.*

" I desire to return thanks (in the name of the Club) for your kindness in sending us the papers. I am very pleased to say that they contain a great deal of useful information and instruction. . . . I am happy to state that the Club has been the means of affording the members a place wherein to meet and enjoy the pleasures of social intercourse, and we (here in the country) have had, till this Club was started, no place for enjoying the society of our fellow-workmen of an evening in the winter without going to a public-house, so that the Club has done a little good in that direction. It was also the means of the members joining together and getting up public entertainments, consisting of readings, glees, songs, and recitations, which have drawn a great number of people together, and who, I think, have derived a great deal of useful information as well as amusement. These entertainments have also been very useful as regards making the Club self supporting, and giving the members more confidence in what they can do. As far as I can speak for my own self, I think that

the Working Men's Club is the best thing that has been yet starte
in this village."—*From Harting.*

"We are now thrown more on our own resources, as several of the
farmers who used to subscribe a trifle yearly have now ceased to do
so, on the ground that as young men get educated they will not
work for such low wages, but leave the parish to better their condition elsewhere. . . . I can truly say, since they have joined the
rooms their behaviour has become more polished, and their understanding much improved. In this village the Temperance Society
was first formed ; men began to meet together to talk of the Temperance movement, and kindred subjects. Next, the Club-rooms
were opened, one of the results being the increased sobriety of the
people, also the formation of a Co-operative Society, which is a great
success."—*From Whitchurch, Dorset.*

"On behalf of our committee, I beg to return you our sincere thanks
for the very valuable hints and suggestions therein contained. . . .
For the short time our Club has been in existence we can with confidence say that there are many parties who were attenders night
after night at beer-houses, in gaming, or other frivolous sports, such
as pigeon flying and the like, who now spend their time at the Club,
anxiously seeking for information which is likely to prove more
beneficial to them in their every-day life. There is one thing that I
must name in particular in connexion with our Club—viz., our
Pleasant Evenings, or, as you please to call them, Free and Easys, have
been a *decided success*, so much so that our room has been much too
small on those occasions. We feel confident that Working Men's
Clubs must be beneficial in large towns, if fully and fairly carried
out, from the success that has attended our efforts in a small village,
with a population of about 300."—*From Taylor Hill.*

"I beg to inform you that at present our Reading Room is in a most
healthy condition. The number of members, both honorary and
ordinary, continues good. During the winter months a class for
reading, writing, and arithmetic was held two evenings in each
week. The attendance was very good. I must also mention that a
greater taste for reading has grown among the junior members, and
also a fondness for chess, &c."—*From Iffley.*

"We are greatly obliged for the valuable 'Hints and Suggestions,'
&c., as well as other valuable papers sent before. Since the formation of the Club in November last, we have had a course of Lectures,
more especially for the benefit of the working men and their wives
—the latter were admitted free of charge. These lectures have been
of a high moral tone and value, and must have been of advantage to
those who listened to them. Many working men—and of these a
goodly number are about from twenty to twenty-five years of age—
who formerly spent much of their leisure time and hard earnings at
the beershop and public-house, have joined the Club, and it is evident
are much improved in habits and general appearance. Perhaps our
bitterest opponents are the publicans, and this is one proof to us we
are doing good. The testimony of the wives of many working men
here is that the Club is making their husbands better husbands, and
their homes happier."—*From Lockwood.*

M

" Our Club is purely agricultural, and is the means of keeping many a hard-working young man from spending his evenings at the public-house. They are beginning to think for themselves." — *From Freckenham.*

" The Club has supplied a want which has long been felt in the village."—*From Great Baddow.*

" With respect to the good done by the Institute, I beg to state that it has been a great benefit to the working men, &c., as it has drawn many from the public-house, dancing-saloons, and theatres. We have a few on the committee that did attend the above places before the Institute opened, and also at present a great many members, who have been persuaded to shun such places."—*From Kirkstall.*

" . . . The anniversary was in every way a success. The Chairman was very gratified to be able to report that the Club appeared to be in a more prosperous state than at any previous time of its existence. . . . The number of members in their Club had so increased that their rooms were scarcely large enough for them. . . . One evening last week when he went in, every chair was occupied. . . . If they went on as they were then doing, it would certainly be necessary for them to have new rooms." [Since the above was written the follow-ing has been received from this Club : " New premises have just been purchased. . . . The Club is entirely self-supporting."]—*From Wisbeach.*

" I beg to acknowledge my best thanks for the advice you give me. . . . I have much, as said above, to be thankful for, although the first year was a trying one, yet I was enabled, by Divine help, to prosecute the work, as you may read. I beg to say, with your kind advice and the help of the Lord, I have been enabled to see the Club established upon a fair principle. . . . We have at present chess, draughts, &c., coffee-room, with all requisites, smoking-room, &c., two bagatelle-rooms, one reading-room, a permanent building society, &c."—*From Bradford, near Manchester.*

" When we first threw open our doors, two years since, few took advantage of our reading-room and library. Gradually others joined us, and the small room we first possessed was soon too small for the members who preferred our reading-room to the public-house. A larger room was hired, our library has gradually increased, more papers and periodicals have been taken, games such as chess and draughts introduced, a second small room added to the larger one, and anyone who enters, at night particularly, will find our rooms well filled with working men. Their wives and families use the library freely. A series of Popular Readings has been given every fortnight through the winter, and competitive reading introduced. At first, St. George's Hall was only very sparsely filled at these readings. A few only came from conviviality, but the hall, though capable of holding 900 people, is now often too small for our requirements. We are endeavouring to add a juvenile library to the Institution, and to establish discussions on interesting subjects."—*From Llandudno.*

" I am happy to say that, through the kindness and liberality of our President, the Rev. James Horsbrugh (vicar), our members have been considerably increased. Upon entering our new premises, the reverend gentleman furnished us with a splendid bagatelle-board at less than half its value ; which has been the means of inducing many young men to join us who would not otherwise have looked at the place. We cleared 6*l*. 9s. 2½d. by our Penny Readings."—*From Ilkeston.*

"As regards the benefits arising from the Institution locally, I may say that it far exceeds our most sanguine expectations. The reading-room is nightly well attended, and the members are evidently seeking for books and periodicals of a higher class than formerly. The cultivation, also, of music does a great deal to refine the taste of members. Productions of a more classical nature are introducing themselves."—*From Hastings.*

"We have a small local museum for the exhibition of natural history and other objects of interest collected within four miles of Hampstead. A band of wind instruments, consisting of members of the rooms, meets twice a-week. A string band also meets twice a-week. Each band numbers about twenty members. In the summer months there is a cricket club in connexion with the Association, which has hitherto been very successful."—*From Hampstead.*

"This Institute is in a highly prosperous state ; gradual increase of members ; and of great benefit to those for whom it is intended." —*From Guildford.*

"The social and moral standing of this Club has greatly improved, and we hope in a short time, not only to be out of debt, but to have premises of our own before long. The members propose to buy the place in shares of 5s. each, the money to be returned as the funds will admit, and distributed by ballot annually."—*From Bridlington Quay.*

"The Club has lately been given up into the hands of the owners of the rooms—the Temperance Hall Company (in December last). Since that time the Club has largely increased, and is still, so that the rooms seem too small."—*From Chippenham.*

"This Reading-room has led to night-schools, lectures, &c., thereby doing much good."—*From Guestling.*

"We are in a very satisfactory state, and progressing very fast. The men are valuing the room."—*From Weymouth.*

"Interest in Club well maintained ; results so far very satisfactory."—*From Croydon.*

"I may say we are in very favourable circumstances . . . We have given about seven entertainments this winter in and about the neighbourhood. We are still self-supporting ; no honorary members. Our subscription 2d. a-week as usual. Having now about 20*l*. in the treasurer's hands, we hope before long to be in another building." —*From Buersil.*

The following is from the annual report (lately received) of one of the largest and best Clubs in the kingdom, Bolton, Lancashire :—

"In presenting the third annual report, the committee have to congratulate the friends and members of the Institution upon its increasing usefulness, as evidenced by the larger receipts and attendance over last year. The number of tickets sold has been—1 annual, 457 quarterly, 6,945 weekly, and 14,367 visitors; total 21,770, an increase over last year of 2,431. Calculating, as in former reports, that each quarterly and weekly member attends the Club three times per week, we have an average weekly attendance of 1,022, exclusive of those who meet in the various rooms for transacting their private club business, and of those who come for refreshment only; the latter may be computed at not less than 250 per week. The reading-room has been well supplied with newspapers and periodicals, and has been largely attended, showing that the members of the Club appreciate this provision made for their intellectual requirements. The various amusements have been attractive to many; and the refreshment department, under its present manager, we have every reason to believe, has given satisfaction to the members and visitors. The rooms set apart for the use of sick and friendly societies continue to be well let, and an additional room, entailing considerable outlay, has had to be provided for these purposes; but the committee, believing that such societies, when rightly conducted, are attended with much good to the working class, by enabling them to make provision for times of sickness, feel that no more effectual effort to promote their success can be made than providing suitable accommodation for transacting the business connected therewith, where each member can feel himself at liberty to come and go without any unnecessary outlay."

Our last extract is also from one of the best Clubs, which has been a thorough financial, as well as social and moral, success :—

"The healthy influence of our Club has been manifested in a *marked manner* in the great change that has taken place in the language and manners of those who frequent the 'Game Rooms.' Their conduct is now much less boisterous, and altogether more civilised, than when the Club was opened; the language used, too, is now much less apt to jar on ears polite; and numbers who at first came for the amusement department solely, have now found their way into the reading-rooms, and are acquiring literary tastes in a small way. But the influence our Club has won is not confined to the members. We have got a hold on the *public mind*, mainly through the medium of the discussion class, where social, sanitary, and other topics are weekly debated, the discussions being *regularly paragraphed*, and sometimes lengthily "reported," in the newspapers. This I believe to be an excellent way of promoting both the usefulness and influence of such institutions. The Industrial Exhibition, which we propose to hold shortly, is causing a considering amount of interest among *bonâ fide* working men, and we have already received quite a number of promises of all manner of things, and expect to be able at once to fill our rooms with a very interesting collection of articles, to give a stimulus to ingenuity and benefit our funds."—*From Sunderland*.

The Club at Great Ancoats, Manchester, referred to at page 122 (and which had had so hard a fight to pay its heavy rent), having changed its manager and made a vigorous effort, was, at the last advice, "thronged, and quite self-supporting."

Copy of Placard Announcing the Meetings there Referred to.

WORKING MEN'S CLUB AND INSTITUTE UNION, 150, STRAND, W.C.

The following is the Syllabus of Subjects for Discussion at the Tuesday Evening Social Meetings, Lower Hall, Exeter Hall, Strand.

DATE.	SUBJECT.	SPEAKER.	CHAIRMAN.
May 16	The Labour Question in Connexion with Strikes and Co-operation.	Thomas Hughes, Esq.	His Grace the Duke of Argyll.
,, 23	Co-operation and Partnership between Masters and Men in a Yorkshire Colliery and Factory	The Secretary	Lord Lyttelton.
,, 30	The Permissive Bill	Wilfrid Lawson, Esq., M.P.	The Earl of Shrewsbury & Talbot.
June 6	Dwellings of the Working Classes — Means and Appliances for Domestic Comfort	Viscount Ingestre	Viscount Enfield, M.P.
,, 13	Extension of the Half-time System of Education to Classes of the Population to which it does not now apply	Lord Lyttelton	Earl Grosvenor, M.P.
,, 20	Duties of Citizenship	Rev. F. D. Maurice, M.A.	His Grace the Duke of Devonshire.
,, 27	Can Arbitration be Successfully used in Disputes between Employers and Workmen?	J. M. Ludlow, Esq.	The Earl of Lichfield.
July 4	Industrial Exhibitions, Museums, and Art Training for the People	Right. Hon. W. F. Cowper, M.P.	The Right Hon. Sir John Pakington, Bart., M.P.

These Meetings are intended to afford to Working Men and persons of higher social position, or eminent in various ways, an opportunity of friendly intercourse and interchange of opinions upon subjects of social and national interest. The Rooms will be open each Evening at 7 P.M. for General Conversation. The Chair will be taken at 8 P.M., when the subject for the Evening will be introduced; after which free discussion will be invited. Each person sending up his name to the Chairman will be called on in turn, ten minutes being allowed to each Speaker. No Resolutions to be moved, nor Votes taken.

Admission to the Public, 6d. for Single Evenings, or 2s. 6d. the Series. Tickets to be obtained at the Office, 150, Strand. Members of Working Men's Clubs and Institutes affiliated to the Union admitted free, by Ticket to be had at their respective Clubs, with liberty to bring a friend at half-price, should there be room.

Refreshments will be supplied during the Evening at very Moderate Charges.

May, 1865.   HENRY SOLLY, *Secretary.*

INDEX.

W. J. JOHNSON, PRINTER, 121, FLEET STREET, LONDON.

For EU product safety concerns, contact us at Calle de José Abascal, 56–1°,
28003 Madrid, Spain or eugpsr@cambridge.org.

www.ingramcontent.com/pod-product-compliance
Ingram Content Group UK Ltd.
Pitfield, Milton Keynes, MK11 3LW, UK
UKHW040617240426
470322UK00010B/176